Cultivating Diversity in Fundraising

JANICE GOW PETTEY

John Wiley & Sons, Inc.

To
Tanya Glazebrook
Joe Valentine
and
Marv

Copyright © 2002 by John Wiley & Sons, Inc., New York. All rights reserved.

Published simultaneously in Canada.

ISBN 0-471-40361-X

Printed in the United States of America.

10 9 8 7 6 5 4 3 2 1

THE AFP/WILEY FUND DEVELOPMENT SERIES

The AFP/Wiley Fund Development Series is intended to provide fund development professionals and volunteers, including board members (and others interested in the not-for-profit sector), with top-quality publications that help advance philanthropy as voluntary action for the public good. Our goal is to provide practical, timely guidance and information on fundraising, charitable giving, and related subjects. AFP and Wiley each bring to this innovative collaboration unique and important resources that result in a whole greater than the sum of its parts.

Association of Fundraising Professionals

AFP is a professional association of fundraising executives that advances philanthropy through its more than 25,000 members in over 159 chapters throughout the United States, Canada, and Mexico. Through its advocacy, research, education, and certification programs, the society fosters development and growth of fundraising professionals, works to advance philanthropy and volunteerism, and promotes high ethical standards in the fundraising profession.

2001–2002 AFP Publishing Advisory Council

Linda A. Chew, CFRE, Chair
Associate Director, Alta Bates Summit Foundation

Nina P. Berkheiser, CFRE
Director of Development, SPCA of Pinellas County

Samuel N. Gough, CFRE
Principal, The AFRAM Group

Guy Mallabone, CFRE
VP, External Relations, Southern Alberta Institute of Technology

Robert Mueller, CFRE
Director of Development, Alliance of Community Hospices & Palliative Care Services

Maria Elena Noriega
Director, Noriega Malo & Associates

R. Michael Patterson, CFRE
Regional Director of Planned Giving, Arthritis Foundation

G. Patrick Williams, MS, ACFRE
Vice Chancellor of Development & Public Affairs, Southern Illinois University—
    Edwardsville

John Wiley & Sons

Susan McDermott
Editor (Professional/Trade Division), John Wiley & Sons, Inc.

AFP Staff

Richard B. Chobot, Ph.D.
Vice President, Professional Advancement, AFP

Jan Alfieri
Manager, AFP Resource Center, AFP

Beyond Fund Raising: New Strategies for Nonprofit Innovation and Investment
Kay Sprinkel Grace, CFRE
ISBN 0-471-16232-9
Inspirational yet practical, this book teaches you how to "put away the tin cup" and take fundraising to a new level. An experienced fundraising consultant and volunteer, Grace shows you how to establish a true relationship between philanthropy, development, and fundraising. You will also get forms, checklists, and flow charts to help you understand, visualize, and incorporate this new philosophy into your own nonprofit organization.

Careers in Fundraising
Lilya Wagner, Ed.D., CFRE
ISBN 0-471-40359-8
Careers in Fundraising provides expert guidance on professional opportunities in the field of fundraising, including topics on professional development, on-the-job issues, and the significance of fundraising as a career. This comprehensive resource covers all aspects of the profession, and also addresses the personal mission and commitment necessary for success in the field.

The Complete Guide to Fundraising Management
Stanley Weinstein, ACFRE
ISBN 0-471-24290-X
This book is a practical management how-to tailored specifically to the needs of fundraisers. Moving beyond theory, it addresses the day-to-day problems faced in these organizations, and offers hands-on advice and practical solutions. The book and accompanying disk include sample forms, checklists, and grids to help the reader plan and execute complicated fundraising campaigns.

Critical Issues in Fundraising
Dwight F. Burlingame, Ph.D., CFRE, editor
ISBN 0-471-17465-3
This book examines the most pressing issues facing fundraising professionals today. Extensive chapters cover donors, innovative fundraising, marketing, financial management, ethics, international philanthropy, and the fundraising professional. Written by a team of highly respected practitioners and educators, this book was developed in conjunction with AFP, the Council for the Advancement and Support of Education, the Association for Research on Nonprofit Organizations and Voluntary Action, and the Indiana University Center on Philanthropy.

Cultivating Diversity in Fundraising

Janice Gow Pettey

ISBN 0-471-40361-X

Cultivating Diversity in Fundraising offers an overview in cultivating successful fundraising and an enhanced understanding of philanthropic motivation in four selected racial/ethnic populations—African American, Asian American (Chinese, Filipino, Japanese, Korean, and South Asian), Hispanic/Latino (Cuban, Dominican, Salvadoran, Mexican, and Puerto Rican), and Native American. By understanding the rich philanthropic traditions of the individuals they are working with and soliciting funds from, fundraisers will be better equipped to serve their communities and their organizations.

Direct Response Fundraising: Mastering New Trends for Results

Michael Johnston

ISBN 0-471-38024-5

This guide offers fundraisers, managers, and volunteers an excellent understanding of how to plan and execute successful direct response campaigns. The success of a nonprofit direct response program requires staying on top of recent trends in the field. These trends include appealing more effectively to aging baby boomers as well as tapping into powerful new databases, the Internet, CD-ROMs, diskettes, and videos. The book includes a CD-ROM, with all the full-color, complete examples from the book as well as many more.

Ethical Decision-Making in fundraising

Marilyn Fischer, Ph.D.

ISBN 0-471-28943-3

A handbook for ethical reasoning and discussion. In her provocative new book, Dr. Fischer provides conceptual tools with which a nonprofit can thoroughly examine the ethics of how and from whom it seeks donations. With the book's Ethical Decision-Making Model, the author explains how fundraisers can use their basic value commitments to organizational mission, relationships, and integrity as day-to-day touchstones for making balanced, ethical fundraising decisions.

The Fund Raiser's Guide to the Internet

Michael Johnston

ISBN 0-471-25365-0

This book presents the issues, technology, and resources involved in online fundraising and donor relations. A practical "how-to" guide, it presents real-world case studies and successful practices from a top consulting firm, as well as guidance, inspiration, and warnings to nonprofits learning to develop this new fundraising technique. It also covers such important factors as determining your market, online solicitation pieces, security issues, and setting up your Web site.

Fundraising Cost Effectiveness: A Self-Assessment Workbook

James M. Greenfield, ACFRE, FAHP

ISBN 0-471-10916-9

A comprehensive, step-by-step guide that will help nonprofit professionals ensure that their department and campaigns are as efficient and cost-effective as possible. It combines a thorough explanation of the issues critical to fundraising self-assessment with easy-to-use worksheets and practical advice. The accompanying disk contains all the sample worksheets plus software for downloading a nonprofit's fundraising data from major software products into charts, graphs, and P&L-like spreadsheet templates.

Fundraising: Evaluating and Managing the Fund Development Process

James M. Greenfield, ACFRE, FAHP

ISBN 0-471-32014-5

Covering initial preparation in 15 areas of fundraising and the ongoing management of the process, this book is designed for fundraising executives of organizations both large and small. Included are numerous examples, case studies, checklists, and a unique evaluation of the audit environment of nonprofit organizations.

International Fundraising for Not-for-Profits: A Country-by-Country Profile

Thomas Harris

ISBN 0-471-24452-X

The only comprehensive book of its kind, it examines and compares the fundraising environments of 18 countries around the world. Each chapter is written by a local expert and details the history and context of fundraising for the country, local and global economic factors, legal and fiscal practices, sources of funding, and what fundraising practices are considered acceptable by the culture and government.

The Legislative Labyrinth: A Map for Not-for-Profits

Walter P. Pidgeon, Jr., Ph.D., CFRE

ISBN 0-471-40069-6

Currently, only a fraction of the nonprofit community takes advantage of the legislative process in representing their members and furthering its missions. Nonprofits are missing a significant way to fulfill their mission of gaining visibility and attracting new members and funding sources. This book answers the questions of nonprofits thinking of starting a lobbying program.

The Nonprofit Handbook: Fundraising, Third Edition

James M. Greenfield, ACFRE, FAHP

ISBN 0-471-40304-0

The third edition of this invaluable handbook provides a complete overview of the entire development function, from management and strategic planning to hands-on, practical guidance for the various kinds of fundraising. Written by leading fundraising professionals, edited by James M. Greenfield, this invaluable resource brings together more than 40 contributors who are vanguard experts and professionals in the field of fundraising.

Nonprofit Investment Policies: Practical Steps for Growing Charitable Funds
Robert P. Fry, Jr., Esq.
ISBN 0-471-17887-X
Written in plain English by an investment manager who specializes in nonprofit organizations, *Nonprofit Investment Policies* explores the unique characteristics of nonprofit investing. Covered topics include endowment management, planned gift assets, socially responsible investing, and more. This book includes charts and graphs to illustrate complex investment concepts, tables and checklists to guide nonprofit managers in decision making, and case studies of organizations of various sizes to show how to successfully develop and implement investment policies.

The NSFRE Fund-Raising Dictionary
ISBN 0-471-14916-0
Developed by NSFRE experts, this book provides clear and concise definitions for nearly 1,400 key fundraising and related nonprofit terms—from development and accounting to marketing and public relations. It also offers additional resource material, including a suggested bibliography.

Planned Giving Simplified: The Gift, the Giver, and the Gift Planner
Robert F. Sharpe, Sr.
ISBN 0-471-16674-X
This resource, written by a well-known veteran of planned giving, is a down-to-earth introduction to the complex world of planned giving, a sophisticated fundraising strategy that involves big money, complex tax laws, and delicate personal politics. This book shows charities, and in particular the charities' planned givers, how to understand the process—both the administration of planned gifts as well as the spirit of giving.

The Universal Benefits of Volunteering
Walter P. Pidgeon, Jr., Ph.D., CFRE
ISBN 0-471-18505-I
Volunteering is good for nonprofits, individuals, and corporations because it builds strong interpersonal and professionals skills that carry over into all sectors. A concise, hands-on guide to maximizing the use of business professionals in the nonprofit volunteer context, this workbook is a vital resource for all those involved in volunteering efforts. Included is a disk with all the worksheets and model documents needed to establish effective, successful, and ongoing volunteer programs.

About the Author

Janice Gow Pettey, CFRE, is the executive director of the Sacramento Regional Foundation (California). She has been a fundraiser for more than 22 years, working for the American Red Cross, YMCA of San Francisco, and the United Way of the Bay Area. Ms. Pettey is an adjunct professor at the University of San Francisco, where she teaches fundraising and philanthropy courses through the Institute of Nonprofit Organization Management. She is a member of the AFP Ethics Committee, and has served on the national AFP board and the Foundation board, and has chaired the Diversity Committee. She is a nationally known speaker and trainer on the subject of diversity and philanthropy. A graduate of Park University (Kansas City, Missouri), Ms. Pettey attended graduate school at Colorado State University. She is a returned Peace Corps volunteer (Korea). She is on the boards of the San Francisco Public Library Foundation and the United Religions Initiative, and has served on the boards of many other community agencies. A third-generation Chinese American, Ms. Pettey lives in San Francisco and Sacramento. She and her husband have three sons.

About the Contributing Authors

Michael Edell has more than 20-years experience in executive management and direction on the front lines of community health education, outreach, and research. He received his master's degree in Human Resources and Organization Development from the University of San Francisco, where he now serves as adjunct professor for its Institute for Nonprofit Organization Management. Michael managed national health information and referral hotlines for the American Social Health Association, including the National AIDS Hotline, STD National Hotline, and Herpes Resource Center Hotline. He managed a community-based infectious diseases clinic for the County of San Mateo, and is currently the executive director for ACRC—a leading Northern California clinical and behavioral research center. Under his direction, ACRC participated in more than 150 clinical trials, which led to FDA approval of more than 20 treatments and devices to fight HIV/AIDS. He is also a well-respected health educator known for developing innovative, grassroots education and outreach programs that focus on empowering traditionally underserved communities.

Samuel N. Gough, Jr., CFRE, a principal with the AFRAM Group, a full-service development firm, is a senior professional with more than 34 years' development experience. Having retired from his alma mater, Howard University, after serving more than 22 years in various advancement positions, he has been a special assistant to the president for development at the National Council of Negro Women, deputy director of development for the Children's Defense Fund, project director for the National Society of Fund Raising Executives, consultant to the Center for Policy Alternatives, and director of development for the Thelonious Monk Institute of Jazz.

He guided the direction of volunteer boards, both as a member of several boards and as a professional employed for that purpose. He managed and supervised annual alumni campaigns and planned giving programs, prospect research and records management, mail and telemarketing programs, and special Ford Foundation–supported programs. He also directed programs, staff, and budgets in university advancement and other nonprofit organizations. He directed Howard University to the conclusion its One Hundred Million Dollar Campaign.

Mr. Gough also is a graduate of the Harvard University Institute for Educational Management, in addition to the dozens of other educational programs in which he has participated as mentor, teacher, and student. He is a founding member of the Association of Fund Raising Officers (AFRO, Inc.). The D.C. Chapter of the National Society of Fund Raising Executives recognized him as the Outstanding Fund Raising Professional in 1992. He is listed in the Year 2001 edition of *Who's Who in America*.

Patrick J. Heryford is assistant director for Corporate and Foundation Relations at the University of San Francisco (USF), a Catholic Jesuit institution. He has worked in the nonprofit sector for six years, predominantly in Roman Catholic organizations. He is currently completing a master's in Nonprofit Administration at USF's Institute for Nonprofit Organization Management.

Prudence Precourt, Ph.D., is vice-president for development at the Experimental Aircraft Association (EAA) Foundation in Oshkosh, Wisconsin. Working together with the EAA, the Foundation preserves the heritage of aviation and reaches out to members and the public alike, bringing aviation-themed science, math, and technology education to students in the classroom, in onsite residential programs, and through distance learning opportunities. With an earned Ph.D. in cultural anthropology and more than 26 years of fundraising experience, she frequently writes and speaks about the issues involved in applying best practices in fundraising to special and diverse groups. Dr. Precourt comes from a family of diverse heritage that includes First Nations people.

Rolando Damian Rodriguez, CFRE, has served for the past nine years as executive director of the Jackson Memorial Foundation, a nonprofit organization dedicated exclusively to raising funds for Jackson Memorial Hospital, one of the largest teaching hospitals in the nation.

Under his direction, the start-up foundation has developed a number of major projects, including raising $28 million for the creation of the Ryder Trauma Center and more than $13 million for the development of Jackson's children's hospital, named the Holtz Center for Maternal & Child Health.

Prior to his arrival at Jackson Memorial Foundation, Mr. Rodriguez spent five years with the Catholic Health and Rehabilitation Foundation, an archdiocesan agency created under his guidance to develop and support a variety of health and elderly care programs in South Florida. He was responsible for the development and funding of Genesis, one of the first comprehensive residential AIDS programs in the nation.

Mr. Rodriguez has been active on local and national levels of the National Society of Fund Raising Executives, having served as president of the local chapter in 1991. Nationally, he was the first Hispanic American to serve on NSFRE national committees and boards, and recently completed his second term on the NSFRE Foundation Board. He has been highly involved in developing diversity efforts aimed at attracting and training more minority fundraising professionals. His latest challenge has been to help foster the development of philanthropy and the fundraising profession in Mexico, including serving as visiting faculty for fundraising courses in Mexico City and Tijuana.

Locally, Mr. Rodriguez serves on the advisory boards for Actor's Playhouse in Coral Gables, is a leadership mentor in the Kellogg Foundation/Dade Community Foundation's Fellowship Program, served as the 2000 chairman of the Greater Miami Chamber's Cutting Edge Award program and is 2001 co-chair of the Chamber's Children's Health Initiative, serves as a board member of the South Florida Leave a Legacy Program and co-chair of its 2001 "Donor Next Door" luncheon, and is involved in civic activities in his home city of Miami Beach through service on various city committees.

Born in Havana, Cuba, Mr. Rodriguez grew up on Miami Beach, where he currently resides. He has B.A. and M.S. degrees in Community Psychology, is married to Patricia Caballero, and has three children, Nicholas, Lauren, and Marcelo.

Norman Sullivan was awarded a Ph.D. in anthropology from the University of Toronto and is an associate professor at Marquette University.

His area of expertise is in the study of population structure in traditional and small-scale societies. He has published two monographs on the demographic consequences of European contact with native peoples and numerous articles and presentations on diseases in prehistoric communities. His current research is concerned with the biological experience of immigrant communities during the late nineteenth century. Dr. Sullivan is the owner of two small cats and two large dogs.

Acknowledgments

I wish to thank the Association of Fundraising Professionals (AFP) for enriching my interest in the area of diversity and philanthropy. Specific thanks go to AFP's Publishing Advisory Council; to the Research Council for their generous grant; to the Diversity Committees I worked with, especially former committee members Sam Gough, Prue Precourt, and Rolando Rodriguez, who are contributing authors to this book, and to colleagues too numerous to mention who agreed to answer interviews and who have supported me in this effort. Thanks to Lori Gusdorf, senior director at AFP, Jan Alfieri, manager, AFP Resource Center, and to Ruby Love, who first encouraged me to chair AFP's Diversity Committee.

I am also grateful to those many scholars, researchers, and professionals whose earlier works add substantially to this book. Thank you to the Council on Foundations for "Cultures of Caring" and to those authors whose research is cited—Joanne Scanlan, Mindy Berry, Jessica Chao, Henry Ramos, and Mary-Frances Winters.

I am grateful to those historians whose works are cited in this book: Sucheng Chan, John Hope Franklin, Manuel E. Gonzales, Harry H. L. Kitano, Karen Leonard, Alfred E. Moss, Jr., Himilce Novas, Ronald Takaki, and Gordon Willey.

My gratitude, to the University of San Francisco, and to Mike Cortés, director of the Institute for Nonprofit Organization Management at USF, for offering the support of the Gleeson Library. Thanks to Patrick Heryford of USF, colleague and former student, for diligent research and for skilled writing and editing. USF colleague Michael Edell wrote the case study "Our Turn" and provided guidance and input on the definition of culture and ethnicity. My grateful appreciation to Mike Zimmerman for his thoughtful edits of the Asian American chapters. Norman Sullivan, associate professor of anthropology, Marquette University (WI), authored the discussion paper on anthropology and the concept of race.

Earlier works done by Bradford Smith and Sylvia Shue in *Philanthropy in Communities of Color*, and Stella Shao in "Asian American Giving Issues: A Practitioner's Perspective" in *New Directions for Philanthropic Fundraising, No. 8* (Summer 1995), are acknowledged for their valuable studies on the subject of diversity in the philanthropic sector.

I wish to acknowledge the wisdom and generosity of all those who have shared their experiences as philanthropists and fundraising practitioners representing diverse cultures. My heart is filled with gratitude for enriching my cultural awareness. From every diversity workshop, seminar, or conference where I've presented has come a greater understanding of diversity, learned from so many of the attendees. Particular thanks to those colleagues who participated in the interviews and so willingly and eloquently shared their philanthropic history, customs, and practices.

I offer my grateful appreciation to Susan McDermott, Martha Cooley, and Sujin Hong, my editors at Wiley, for their encouragement and advice.

Finally, thanks to Jen Orr for reassurance and e-mail diversions offered during the writing of this book. To aforementioned Sam Gough, Prue Precourt, Patrick Heryford, and Michael Edell, who wrote, read, edited, advised, and encouraged me throughout—my grateful thanks. And to my husband, Marv, and our sons, Jonathan, Matthew, and Marvin Aaron, for their support and patience—thank you.

Contents

Preface

We cannot live for ourselves alone. Our lives are connected by a thousand invisible threads, and along these sympathetic fibers, our actions run as causes and return to use as results.

—Herman Melville

Cultivating Diversity in Fundraising is a source book, a collection of strategies and successes for fundraising among the four largest racial/ethnic minority groups in the United States. This book offers a review of history and customs, necessary to increase effective philanthropy in diverse communities. It is about people, and the intent is to stimulate further dialog based on research, discussion, and practice.

Those who have contributed to this book along with the author bring individual perspectives on diversity and philanthropy. The content of the book is the responsibility of the author; the message of the book is that we share in the responsibility for shaping philanthropic practices that embrace sensitivity to those we call our donors and prospects.

Some of the perspectives contained in this book reflect pain, others pride, but all are connected by the fiber of hope. It is with that sense of hope that this book is written.

JGP
San Francisco, CA

Introduction

A story is told about a southern gentleman who owned a grove of beautiful oak trees. Well established and much admired, these oak trees were a source of great pride. On a trip to another part of the country, the man discovered peach trees. Taken with their lovely blossoms and sweet fruit, he decided that peaches would be a good addition to his grove. Because the grove was filled with oaks, he decided to graft a peach branch onto an existing oak. He studied grafting, soil and climate conditions, and carefully grafted a peach branch onto one of his oak trees. He tended to the grafted tree and patiently waited for the fruits of his work. Spring came and passed, and there was no sign of peach blossoms on the oak tree. After repeated attempts, the man finally admitted that his efforts to graft a fruit tree onto an oak were futile.

Philanthropy in America is well cultivated and bears deep roots. These philanthropic practices as they are known to us have evolved through the growth of the nation reflecting the traditions and interests of the early settlers. The increasing numbers of racially and ethnically diverse people living in the United States now gives us the opportunity to develop new and distinct forms of philanthropy. Our fields of philanthropy will be enriched through the cultivation and appreciation of diversity yielding promise for generations to come.

Scores of books have been written on fundraising theory and techniques, not to mention the voluminous number of articles in professional journals. From Henry Rosso, Jim Greenfield, Jerold Panas, and Harold Seymour, among many others, we are taught the best practices in fundraising. Books specific to major gifts, planned giving, capital campaigns, and special events are accepted as necessary tools for those in the profession. Judith Nichols and others have provided us with current demographic information to assist us in our work. Sandra Shaw and Martha Taylor, in their book *Reinventing Fundraising*, have addressed the subject of women in philanthropy. The history of philanthropy has been well chronicled by Robert Bremner in *Giving* and *American Philanthropy*. Robert Payton, in *Philanthropy Voluntary Action for the Public Good*, has enriched our knowledge of the foundation of our work—philanthropic motivation. The subject of ethics in fundraising is both timely and necessary, and Albert Anderson in *Ethics for Fundraisers* and Marilyn Fischer in *Ethical Decision Making in Fund Raising* address this critical component of fundraising.

We are fortunate to have a growing body of research and literature on racial/ethnic traditions in philanthropy. The 1999 study *Cultures of Caring* produced by the Council on Foundations covers in detail the issue of motivation for major donors in African American, Asian American/Pacific Islander, Hispanic/Latino, and Native American communities. Each section of this thorough report was researched and written by a professional with strong ties to the specific community. This report is available from the Council on Foundations. A book originally produced as a study sponsored by the University of San Francisco, and published in 1999 by the Indiana University Press, *Philanthropy in Communities of Color* by Bradford Smith, Sylvia Shue, Jennifer Lisa Vest, and Joseph Villarreal, is a cross-cultural ethnography focused on giving and volunteering in eight communities of color in the San Francisco Bay Area. In his book *Remaking America*, James Joseph looks at the benevolent traditions of culturally diverse Americans and the transforming effect these traditions have on our national life.

None of these works, however, merges the elements of history, tradition, and motivation with the components of successful fundraising within and among diverse communities. We are left to piece together the available data on demographics, history and traditions, and cultural patterns to assemble some understanding of what is necessary and appropriate to both fundraise and increase philanthropic awareness in racially and ethnically diverse communities.

Cultivating Diversity in Fundraising is written as an introduction for those who are interested in fundraising in diverse communities. The purpose of this book is to provide an overview in cultivating successful fundraising and an enhanced understanding of philanthropic motivation in four selected racial/ethnic populations—African American, Asian American (Chinese, Filipino, Japanese, Korean, and South Asian), Hispanic/Latino (Cuban, Dominican, Salvadoran, Mexican, and Puerto Rican), and Native American. The book is organized in several sections, including an overview of the history and immigration for each population; cultural traditions; recent demographic data; a review of fundraising practices; and highlights of philanthropic practice from within each population. Case studies with discussion questions are included to promote further discussion and insight into specific components of diversity in fundraising. They are written by professionals with first hand experience in fundraising among diverse populations. This book responds to the following questions:

- Who are diverse donors?
- What are their charitable traditions and interests?
- What fundraising methods will be successful in diverse communities?
- What can we do to include more diversity in our fundraising efforts?

Fundraisers work in an ever-changing environment, and we are called upon to address future challenges while responding to current needs. The fast-moving population changes in America require thoughtfulness and creativity from fundraisers in order for the nonprofit sector to remain balanced in delivering services and securing funding constituencies. Creating a vibrant and expanded nonprofit sector is possible through individual and collective effort. Raising more money from diverse communities is the by-product of successful collaborations, understanding, and respect of differences. People will support what they help create.

A portion of this book brings to question the issue of racial and ethnic classifications. What are the characteristics that define race and ethnicity? How many races are there, and what are they? What are the generic and cultural differences between people?

The Association of Fundraising Professionals (AFP) defines diversity as "the state of being different among others." By definition, diversity is limitless, and an understanding of the diversity of religious preference, racial/ethnic populations, lifestyle, economic level, education, gender, and age will add to our understanding of prospects, donors, and philanthropists. All of this is required for successful cultivation of diversity in the field of philanthropy and fundraising.

DIVERSITY

There is an abiding need to recognize the value of cultivating diversity in the field of philanthropy as in every other aspect of our national lives. Demographics alone validate this need. In the year 2000, the state of California was the first state to become a "minority majority." The "minority" population is greater than non-Hispanic white Californians. It is expected that Texas will become the second "minority majority" state in 2001. Demographers forecast that the population of the United States will become a majority population of "minorities" by the middle of the twenty-first century. Historically, most of the population growth from Asian Pacific Islanders and Latinos resulted from immigration. Now for the first time, the birth rate is the leading factor in the increased numbers of Latinos and Asians. The white population is aging and having fewer children, while Latinos and Asians are younger and are bearing more children.

From an article "American Dreamers" in *U.S. News and World Report* comes this comparison: "We are not in a wholly new place in American history. We've been here before."[1] The article compares the status of African Americans in 2000 to that of the Irish Americans in 1900. Both Irish Catholic immigrants and blacks who left the South in the 1940s were denied by law and custom certain rights and economic privileges afforded others. Both groups had high rates of crime and substance abuse, both produced large numbers of police. Both performed poorly economically and excelled in politics. Both groups participated in riots, and both groups were subjected to discrimination. Both had strong ties to their churches. "Slowly Irish crime fell and incomes rose, by the 1950s to above the national average. Blacks are moving in the same direction. Crime was sharply down in the 1990s and . . . black incomes have been rising so that now two-parent black families have incomes about equal to two-parent white families with similar levels of educational achievement."[2]

Fundraising as it is practiced today will not be as effective without attention to the needs and interests of our changing population. We don't need to look far to find ways to enhance our fundraising sensitivities. It is a fundamental matter of willingness to learn and adapt. In "Respecting the Individual, Valuing Diversity," Marilyn Fischer writes:

> To overlook traditions of giving in ethnic communities while collecting data on philanthropy is to impose cultural patterns of the dominant society

on communities where these do not fit. When giving through voluntary organizations is assumed to be normal and definitional, rather than as "one" way of being philanthropic, other patterns are judged deficient or not even seen.[3]

I agree with Fischer and others who defend the significance of "informal giving" practiced by many ethnic groups, yet not documented or counted in so many surveys measuring time and money given to charitable organizations. In a report issued by the University of San Francisco, Michael O'Neill and William L. Roberts note the "disparity between the findings of survey research on minority giving and volunteering and qualitative studies of this issue." O'Neill and Roberts state, "The latter report extensive and diverse charitable behavior in communities of color, but the former report levels of giving and volunteering substantially below those of whites."[4]

Among the challenges in creating successful models of fundraising in diverse communities is one of definition. AFP's definition of diversity is "the quality or state of being different."[5]

To cite a personal example, my experiences as a Peace Corps volunteer prompted my personal interest in diversity. I was sent to Korea as a public health worker in an isolated fishing village where I was the only American for miles. The program was designed for pairs of volunteers to develop health clinics in the rural Korea of the late 1960s. I was assigned alone, in a particularly isolated area with no paved roads, electricity, or plumbing. There was only one phone in the village, which worked occasionally. I knew I did not earn this assignment because of my Korean language skills, as I had, at best, a marginal grasp of the language. It was not because I possessed technical public health skills, as my degree was in American Literature. It might have had more to do with appearance—an Asian in an Asian country. Korean society, particularly rural Korea at that time, was male dominated and very traditional. This was not a situation where a Chinese-American female could easily and effectively lead others without establishing mutual trust, understanding, and acceptance.

In *Remaking America* author James Joseph says, "the theologian Reinhold Niebuhr suggested that the chief cause of our inhumanity to each other is the tendency to set up 'we' groups and to place them over and against 'they' groups that we assume are outside the pale of our community."[6] Mr. Joseph goes on to suggest, "Whatever cohesion early Americans enjoyed, much of it was based on mutual respect. And that, not surprisingly, is today's missing element. Unless mutual respect is restored, the American society will continue to unravel. . . . Few Americans are aware of the extent to which voluntary groups provided a means of economic survival for racial minorities and helped them to make sense of their realities by serving as vehicles for self-help, social cohesion, and a positive group identity."[7] We can and should be proud of the American contributions to the field of philanthropy; but we must not ignore the legacies of the benevolent societies created by Chinese immigrants in the 1800s, or the impact of organized religion on philanthropy evidenced by the acts of charity practiced in African-American churches throughout the South during the same time. Philanthropy has a rich heritage, which, if studied and practiced, would only strengthen the fundraising profession. Organizations with interest in the successful cultivation of diverse donor relationships will benefit from enriched understanding and appreciation of others' cultural, ethnic, religious, and other practices. Fundraisers with an enhanced awareness and empathy for other cultures and lifestyles will assist in cultivating that field of philanthropy that thrives on diversity.

Oseola McCarty, the Mississippi laundress turned philanthropist in 1995, was somewhat amazed at the fuss made over her gift to a university she never attended. She inspired many with the generous donation of her life savings, $150,000, to the University of Southern Mississippi. This was not the largest donation the school had ever received, but what distinguished this gift from others was that she had saved the money over the course of a lifetime from her modest earnings ironing other people's laundry. Ms. McCarty had no family to inherit her nest egg, so she chose USM because she herself had dropped out of high school to take care of her family. She wanted to give youth of limited means the opportunity to go to college. Her gift is being used for scholarships. Interviewed by many, her response was modest. She just wanted to help. "I just want the scholarship to go to some child who needs it, to whoever is not able to help their children. I'm too old to get an education, but they can."[8]

In my career as a fundraiser, I worked for a disaster relief organization, assisting at several large disasters. It was energizing to see the philanthropic spirit of the many diverse ethnic groups in Guam following a major typhoon. Their approach was culturally appropriate and successful. There was support for one another without sacrificing individuality. Neighborhood fiestas—we would call them potlucks—created to support one another, and the practice of neighbor helping neighbor, are examples of a comfortable blending of customs used for charitable ends. I have learned to wear the shoes of the residents of the communities I am in, as it is their footprints that will lead the way to successful fundraising.

In choosing to work as fundraisers, we are expected to raise the money, serve as effective administrators, be good with numbers, communicate well, and serve as faithful stewards of the gifts and grants that our organizations receive. Good social work skills can come in handy, too. I believe it is the soul of fundraising that makes the difference. Arthur Frantzreb says this about philanthropy: "The word *philanthropy* has its roots in the Greek language meaning 'love for mankind.' It was never meant to apply only to donors of thousands or millions of dollars." John Gardner's analogy of giving in America being a Mississippi River of small gifts suggests that this flow of generosity comes from many sources composed of large and small gifts, from major donors to those who give less, yet equal in compassion.

The opportunities that exist for us to increase the numbers of donors among diverse constituencies are at the same time challenging and necessary. First, we must understand each other better, and be prepared to learn from others, including those from other cultures that have practiced philanthropy longer than the United States has been a nation.

Evidence that our efforts to support diversity and inclusiveness in fundraising are apparent, but one has only to look at the lack of diversity within the fundraising profession to understand the challenge. The number of diverse fundraisers has not changed significantly in the last 10 years, and yet we are looking at an increasingly diverse donor prospect base. Fundraising in the United States has mainly been driven by Western traditions that have shaped philanthropy. It is time for us to broaden our understanding of philanthropic motivation by learning from all those we wish to engage.

What can we do to successfully embrace diversity and overcome the challenges of isolation, myth, and perception? We need to continue to move from isolation to collaboration. Albert Schweitzer said, "Only those who respect the personality of others can be of real use to them." Myth and perception will continue to challenge us as long as we choose to apply general behavioral responses to unique situations. As we grow in our ability to learn from each other, myth and perception will be replaced by knowledge that comes from experiential learning. People will support what they help create.

We are all diverse. As you read this book, consider the implications for cultivating diversity and inclusiveness in fundraising. Successful diverse philanthropic efforts will be more than institutional, value-added opportunities designed to raise more money. It will be what Roosevelt Thomas, an organizational expert on diversity in the workplace, refers to as the changing of the "root culture" that will ensure our ability to cultivate diversity in the field of philanthropy.

2000 CENSUS

The U.S. federal government requires a census every 10 years. The 2000 Census included for the first time the opportunity for selection of one or more race categories to indicate racial identity. For the first time, a person could choose from 63 combinations. The government considers race and Hispanic origin to be separate and distinct (see Exhibit I-1). For Census 2000, the questions on race and Hispanic origin were asked of every individual living in the United States. The question on Hispanic origin asked

EXHIBIT I-I	CENSUS SELECTION BY RACE AND HISPANIC ORIGIN, 2000	

Selection	Number	Percent
RACE		
Total population	281,421,906	100.0
One race	274,595,678	97.6
White	211,460,626	75.1
Black or African American	34,658,190	12.3
American Indian and Alaska Native	2,475,956	0.9
Asian	10,242,998	3.6
Native Hawaiian and Other Pacific Islander	398,835	0.1
Some other race	15,359,073	5.5
Two or more races	6,826,228	2.4
HISPANIC OR LATINO		
Total population	281,421,906	100.0
Hispanic or Latino	35,305,818	12.5
Not Hispanic or Latino	246,116,088	87.5

Source: U.S. Census Bureau, Census 2000 Redistricting (Public Law 94-171) Summary File, Table PL1 and PL2.

respondents if they were Spanish, Hispanic, or Latino. The question on race asked respondents to report the race or races they considered themselves to be. Hispanic or Latino is a cultural classification, not a race or ethnic distinction. There are Hispanics and Latinos who have European, African, and/or Asian backgrounds.

How are the race categories used in Census 2000 defined?

- *White* refers to people having origins in any of the original peoples of Europe, the Middle East, or North Africa. It includes people who indicated their race or races as "White" or wrote in entries such as Irish, German, Italian, Lebanese, Near Easterner, Arab, or Polish.

- *Black or African American* refers to people having origins in any of the black racial groups of Africa. It includes people who indicated their race or races as "Black, African Am[erican] or Negro," or wrote in entries such as African American, Afro-American, Nigerian, or Haitian.

- *American Indian and Alaska Native* refers to people having origins in any of the original peoples of North and South America (including Central America), and who maintain tribal affiliation or community attachment. It includes people who indicated their race or races by marking this category or writing in their principal or enrolled tribe, such as Rosebud, Sioux, Chippewa, or Navajo.

- *Asian* refers to people having origins in any of the original peoples of the Far East, Southeast Asia, or the Indian subcontinent. It includes people who indicated their race or races as "Asian Indian," "Chinese," "Filipino," "Korean," "Japanese," "Vietnamese," or "Other Asian," or wrote in entries such as Burmese, Hmong, Pakistani, or Thai.

- *Native Hawaiian and Other Pacific Islander* refers to people tracing ancestry to the original peoples of Hawaii, Guam, Samoa, or other Pacific Islands. It includes people who indicated their race or races as "Native Hawaiian," "Guamanian, or Chamorro," "Samoan," or "Other Pacific Islander," or wrote in entries such as Tahitian or Mariana Islander.

- *Some other race* was included in Census 2000 for respondents who were unable to identify with the five race categories. Respondents who provided write-in entries such as Moroccan, South African Belizean, or a Hispanic origin (for example, Mexican, Puerto Rican, or Cuban) are included in the "Some Other Race" category.[9]

Initial summaries of Census 2000 became available in Spring 2001; some highlights follow. Selected charts on racial/ethnic census shifts can be found in the appendices.

- There are more than 281 million people living in the United States, an increase of 13 percent, or nearly 33 million, from 1990. That surpassed the previous 10-year growth record of 28 million between 1950 and 1960, the post–World War II baby boom.

- Metropolitan areas in the South and West experienced the biggest percentage increases, led by an 83 percent growth in Las Vegas.

- Three metropolitan areas in Texas are among the 10 fastest growing. Two of them—McAllen–Edinburg–Mission and Laredo—are on the U.S.–Mexico border. The third—Austin–San Marcos—is within an economically booming central Texas corridor that includes Dallas.

- Much of the population gain in 2000 was due to higher-than-expected birth rates, especially among Hispanics.

- Retirees account for population increases in fast-growing metropolitan areas, such as Naples, Florida, which saw a 65 percent increase over the last decade.

CHAPTER 1

African Americans

SAMUEL N. GOUGH, JR., CFRE

INTRODUCTION

Philanthropy in the African-American community includes gifts of time, service, knowledge, and love. According to James A. Joseph:

> The communal tradition of caring for each other has deep historical and metaphysical roots. *Homo communalis*, the idea that we live and have our being in a caring society, is at the heart of African metaphysics. . . . This cosmology of connectedness provided the first principle of early black philanthropy.[1]

The tradition can be traced back at least as far as the seventh century in West Africa. The first African Americans were captured, traded, transported, and forced into slavery with little more than what they had on their backs, in their heads, and in their hearts. In America, slaves were subjected to the will of people who used them for economic gain and for personal comfort. There was no respect for the family structure, the religion, knowledge, or humanity of African-American slaves.

As families were broken up—husbands and wives separated, children taken from parents—new families were formed. Women with children and orphaned children became members of the family of other enslaved people, and all shared their meager resources.

African-American churches, mutual aid societies, and fraternal groups were the early organizations through which African Americans could practice philanthropy. Because these people had little to give in tangible goods, volunteerism became an important aspect of black philanthropy. The help that these early African-American institutions provided was most often in response to an immediate need. As Dr. Emmett D. Carson describes it, "for 200 years most black giving was crisis driven."[2]

As the socioeconomic position of African Americans improved, their view of philanthropy broadened. Carson calls the new group of emerging philanthropists *strategic givers*: "These are people who want to see, and perhaps influence how their money is being used." Volunteerism remains an important element of African-American philanthropy. Involvement with causes to which they give is a determinant when African Americans decide how much and where they will give their time and money.

AFRICAN HISTORY

John Hope Franklin's and Alfred A. Moss Jr.'s book *From Slavery to Freedom: A History of African Americans* records 11 centuries of African history. It is from that book that the following synopsis of African history is taken.[3]

Ghana is known as the first West African state. Its history dates back to the seventh century, and it is recorded that farming was the primary occupation until droughts devastated the country. A later form of economic sustenance developed through trading. By the tenth century, Arabian settlers created a Muslim influence, and in the eleventh century, the King of Ghana became a Muslim. Religion during this period was based on a belief that everything living possessed good and evil spirits, which had to be satisfied in order for the country to prosper. Muslim invasion of the Almoravids established Islam as the kingdom's religion in 1076. Ghana gradually went into an economic decline precipitated by a lengthy drought, and the kingdom was destroyed during the twelfth and thirteenth centuries.

The kingdom of Mali arose as Ghana went into decline. This Mali was located west of the modern-day country of Mali, and was sometimes called Melle. Mali emerged as the strongest West African kingdom.

By the fifteenth century, the kingdom of Songhay arose to challenge the power of the Malians. Sonni Ali emerged as ruler of this new kingdom, and ruled for almost 30 years. An Islam follower, Askia Mohammed, overthrew Ali and became Songhay's most brilliant ruler. He was noted for establishing schools and creating political reform. Later developments included the

Moroccan conquest of Songhay in 1591, which pushed trans-Siberian trade east to the Hausa states and Bornu empires in Africa.

By the early twentieth century, Great Britain, France, and Germany were completing their conquest of West African states, and the power in Africa moved to the south.

Portuguese explorers sailed down the West African coast in the fifteenth century and discovered Benin and Congo, prosperous and substantial communities. The Portuguese bought slaves, beads, and cloth, and exchanged these goods with Africans living farther west. European traders were so taken with these products that they named sections of the West African coast after them—pepper, ivory, gold, slaves.

Slave trade was an important form of commerce. The most powerful people of the region were the Oyo, who—following the dissolution of the Songhay empire in the nineteenth century, and the ensuing conditions of war and disorder—became renowned transatlantic slave traders. A highly centralized state with successful commercial enterprises in palm oil followed as a premier economic center. Europeans, however, used the image of a barbaric society to justify their invasions and conquests in the 1890s.

Social organization within African culture was a family-based society. Focused on matrilineal relationships, familial relationships were traced through the mother rather than the father. Social stratification existed; nobility ranked highest, followed by workers, then slaves and war captives who had no political or social rights. Franklin writes that slavery was an important component of the social and economic life in Africa.

> The institution was widespread and was perhaps as old as African society itself. Slaves were predominantly people captured in war and could be sold or kept by those who captured them. Slaves were usually regarded as the property of the chief of the tribe or the head of the family. In law, slaves were chattel property, but in practice they often became trusted associates of their owners and enjoyed virtual freedom.[4]

Prior to European conquests of the continent, religion in Africa centered on ancestor worship. Islamic influences included the acceptance of Africans as social equals, advantages of education, and consideration of slaves as brothers. The cohesive influence of the family was the basis of social influence in Africa, reflecting a deep loyalty and attachment to family as a core social value.

Migration

The extent of migration of African culture has been studied and is varied in its findings. Franklin notes that slaves came from complex social and economic lives in Africa, and therefore were not overwhelmed by the New World. Other observations regarding acculturation include the African-to-African dynamic, where peoples of the same continent but different regions were now living together; and African-to-Western cultures. European institutions did not exist throughout the New World, so where European practices were weak, the opportunities for African survival were increased.

Africans in the New World

According to Claud Anderson in *Dirty Little Secrets About Black History, Its Heroes, and Other Troublemakers,* some historians believe the Folsom people of the southwestern United States were of African origin. The Folsom people were the oldest group of inhabitants in the Americas. Anderson suggests that might explain why the early Native Americans had dark complexions and African features. The Native Americans, whose forebears crossed the Bering Straits from Asia, had characteristics more similar to Asians. He therefore hypothesizes an intertwining of ancestry between Africans, Asians, and Native Americans.[5]

Slave trading in the New World began in Haiti, where European brutality almost exterminated the Indian population of the area. New sources of labor were needed, and Africans became the primary source of slave labor for Portuguese, French, Dutch, and English settlers. Africans were first used to work the tobacco plantations of the Caribbean Islands and later for the cultivation of sugarcane. Many African slaves in Jamaica fled to the mountains following the British takeover. These runaways banded together to terrorize the white landowners.

There is also evidence that *maroons,* so named by the Spaniards, were among the first black enslaved people brought to America as early as 1526. That year 500 Spaniards and 100 Africans founded a town near the mouth of the Pee Dee River in South Carolina. Disease and warfare with Native Americans killed many of the settlers. Later that year, the Africans rebelled, killing many of their slave masters and escaping into the woods to live with the Native Americans.

Living together created a symbiotic relationship between the Africans and Native Americans. Although the Africans were primarily on the receiving end of the goodwill, they brought with them skills and knowledge of African and European medicines, building, and tool-making skills, which they shared with the Native Americans in exchange for the opportunity to be part of their community.

In 1619, Dutch ships brought 20 Africans to Jamestown, Virginia. The Africans were traded for food, water, and supplies for the ship. However, these Africans were not slaves; they were indentured servants who would eventually be released. Formal slavery was not introduced in America until 1659.

Africans were brought forcibly into the Americas, mistreated, and exploited, primarily for economic reasons. The majority of enslaved Africans lived in conditions that were deplorable. These conditions led them to develop survival skills and other means of helping one another, using whatever limited resources they had available.

Early African-American Philanthropy

As Dr. Emmett Carson wrote in his book *A Hand Up: Black Philanthropy and Self-Help in America:*

> The foundations for black philanthropy were laid during the colonial period with the establishment of black churches and virtually simultaneously, the growth of mutual aid societies and fraternal orders. The relationships among these institutions were closed indeed. It was not unusual for black churches to have their own aid societies or fraternal organizations. It was through these benevolent institutions that the churches were able to address the social and material needs of parishioners and the larger community; in that sense, these societies were the secular arm of the church, albeit a separate and independent one, in the black community.[6]

In 1786, Richard Allen and Absalom Jones founded the Free African Society in Philadelphia. The society was founded as a direct result of their exclusion from praying at a local white church. Although founded primarily to aid blacks, the society helped the larger community of Philadelphia when a plague struck in 1793. Members of the society voluntarily aided the sick and buried the dead, regardless of race.

Two years later, Boston's Sons of the African Society was founded to provide burial services for its members and to assist widows and children. Mutual-aid societies continued to flourish in the late 1700s and well into the 1800s. Their missions were expanded to include assistance to widows and children and support of the abolition movement. Several mutual-aid societies and fraternities were organized throughout the country, including the Grand United Order of Odd Fellows, the Independent Order of Good Samaritans, the International Order of Twelve Knights, and the Daughters of Tabor.

Prior to the start of the Civil War, thousands of enslaved Africans escaped slavery by way of the Underground Railroad, a network of people. Blacks, Native Americans, and whites helped the enslaved people who were burned out of their homes and run off their land. Once the passengers on the Underground Railroad reached the free states or Canada, many eventually returned to help others escape.

Carson calls this movement "Philanthropy for Social Change." He notes this movement began in 1804 and continued until the outbreak of the Civil War. Not only did the members of the movement help the enslaved people escape, but they also helped them adapt to new, hostile environments. There were also "national and international fundraising campaigns, and black business people were among those who regularly contributed time and money" to help the Underground Railroad.[7]

At the beginning of the twentieth century, black Greek-letter fraternities and sororities were founded—not only to advance academic goals, but also to initiate social action. Precursors to these collegiate organizations were the American Negro Business League in 1900, the National Afro-American Council in 1903, and the National Urban League in 1905.

Also, there was the Niagara Movement in 1905, which had support from professional groups, teachers, ministers, physicians, lawyers, dentists, and businesspeople. Its declaration of principles addressed the injustices that African-American men were suffering, and it was one of the forerunners of the National Association for the Advancement of Colored People (NAACP).

The first black Greek-letter fraternity was Alpha Phi Alpha, founded by seven young African-American men (later called Jewels) at Cornell University in Ithaca, New York, in 1906. As Dr. Charles H. Wesley, author of *The History of Alpha Phi Alpha: A Development in College Life,* states:

Pressures of segregation, discrimination, mistreatment, prejudice, caste, and neglect of consideration were being exerted on the Negro people in many places, as they were endeavoring to advance and improve their status. Books, magazines, and newspapers were used to spread unworthy and false opinions about them. Scholarly writers among Negroes endeavored to combat these views with their writings. These opinions pro and con were criticized, praised and condemned by readers in various parts of the country.[8]

There is considerable evidence that students at Cornell University, who formed the Social Club and later the fraternity, were seriously concerned about negative conditions affecting blacks. The programs presented at their meetings demonstrated their concern. Jewel Henry Arthur Callis says of his early fraternity days, "Society offered us narrowly circumscribed opportunity and no security. Out of our need, our fraternity brought social purpose and social action."[9]

Early Education

The close of the Civil War and the abolition of slavery brought forth the Reconstruction Era, a period of deep political unrest. The partisan politics of the Republicans and Democrats were extended to African Americans living in both the North and the South. Leagues were organized in the North during the war to increase Republican support, and the league grew in popularity among southern blacks, bringing a large number of black votes to the Republican Party, both locally and nationally. Southern whites believed they could control the blacks, and the Ku Klux Klan was formed as a result of that violence in 1867. The struggle for white superiority in the South continued well into the twentieth century.

The Reconstruction Era brought little improvement to the socioeconomic state of African Americans. Education was the hope for African Americans to advance and improve the quality of their lives. Fueled by the desire for adequate education for their children, African Americans were resolute in achieving this dream for future generations. The pursuit of education came to be one of the great preoccupations of African Americans, and enlightenment was viewed by many as the greatest single opportunity to escape the indignities that whites heaped upon blacks. Small wonder that black children were sent to school even when it was a great inconvenience to their parents. Black fathers and mothers made untold sacrifices to secure for their children the learning that they had been denied.

Northern churches did provide assistance for furthering the educational needs of African Americans in the South, but African Americans themselves created institutions of learning. The Freedmen's Aid Society of the Methodist Episcopal Church created secondary schools and colleges, as well as two medical colleges and three theological institutions. Between 1860 and 1900 wealthy philanthropists established 260 institutions of higher learning, **among** them Vanderbilt, Johns Hopkins, Stanford, and the University of Chicago, all financed by private philanthropy. One of the major differences between church philanthropy and the large educational foundations—aside from the much larger amounts of money available for the direct funding of education—was one of motive. Although church philanthropy either served some recognized social need or supported agencies for the promotion of its own interests, the educational foundations usually were interested in stimulating the public to recognize certain existent needs as yet unfelt by society. These new agencies hoped to establish the principle of self-help for the individual as well as for the state.

Philanthropy did create greater support for education in the South, but it did not encourage equitable distribution of public funds for all southern children. Inequities were noted in the amount of state tax dollars spent on white children and those spent on black children. African Americans made a special effort to train African-American teachers and to raise money to support the education of their children. In 1900 there were 28,560 black teachers. At the same time there were more than 1.5 million black children in school. By 1900, more than 2,000 African Americans were college graduates.

African-American achievements in education are numerous, and the durability of some of the oldest African-American–founded institutions adds to the significance of these achievements. Predominantly black colleges and universities increased from 1 in 1854 to more than 100 by the mid-1900s. Financial constraints caused some black colleges to merge. In 1929, Morehouse College, Spelman College, and Atlanta University combined to become the Atlanta University system. A few years later, Straight College and New Orleans University merged to become Dillard University, receiving financial support from the Rosenwald Fund and the General Education Board to combine the schools. By 1943, operating costs escalated to the point that 33 schools formed a joint fundraising effort, the United Negro College Fund.

AFRICAN-AMERICAN CULTURAL GIVING PATTERNS

In *New Directions for Philanthropy*, Jean E. Fairfax, consultant to grant makers on diversity and multiculturalism, states:

> Patterns of black giving and volunteering in the twentieth century have been documented . . . [in] "Black Volunteers as Givers and Fundraisers" (working paper prepared for the Study of Philanthropy, City University of New York, 1990), . . . [which] states that in 1989, 69.7 percent of black households with incomes under $20,000 were givers; 29.7 percent were both givers and volunteers. Blacks give and volunteer disproportionately to black organizations. Carson observed that traditionally black organizations have relied on their members to be active contributors, volunteers, and fundraisers; this remains the case today.[10]

Fairfax explains:

> Blacks have been very generous, and their giving has often been unplanned and spontaneous. Charity is as likely to take the form of spontaneous assistance to persons in need who are taken into one's home or helped in some other way. Although some may criticize spontaneous giving, let us remember that it has been an important way for blacks of all socioeconomic levels to give back—to give through a special collection at church, to respond to an appeal to help a poor bright student get to college, to show solidarity to a community terrorized by lynching or a cross burning, or to support civil rights movements when even nonviolent challenges to unjust laws were not funded by mainstream foundations.[11]

African Americans are becoming more sophisticated in their philanthropic decision making. Almost weekly, stories appear, especially in the black media, about African-American generosity. This generosity runs the gamut of nonprofit causes.

The black church is historically the main recipient of black philanthropy and the catalyst for social, civic, educational, and economic action, as well as the center for religious activity. It is the institution that has been traditionally owned and controlled by blacks. Ownership and control are the elements of trust that result in the strong financial support for these churches.

Fairfax points out:

> Although we tend to focus on Christian churches when we think of black religious institutions, the Muslim community in America is diverse and important. It encompasses immigrants, diplomats, students, employees of multinational corporations who are temporarily assigned here, and African Americans. The American-Muslim community is considered one of the most important and rapidly growing in the world of Islam. As Islam has grown over the centuries, indigenous cultures have often shaped the ways in which the faithful fulfill their religious obligations. Charity is one of the five pillars of Islam. Consideration of how American Muslims, and especially African-American Muslims, fulfill this religious duty should be included in any discussion about pluralism in philanthropy. We still have so much to learn about all cultures of giving.[12]

Support of the church has been the impetus for a broad range of other philanthropic interests. Historically, religion and education have been the major areas of philanthropic support for African Americans. Slave masters went to great lengths to deny slaves access to education. In fact, national public policy forbade teaching slaves to read and write. Claud Anderson quotes an unnamed member of the Virginia House of Delegates in 1832, "We have, as far as possible, closed every avenue by which light might enter their minds. If we could extinguish the capacity to see the light, our work would be completed; they would be on the level with the beasts of the field, and we would be safe . . . to use them to build wealth, power and personal comfort."[13]

A letter from Colonel Auld, the owner of Frederick Douglass, to his wife after he learned she had been teaching Douglass to read and write, is further proof. In it, he tells her, "It would forever unfit him to be a slave."[14]

African Americans learned the importance and power of education in spite of the efforts of their enslavers to keep it from them. To this day, support of religious and educational institutions remains strong in African-American communities throughout the United States. Philanthropic impulses have been fueled by recent increased economic opportunities for African Americans. Increased disposable income can be channeled into philanthropic areas.

CURRENT STATE OF AFRICAN-AMERICAN PHILANTHROPY

Although there is not much formal research on African-American philanthropy, one of the works worth noting is *African-American Traditions of Giving and Serving: A Midwest Perspective*, by Cheryl Hall-Russell and Robert H. Kasberg, published by The Indiana Center on Philanthropy in 1997. The authors studied the cultural and historical importance of the African-American tradition in the states of Indiana, Michigan, and Ohio. They state, "The goal of this research is to identify African-American patterns of giving and serving, to determine how these traditions are transmitted from generation to generation, and to estimate the incidence and scope of African-American philanthropic behavior."[15] Their data were gathered from literature reviews and interviews of more than 800 individuals.

Their 10 most important findings are:

1. "The foundation of African-American philanthropy is derived from a distinctive notion of family as an inclusive and permeable institution.

2. African Americans frequently express their giving and serving through the idiom of kinship.

3. African Americans consider much of their giving and serving to family, neighbors, and needy strangers as a general obligation rather than philanthropy.

4. African-American philanthropy is community based. Helping any part of the community is viewed as improving the whole.

5. Generally, African Americans prefer to make donations and volunteer time on a situational and personal basis, rather than an abstract or organizational level.

6. African Americans value contributions of time more highly than donations of money.

7. When formal contributions of time and money are made, African Americans prefer giving through the church.

8. African Americans of southern origin are inclined to be more charitable in donating time and money and are more likely to participate than their northern counterparts.

9. African-American females tend to pattern their charitable behavior after the example of their mothers. Males interviewed often cite a male role model other than their fathers as influential in their charitable activities.

10. The concept of the "deserving poor" does not exist in the African-American community as a whole, but rather a sense of helping one another cope in a world generally seen as unfair."[16]

Although this nonrandom study centered only on the people in a specific region of the United States, there is value in testing these conclusions with a broader range of people to measure the efforts to recruit greater numbers of African Americans as donors and as volunteers.

AFRICAN AMERICANS TODAY

The 1990 Census reported the black population was about 30 million, or 12 percent of the total population. Census projections predict the population will grow to 37.6 million by 2010, or 13.1 percent, and the change between 2000 and 2050 will be a 60 percent increase to 53.5 million African Americans.

- New York had the highest number of African Americans with 3.2 million, but is the tenth state by percentage.
- The states with the highest percentage of African Americans were Mississippi (36 percent), Louisiana (32 percent), South Carolina (30 percent), Georgia (29 percent), Maryland (28 percent), Alabama (26 percent), North Carolina (22 percent), Virginia (20 percent), Delaware (20 percent), and New York (18 percent).
- The District of Columbia's African-American population is 61 percent.[17]

Additional facts about African Americans today include the following:

- According to a census update, by 1998, the nation's African-American population totaled an estimated 34.5 million people, 13 percent of the nation's total population.
- The African-American population has grown faster than either the total or the white population since 1990 and is projected to reach 45.1 million by 2020.

- In 1998, 55 percent of African Americans lived in the South, which accounted for one-fifth of that region's population. Nationwide, 54 percent of African Americans lived in central cities of metropolitan areas.

- In 1998, there were 8.4 million African–American families, nearly half being married-couple families.

- The typical African-American family consisted of 3.4 members. The typical white family consisted of 3.0 members and the typical Hispanic family had 3.92 members.

- In 1998, nearly 6 in 10 African-American families had children under the age of 18.

- Thirty-six percent of those children lived with both parents, while 12 percent lived with grandparents, with or without their parents present.

- By 1998, the median age of the African-American population was 30 years old, five years younger than the total U.S. population.

- Between 1987 and 1992, the number of African-American–owned businesses increased by 46 percent.

- In 1998, nearly 23 percent of African-American women and 17 percent of African-American men worked in managerial and professional positions.

- In 1998, 41 percent of African-American men ages 18 and over had never been married, 45 percent currently were married, 10 percent were divorced, and 4 percent were widowed. Among African-American women 18 and older, 37 percent had never been married, 39 percent currently were married, 13 percent were divorced, and 11 percent were widowed.

- Between 1996 and 1997, the household income for African-American families increased by 4.3 percent. The median income for African-American families rose from $24,021 to $25,050.

- Between 1993 and 1998, the wealth gap closed among African Americans in relation to whites and Hispanics (see Exhibit 1-1).

- Between 1989 and 1998, an average, middle-class, married couple's income rose 9.2 percent. However, the family had to work an additional 182 hours per year (4.5 work weeks), for a total of 3,600 hours.

EXHIBIT I-I   THE RACIAL WEALTH GAP, 1983–1998

Categories	1983	1989	1992	1995	1998
Median Net Worth					
White	$71,500	$84,900	$71,300	$65,200	$81,700
African American	4,800	2,200	12,000	7,900	10,000
Hispanic	2,800	1,800	4,300	5,300	3,000
Median Financial Wealth					
White	$19,900	$26,900	$21,900	$19,300	$37,600
African American	0	0	200	200	1,200
Hispanic	0	0	0	0	0
Homeownership Rate					
White	68.1%	69.3%	69.0%	69.4%	71.8%
African American	44.3%	41.7%	48.5%	46.8%	46.3%
Hispanic	32.6%	39.8%	43.1%	44.4%	44.2%

Note: Financial wealth is net worth minus the value of owner-occupied housing.

Source: Edward N. Wolff, "Recent Trends in Wealth Ownership, 1983–1998" (April 2000), Tables 8 and 9.

The average, middle-class African-American family worked 4,278 hours per year, an increase of nearly 500 hours. In those same years, poverty rates fell faster for Hispanics (4.7 percent) and African Americans (3.2 percent) than they did for whites (0.7 percent). Yet minorities continued to have much higher overall poverty rates: African Americans, 26.1 percent; Hispanics, 25.6 percent; whites, 10.5 percent.

- Eighty-eight percent of African Americans, ages 25 to 29, were high school graduates.

- In 1998, nearly 3 million or 15 percent of African Americans age 25 or older held at least a bachelor's degree. Of these degree holders, more than 800,000 had an advanced degree.[18]

CHAPTER 2

Asian Americans

INTRODUCTION

Asians in America are a growing and diverse group. According to a 1998 Census report, Asians were less than 4 percent of the U.S. population in 1990, and the current estimate is that there will be 20 million Asians representing 6 percent of the total U.S. population by the year 2020 (see Exhibit 2-1).

The majority of Asians live in California, Hawaii, New York, Texas, and Illinois. Asian Americans live in urban, suburban, and rural communities. However, the largest numbers of Asians can be found in urban centers on the West and East coasts (see Exhibit 2-2). There are growing numbers of Asian populations across the country (see Exhibit 2-3).[1]

EXHIBIT 2-1	ASIAN AND PACIFIC ISLANDER GROUPS, BY ETHNICITY

Asian	Pacific Islander
Chinese	Polynesian
Filipino	Hawaiian
Japanese	Samoan
Asian Indian/South Asian	Tongan
Korean	Other Polynesian
Vietnamese	Micronesian
Cambodian	Guamanian
Hmong	Other Micronesian
Laotian	Melanesian
Thai	Other Pacific Islander
Other Asians	

Source: "Asian American Giving," *Cultures of Giving* (Summer 1995), p. 54.

EXHIBIT 2-2   BIGGEST ASIAN METROS

(Metropolitan statistical areas ranked by Asian-American population, 1990)

Los Angeles–Long Beach, California	954,485
New York, New York	556,399
Honolulu, Hawaii	526,549
San Francisco, California	329,999
Oakland, California	269,566
San Jose, California	261,466
Anaheim-Santa Ana, California	249,192
Chicago, Illinois	229,492
Washington DC–Maryland–Virginia	202,437
San Diego, California	198,311
Seattle, Washington	135,251
Houston, Texas	126,501
Boston–Lawrence–Salem–Lowell–Brockton, Massachusetts	116,597
Sacramento, California	114,520
Philadelphia, Pennsylvania–New Jersey	104,595
Riverside–San Bernardino, California	100,792
Dallas, Texas	67,195
Bergen–Passaic, New Jersey	66,743
Minneapolis–St. Paul, Minnesota–Wisconsin	65,204
Nassau–Suffolk, New York	62,399
Stockton, California	59,690
Detroit, Michigan	57,730
Fresno, California	57,239
Middlesex–Somerset–Hunterdon, New Jersey	56,804
Newark, New Jersey	52,898
Atlanta, Georgia	51,486
Vallejo–Fairfield–Napa, California	47,044
Portland, Oregon	46,360
Baltimore, Maryland	42,634
Denver, Colorado	37,134

Source: This chart first appeared in the June 1991 issue of *American Demographics Magazine*. It is reprinted with permission.

Asians speak different languages. As an example, Chinese and Filipinos have multiple dialects as subsets of their languages. Cantonese and Mandarin are the major Chinese languages, and Ilocano and Pilipino are widely spoken by Filipinos. Different religions are practiced, and customs and traditions vary from group to group. Yet, until 2000, the U.S. Census Bureau considered Asian/Pacific Islanders to be of one classification. Asians in the United States include pioneers—the first generation who immigrated and settled in

EXHIBIT 2-3   THE MOST ASIAN COUNTIES

(Counties with an Asian-American population of 5 percent or more, 1990)

Rank/County	State	% Asian
Kalawao	Hawaii	76.9
Honolulu	Hawaii	63.0
Kauai	Hawaii	62.7
Hawaii	Hawaii	57.1
San Francisco	California	29.1
Aleutians East Borough	Alaska	18.8
Santa Clara	California	17.5
San Mateo	California	16.8
Alameda	California	15.1
Solano	California	12.8
San Joaquin	California	12.4
Queens	New York	12.2
Kodiak Island Borough	Alaska	11.2
Los Angeles	California	10.8
Orange	California	10.3
Aleutians West Census Area	Alaska	10.3
Contra Costa	California	9.6
Sutter	California	9.4
Sacramento	California	9.3
Fresno	California	8.6
Merced	California	8.5
Fairfax	Virginia	8.5
Yuba	California	8.4
Yolo	California	8.4
Montgomery	Maryland	8.2
San Diego	California	7.9
King	Washington	7.9
Monterey	California	7.8
New York	New York	7.4
Fairfax (city)	Virginia	6.8
Arlington	Virginia	6.8
Middlesex	New Jersey	6.6
Hudson	New Jersey	6.7
Bergen	New Jersey	6.6
Fort Bend	Texas	6.4
Benton	Oregon	5.5
Tompkins	New York	5.5
Whitman	Washington	5.4
Stanislaus	California	5.2
Ventura	California	5.2
Ramsey	Minnesota	5.1
DuPage	Illinois	5.1
Suffolk	Massachusetts	5.0

Source: This chart first appeared in the June 1991 issue of *American Demographics Magazine*. It is reprinted with permission.

the United States; "1.5"—those who were born and lived their early youth in Asia and then came to the United States as a youth; and the American born. Asian Americans represent immigrant and refugee populations, as well as a significant number of U.S. nationals. In a keynote presentation at the 1997 Conference on Asian Pacific Americans and the Nonprofit Sector sponsored by the University of San Francisco, Juanita Tamayo Lott, advisor to the U.S. Census, said:

> In addition to Asian immigrants and their descendants there are two demographic groups in the Asian Pacific American population. These are the Southeast Asian refugees and their children, who comprise about 10 percent of the Asian Pacific American population, and the native or indigenous Pacific Islanders, who make up about 5 percent. The major distinction of Asian immigrants from refugees and natives is that Asian immigrants are persons who have voluntarily entered the United States to improve their livelihood and that of their children.
>
> By contrast, refugees and native peoples are not voluntary settlers to the United States. Pacific Islander groups are indigenous to the Americas. Hawaiians and Guamanians are U.S. citizens; American Samoans are nationals. They are Americans by conquest.[2]

The historical impact of Asian American immigration varies, as does the amount of data on immigration patterns. Because the Chinese and Japanese immigrated earlier, more information is available than with recent Asian immigrant populations such as Southeast Asians, South Asians, and Koreans.

OVERVIEW

To appreciate the diversity of the Asian/Pacific Islanders in the United States, it is necessary to have some knowledge of their histories and cultural traditions. This chapter reviews the history and immigration patterns of Asians in America. The historic overview includes the traditions of giving and sharing within Asian-American communities, derived from cultural patterns developed over many generations influenced heavily by behavior, values, and the religious teachings found in Buddhism, Taoism, Confucianism, Islam, Hinduism, and Roman Catholicism, the major Asian religions. The teachings of Buddha, for example, are so ingrained into Chinese culture that it is believed that some Chinese practice Buddhist teachings without a conscious understanding of Buddhism's central role at the root of the culture. The teachings of Buddha emphasize compassion and service to others; from Confucius comes benevolence and filial piety; and Lao Tzu teaches the relatedness of all things, and the reciprocity that characterizes all human relationships. The precepts of Sikhism practiced by many Indians from the Punjab region of India stress sharing with those in need outside of the Sikh community, and giving both money and time to charity.

The Chinese were the first group to immigrate to the United States in large numbers. The initial major influx occurred during the Gold Rush in California in the mid-1800s. Communities of Chinese Americans were established in San Francisco, as well as in the gold mine camps of the Sierras, lumber towns along the coast, and in the farming communities of central California. Assimilation and acceptance did not come easily for many early Chinese immigrants. Language barriers, long separation from families in China, low wages, and harsh working and living conditions were among the challenges facing early immigrants. As time passed, an increasing number of Chinese-owned small businesses proliferated throughout the West. Most of the immigrants from China through the mid-twentieth century were Cantonese speaking, coming primarily from the southeastern region of China near Canton (Xian). When the Immigration Act of 1965 was passed, ethnic Chinese from many other areas of Asia came to the United States, creating tremendous diversity within the Chinese immigrant communities. Chinese from Southeast Asia and Hong Kong immigrated in larger numbers from 1965 on, more than those emigrating from the central regions of China. The new immigrants spoke languages other than Cantonese—Mandarin, Vietnamese, and Thai among them. The Chinese-American population now spans several generations.

Japanese were the next large wave of Asian immigrants. The first wave settled in Hawaii as workers on the sugar plantations. A significant (but smaller number) of Japanese immigrants came to the U.S. mainland following the lure of gold, as did the Chinese immigrants. Japanese Americans settled in the farming areas of the West, and many small farms were run and worked by Japanese farmers until World War II. Following the bombing of Pearl Harbor on December 7, 1941, life for Japanese Americans changed radically. Executive Order 9066 created relocation camps for all persons of Japanese ancestry. Loss of personal property, privacy, and dignity irrevocably changed the lifestyle of Japanese Americans. Following the close of the war, first-generation (*Issei*) Japanese found work as domestics and garden-ers. The second generation (*Nisei*) was of school age, and turned to com-pleting their American education. Unlike the Chinese, Japanese-American neighborhoods did not continue to grow after the war. Japanese churches, sports leagues, and ethnic associations continued to thrive, but Japanese Americans became more dispersed throughout the country. Like the Chi-nese, there are now more than five generations of Japanese Americans liv-ing in the United States.

The Philippine Islands were held as a territory of the United States for part of the twentieth century, giving Filipino immigrants a unique status among Asian immigrants—as nationals, not aliens, according to immigration status. Filipinos, like the Japanese, settled in Hawaii to work on the plan-tations. The *pensionados* program sponsored by the United States gave Fil-ipino students the opportunity to attend college in the United States. Many intended to return to the Philippines after graduation. Some students elected to stay in the United States, and they found work as skilled labor-ers or in lower levels of their chosen professions. Unlike earlier Asian immi-grants, Filipino men actively sought non-Filipino female companionship, and intermarriage between Filipinos and non-Filipinos grew until anti-miscegenation laws were amended in 1933, to forbid marriages with mem-bers of the "Malay race" in addition to other Asian immigrant groups included in earlier miscegenation laws.

Since 1965, not only has the number of Filipinos immigrating grown rapidly, but the composition of the population has also changed. In his book *Asian Americans: Emerging Minorities,* Harry H. L. Kitano estimates that up to two-thirds of the immigrants from the Philippines (since 1965) have rep-resented professional classes.[3] The health industry in particular has bene-fited from the educated Filipino workforce. Filipino women represented the largest percentage of Asian women in the workforce in 1980. In the 1990s, census estimates for 2000 called for Filipinos to be the fastest-grow-ing Asian population in the United States.

The history of Koreans immigrating to the United States is a fairly recent occurrence. Some Koreans went to Hawaii in the late 1800s mainly as a re-placement for Chinese and Japanese laborers. A severe famine in the early 1900s prompted Koreans to leave Korea for the United States, as well as Manchuria, Japan, and Russia. The second wave of Korean immigration was between 1951 and 1964, the period of time following the Korean conflict.

Many U.S. servicemen brought home Korean wives (an estimated 28,205 "war brides" arrived in the United States between 1950 and 1975).[4] In addition to the war brides were a large number of Korean children, orphaned during the war and adopted by U.S. families. The last group in this second wave of Korean immigrants was 5,000 Korean students who came to study.

As with earlier Asian immigrants, the Immigration and Naturalization Act of 1965 resulted in dramatic changes in Korean immigration. The Korean share of total U.S. immigration rose from 0.7 percent to 3.8 percent between 1969 and 1973.[5] Many Korean families in the United States still include first-generation heads of household, with children born in Korea now living in the United States. This younger generation is often referred to as "1.5," acknowledging their early years in Korea and their current life in America.

Asian immigration has been refugee centered since the mid-1970s. Southeast Asians who have entered the United States as refugees include Vietnamese, Laotians, Cambodians (Kampucheans), Hmong, and ethnic Chinese. The Refugee Assistance Act of 1980 provided a specific policy for refugees, establishing annual admission levels of 50,000 and more, and further recognized the principle of asylum and the social, economic, and educational needs of refugees.

> Southeast Asian refugees are extraordinarily diverse. They bring a variety of backgrounds, differences in culture and history, and a heterogeneity of skills and experiences. Yet there is a tendency to lump them together as "refugees from Southeast Asia." . . . They do share some commonalities, however. The usual combination of variables that have affected all newcomers to the United States—motivations, skills and aspirations, and the strength of community and family—will determine part of their future.[6]

Pacific Islanders were not measured as a specific Census group until 1980, when the census created the following Pacific Islander categories: Polynesian, Micronesian, and Melanesian. By 1990, there was an increase of 35 percent in the number of Pacific Islanders in the United States. Hawaiians, identified as persons with native Hawaiian ancestry, represent the largest of the Pacific Islander populations. Hawaiian history has witnessed Western influence since the mid-1800s. Christian missionaries from many denominations—Mormon, Protestant, Catholic, among them—introduced Hawaiians to a Western way of life. Western sugar plantation owners later introduced other Asian populations to the laborers' workforce. Today, Hawaii is an Asian-

American majority population with significant blending of Asian cultures through intermarriage. There are very few native Hawaiians left.

Samoans are the next largest Asian-Pacific Islander (API) population. Samoans from American Samoa are nationals as American Samoa has been a U.S. territory for 100 years. Western Samoa is an independent country. The Mormon Church brought the first Samoans to the United States in the 1920s to help build the Hawaiian Mormon Temple. The next wave of Samoan migration occurred after the U.S. Navy transferred administration of American Samoa to the Department of the Interior in 1950, causing many Samoans to follow the Navy to Hawaii and then onto the mainland.

Residents of Guam, a U.S. territory, are Guamanians. The native Guamanians are Chamorros, but Guamanians today include those with Filipino, Chinese, Japanese, and Mexican heritage. The Organic Act of 1950 conferred U.S. citizenship on citizens of Guam. Migration has been a two-way street, with Guamanians moving back and forth, making it difficult to track numbers.

Chamorro values are family centered and matriarchal, and the Guamanian migrants have struggled (along with other Pacific Islander immigrants) in moving from isolation to integration in the U.S. mainland life.

Asian Indians, or South Asians, are immigrants from India and surrounding areas. The first phase of South Asian immigration was from 1900 to 1947, and consisted mainly of men from the British Indian province of Punjab. Primarily from farming backgrounds, these Punjabi men came to the West Coast at the end of the Asian migration of the early twentieth century. This phase of immigration essentially ended in 1917, when U.S. immigration laws were changed. Asian immigration was further limited in 1924.

The second phase of South Asian immigration followed the 1965 Immigration and Naturalization Act that gave preference to Asian immigrants with necessary skills. South Asian immigration in this second wave came from all over India, Pakistan, Bangladesh, Sri Lanka, Afghanistan, and Nepal. In 1970, there were an estimated 75,000 Asian Indians in the United States. In 1990, the number grew to 815,000. South Asians are more geographically dispersed than other Asian-American groups. "In 1990, when nearly 52 percent of Asian Americans lived in the Far West, only 21 percent of Asian Indians did."[7]

The 1990 Census also pointed out some striking characteristics of the South Asian immigrant population:

- 58 percent were college graduates (vs. U.S. 20 percent)

- 47 percent were managers, professionals, executives (vs. 24 percent white)

- 92.7 percent of all Asian Indian children under 18 lived in a two-parent household (vs. 82.9 percent white, and higher than any other Asian-American group)

- Asian Indian households are small on average—2.9 persons

CHINESE-AMERICAN HISTORY

The Chinese have the longest history of any Asian immigrant population in the United States. Many Americans believe that the earliest Chinese immigrants were those who followed the quest for wealth during California's Gold Rush in the 1800s. Indeed, many Chinese did sail across the Pacific Ocean headed for the Mother Lode region, but the first Chinese immigrants are believed to have arrived in the United States soon after the signing of the Declaration of Independence.

Deteriorating economic conditions in China caused by increasing population and decreasing food production and flooding of the Yangtze River caused many Chinese men to journey to the United States in the mid-1800s, as news of the Gold Rush and the need for laborers reached them. A contributing social factor influencing the Chinese migration can be traced to the Opium War of 1839 to 1842 between China, where use of opium had grown rapidly, and England, whose colonies made it the leading supplier. The British prevailed and forced China to cede Hong Kong to Great Britain, creating even more unrest in China. The Taiping Uprising of 1851 to 1864, in which an estimated 20 million Chinese died,[8] was another reason borne of despair that caused many to leave China.

Small in number on a national basis, a substantial number of Chinese sojourners settled in Mississippi after the completion of the work on the Transcontinental Railroad in 1869. The Chinese men, who found themselves in the South and unemployed after the railroad work was done, moved to the sugarcane plantations and shrimp farms of Louisiana. The overflow of Chinese workers migrated to the delta region of Mississippi. Unlike many other Chinese in the western part of the United States, the Mississippi Chinese intended to be temporary residents, with the goal of returning to China when their work was done.[9] The largest early migration of Chinese immigrants was in the nineteenth century. By 1870, there were 63,000 Chinese in the United States. Most settled in California, while others established themselves in other parts of the West as well as in the Southwest, New England, and the South. The Chinese constituted a sizable proportion of the population in certain areas—29 percent in Idaho and 10 percent in Montana.[10]

China's coastline is more than 5,000 miles long, so it is not surprising that the Chinese were experienced mariners. The common form of transport from China to California was by small boat, sometimes referred to as *junks* or *sampans*. The trip was often treacherous and the conditions miserable, and not all survived the trip. The earlier Chinese immigrants were over-whelmingly males, so families were separated for long periods of time. The majority of immigrants came from the same province near Canton, a major port city in China. In spite of the danger and hardships involved in the voyage, Chinese were not deterred in their desire to seek a better life. H. H. Bancroft, in 1888, made this comment about the interest among Chinese to come to America: "Among Asiatic nations, the most severely affected by this western malady were the Chinese . . . they turned over the tidings in their minds with feverish impatience, whilst their neighbors, the Japanese, heard of the gold discovery with stolid indifference."[11]

Chinese immigrants found work as laborers. They were cooks and laundry persons, worked in the lumber mills, and were a major part of the workforce that built the Transcontinental Railroad. Despite their contributions to the economic growth in the West, Chinese immigrants were often targets of discrimination and racism. In 1850, the California legislature passed a foreign miner's tax designed to reduce the number of Mexican miners. This law was repealed in 1852, and replaced with another foreign miner's tax, this time aimed mainly at Chinese laborers. It required a monthly payment of three dollars from every foreign miner who did not desire to become a citizen. But Chinese could not have become citizens as a 1790 federal law reserved naturalized citizenship for "white" persons. This foreign miner's tax remained in effect until the 1870 Civil Rights Act voided it. By then, California had collected $5 million from the Chinese, a sum representing 25 to 50 percent of all state revenue.[12]

Throughout the late 1800s, the Chinese were victimized by acts of racial violence and laws designed to harass them. Difficult economic conditions during this time caused Chinese workers to become the targets of white labor resentment. "Protests became violent as economic depression led to anti-Chinese riots . . . throughout California. . . . Chinese were beaten and shot by white workers and often loaded onto trains and shipped out of town."[13] President Rutherford Hayes warned Americans about the "Chinese problem." The "present Chinese invasion," he argued in 1879, was "pernicious and should be discouraged. Our experience in dealing with the weaker races—the Negroes and Indians . . . is not encouraging. . . . I would consider with favor any suitable measures to discourage the Chinese from coming to our shores."[14]

In 1882, Congress enacted the Chinese Exclusion Act, marking the first time in U.S. history that members of a specific ethnic group were denied entry to the United States. This exclusion act was renewed in 1892 and extended indefinitely in 1902.

Angel Island, now a state park in San Francisco Bay not far from Alcatraz, was the point of entry for the majority of the approximately 175,000 Chinese immigrants who came to America between 1910 and 1940. Modeled after New York's Ellis Island, the site was used as the immigration detention headquarters for Chinese awaiting jurisdiction on the outcomes of medical examinations and immigration papers. These Chinese detainees resented their long confinements on Angel Island. They were well aware that immigrants from other countries were processed and released within much shorter periods.[15] This ordeal of prolonged detention left an indelible mark on many of the detainees, and they wrote poetry describing their impressions on the walls of the barracks. Some of these poems eloquently describe the emotions of the writers, and today, more than 135 poems penned on the barracks' walls have been recorded in the book *Island: Poetry and History of Chinese Immigrants on Angel Island, 1910–1940*. The former barracks are now part of the California State Parks system, and many of the poems have been carefully uncovered and are available for visitors to read in their original form. Most of the poems are written in the classical Chinese form. An example follows:

This place is called an island of immortals,
When, in fact, this mountain wilderness is a prison.
Once you see the open net, why throw yourself in?
It is only because of empty pockets I can do nothing else.[16]

In 1965, Congress passed a more liberal immigration law, relaxing quotas and ultimately allowing for increased numbers of Asians to immigrate. Since the relaxation of immigration laws in 1965, the number of immigrants from Asian and Pacific Island countries has grown dramatically. Recent Asian immigrants can be categorized into two groups—family reunification and refugees immigrating after the Vietnam War. Chinese immigrants seeking family reunification came from Hong Kong, China, and Macao. The refugee resettlement movement, which began in 1975, included many ethnic Chinese leaving Southeast Asian countries seeking refugee status in the United States. The circumstances of refugee resettlement were in stark contrast to other Asians who chose to leave their homeland to live in the United States. Chinese-speaking refugees not only found themselves in a foreign environment; they often arrived with little in terms of preparation.

Even more recent changes in the immigration pattern occurred with the return of Hong Kong from British control to the People's Republic of China in 1998. Many Chinese chose to leave Hong Kong for economic reasons, and immigrated to the United States, Canada, and other countries. The West Coast saw many wealthy immigrant Chinese moving to the Bay Area, Seattle, and Southern California. As investors, they acquired hotels, real estate, and banks throughout the United States and provided capital for start-up business ventures, many located in Silicon Valley. The recent immigration of wealthy Chinese marked a visible change in immigration demographics, as people of substantial economic means were coming to live in the United States.

However, the notion that Chinese are a "model minority"[17] is shown to be untrue when poverty, poor education, and crime are noted as important issues for Chinese Americans. Nevertheless, there are examples of spectacular achievement by Chinese. Two of the first 100 people on *Forbes*'s 1983 list of the richest Americans were Chinese: An Wang, the founder of Wang Laboratories, was fifth, worth about $1.6 billion, and Kyupin Philip Hwang, the 46-year-old head of TeleVideo Systems, was worth about $575 million.[18] Many more wealthy Chinese Americans have now joined these two businessmen.

FILIPINO-AMERICAN HISTORY

The history of Filipinos in the United States differs significantly from any other Asian-American ethnic group. As a result of U.S. control in the early twentieth century, Filipinos are considered nationals, a status not afforded other Asian Americans. In many other ways, however, Filipino Americans were treated as other Asian Americans.

The Philippine Islands are more than 7,000 in number and lie off the coast of Southeast Asia. In 1521, Ferdinand Magellan was the first European explorer to visit the islands. Spain acquired the islands in 1565, and Spanish colonial rule of the Philippines lasted 333 years. Most of the Filipinos, mainly Malay and Negrito, converted to Roman Catholicism while the islands were under Spanish control. A notable exception are the residents of a southern island, Mindanao, who are Muslim. The major languages indigenous to the Philippines are Visayan (Cebano and Ilongo), spoken in the central Philippines; Pilipino, the official language, spoken in central Luzon; and Ilocano, a language of northern Luzon. Most Filipino immigrants speak English in addition to Ilocano or Pilipino.

Under Spanish rule there was little motivation for the islanders to emigrate—due primarily to strong family ties, high cost and difficulty of transportation, satisfaction with the status quo, and the repressive rule of Spain. In 1898, the United States and Spain entered into the Spanish American War, a war that lasted only 90 days. As a result of the U.S. victory, the Philippines became a U.S. possession, as did Puerto Rico and Guam. The subsequent Philippine–American War resulted from the Philippine desire to be independent of colonial rule. More than 100,000 American soldiers were sent to the Philippines to suppress the insurrection. The era of U.S. occupation in the Philippines (1898–1946) did bring democratic government and public education to the islands, and the influence of public education widened the opportunities for native Filipinos.

The U.S.-sponsored *pensionados* program allowed chosen Filipino students to study in the United States. Thousands of young Filipinos came to study in colleges and universities, primarily in the Midwest. An estimated 14,000 Filipinos enrolled in American educational institutions between 1910 and 1938. Although many did not complete their studies, those who did typically returned to the Philippines after graduation. Those who stayed in the United States generally became a part of the manual labor force.

The dire need for workers on Hawaiian sugar plantations also prompted a surge of immigration in the early 1900s. Many Filipinos responded to the opportunity. The advent of steamship travel, the desire for further educational opportunities, and economic conditions in the Philippines added to the numbers of Filipino immigrants. The lure of the opportunity to make more money and find a better quality of life was irresistible for many, and Filipinos joined the Chinese in the new labor force. In a manner similar to many Japanese immigrants, the Filipino laborers in Hawaii worked in the sugarcane fields for low wages and under sparse living conditions. Until World War II, work in the United States for Filipinos meant primarily agricultural and unskilled labor work. The Tydings–McDuffie Act of 1934 halted the immigration of Filipino wives and children desiring to join their husbands and fathers in the United States. Ronald Takaki writes, "The Filipino exclusion law was even more severe than the restrictions on Chinese and Japanese immigration. The Chinese Exclusion Law of 1882 had allowed Chinese merchants to bring their wives to America, and the Japanese Exclusion Law of 1908 had permitted family members to join immigrants as well. . . . The only way for an [Filipino] immigrant man to see his family again was for him to go back to the Philippines."[19] This restriction resulted in increased intermarriage among Filipino men and non-Filipino women. "Californians discovered, to their horror, that the existing miscegenation statutes forbade marriages only between white persons and Negroes, mulattoes, and Mongolians. . . . So in 1933, California amended the statute to include 'members of the Malay race,' and within four years, Filipino–white marriages were also forbidden in Oregon, Nevada, and Washington."[20]

It was the 1965 Immigration Law that ended the old system of different quotas for each country of origin, and the new law allowed for 20,000 people from each Asian country to enter the United States annually, up to a total of 170,000 a year. Family members of U.S. citizens were not included in the totals and were free to enter the country. Between 1965 and 1984, 665,000 Filipinos immigrated to the United States, compared to 465,000 Chinese. Ferdinand Marcos's rule in the Philippines was a major factor in the increased numbers of Filipinos immigrating to the United States in the 1980s. In 1990, the total number of Filipino Americans identified through the Census was 1,419,711. The 2000 Census projects that Filipinos will be the largest Asian-American group by the early twenty-first century.

Currently, the population of Filipino Americans is the fastest-growing Asian population in the country. Many first-generation Filipino immigrants were highly educated in the Philippines. Filipino nurses have made up for the deficit of skilled and trained nurses in the United States and have become a mainstay of the American health care system. Similarly, Filipinos trained as doctors and teachers in the Philippines have made substantial contributions to those professions in the United States. However, the requirements of credentialing for these professions in the United States have caused many Philippine-licensed professionals to seek alternative vocational positions in the United States.

> The new immigrants face a variety of problems, including education, finances, unemployment, child guidance, and the elderly. Culture shock, racism, credentials and licensing are other issues. Perhaps the major problem of the Filipinos has been their lack of cohesion. There are island differences, different languages, ideological rifts, and subgroup cultures that separate the community.[21]

JAPANESE-AMERICAN HISTORY

Japanese immigration to the United States and Hawaii began in earnest in the 1880s some 30 years after Commodore Matthew C. Perry sailed into Japan with the purpose of opening trade relationships between the United States and Japan. Fearful that they would follow China in a capitulation to Western colonization, the Japanese government restored the Meiji Empire in 1868 and created a strong centralized government, which pushed for internal industrialization and heavy taxes to support this program. Farmers became victims of the heavy taxation, and many lost their farmlands while hunger spread throughout Japan.

At the same time, word of financial opportunities in Hawaii and the United States reached the struggling Japanese farmers. They, too, heard that wealth could be theirs as plantation workers in the fields of Hawaii. A plantation worker's salary could be six times more than their current wage; in three years a worker could save the equivalent of ten years of earnings in Japan. So, when the Japanese government announced 600 emigrant slots destined for the plantations in Hawaii, more than 28,000 applications were received. Between 1884 and 1924, 200,000 Japanese left for Hawaii, and another 180,000 headed for the U.S. mainland.

Plantation owners viewed their Asian workers as a commodity. These planters were also keenly aware of the nationalities of their workers. "The employers were systematically developing an ethnically diverse labor force in order to create divisions among their workers and reinforce management control."[22] Chinese laborers were thus pitted against the Japanese laborers, and after the Japanese workers demanded higher wages, Koreans were imported to replace the Japanese workforce. After the Spanish–American War, planters brought in laborers from the Philippines, now a U.S. territory. Into the 1900s, planters continued to maintain competition between the Japanese, Chinese, Korean, and Filipino workers. Ronald Takaki in *A Different Mirror* maintains that the Japanese workers were not passive victims of exploitation. "Contrary to the stereotype of the Japanese immigrants as quiet and accommodating, they aggressively protested against the unfair labor conditions and often engaged in strikes."[23] In juxtaposition to Takaki's statement, Harry H. L. Kitano writes in *Japanese Americans: Evolution of a Subculture,* "Japanese compare their strategy of adaptation to a small stream; like a stream they have followed the contours of the land, followed the lines of least resistance, avoided direct confrontation and developed at their own pace, always shaped by the external realities of the larger society."[24]

Japanese workers on the plantations organized into *blood unions*, determined by ethnic membership. In 1909, the Japanese union led a strike for higher wages and equal pay for equal work. They cited the higher wages paid to Portuguese workers for the same work. Several thousand Japanese laborers, representing 70 percent of the plantation labor force, participated in the strike, and they found substantial support from Japanese businesses throughout the islands. After the strike was broken, planters imported a large number of Filipino workers to weaken the Japanese union. Within 10 years the Japanese and Filipino workers were about equal in numbers and separately organized into their own blood unions. Workers from both nationalities began to realize that their successes needed to be based on interethnic working-class unity. In 1919, the two unions issued separate demands for higher wages and better benefits: 3,000 Filipino workers went on strike, along with 5,000 Japanese laborers, amounting to 77 percent of Oahu's entire plantation workforce. In the interest of encouraging multiethnic camaraderie, the Japanese Federation of Labor formed the Hawaii Laborers' Association, which insisted that workers, regardless of ethnicity, should cooperate in the struggle for a higher standard of living. This event marked the first major interethnic working-class struggle in Hawaii.

Living arrangements in the plantation camps were organized around nationality and class hierarchy. The Japanese established Buddhist temples and Japanese-language schools. Traditional Japanese holidays were celebrated within the camps. Public education for workers' children brought the different nationalities together, and interethnic sharing was not uncommon. The Japanese children traded sushi for fish from their Hawaiian school-mates, who swapped lunch items with Portuguese children in return for peanut butter and jelly sandwiches. Food sharing was not the only inter-ethnic activity. The planters wanted the laborers to learn a functional spoken English, so that they could give commands to their multilingual workforce. Over the years, "pidgin English"—a simple English incorporating Chinese, Japanese, Hawaiian, and Portuguese phrases—evolved, and is still com-monly used in Hawaii today.

The multiethnic existence in Hawaii was nothing like the experience Japanese immigrants were finding on the West Coast. Japanese were only 2 percent of the California population in 1920. Many felt isolated, and were victims of racial hostilities perpetrated by white workers. Farmers by back-ground, the Japanese immigrants dreamed of owning farmland. To obtain land, the Japanese used four methods—contract, share, lease, and owner-ship.[25] As early as 1910, Japanese farmers produced 70 percent of Califor-nia's strawberry crop, and by 1940 they grew 95 percent of the fresh snap beans, 67 percent of the tomatoes, 95 percent of the celery, 44 percent of onions, and 40 percent of the green peas. In 1900, Japanese farmers in Cal-ifornia worked or owned 4,698 acres. Five years later, the acreage grew to 61,858, and then to 458,056 acres by 1920.

Many Japanese farmers believed that their agricultural successes would help them become accepted in American society. Various strategies to for-ward this premise were thwarted. In 1908, the U.S. government pressured Japan to prohibit further emigration of Japanese laborers. Soon after, Cal-ifornia, along with other states, passed legislation prohibiting Japanese immigrants from owning and leasing land. In 1924, Congress enacted a general immigration law that included a phrase denying entry of "aliens in-eligible to citizenship," the code phrase for the Japanese.[26]

Excluded by law from owning land and obtaining citizenship, first-generation Japanese immigrants looked to their U.S.-born children to re-alize their dreams. This generation, the *Nisei*, constituted 27 percent of the mainland Japanese population in the United States in 1920 and 63 percent in 1940. Citizenship and education did not immunize the *Nisei* from racial discrimination. Additionally, many of the second generation came of age during the Depression, a time of massive unemployment throughout the country. In his essay "The Rising Son of the Rising Sun," Aiji Tashiro offered this explanation for the exclusion of Japanese Americans, maintaining that the problems of the *Nisei* went far beyond jobs; it was profoundly cultural, involving who was American. "The Jablioskis, Idovitches, and Johannsmanns streaming over from Europe," he pointed out, "[were able] to slip unobtrusively into the clothes of 'dyed-in-the-wool' Americans by the simple expedient of dropping their guttural speech and changing their names to Jones, Brown, or Smith." Tashiro knew it would make no difference for him if he changed his name to Taylor. He spoke English fluently and had even adopted American slang, dress, and mannerisms. But outwardly, he "possessed the marked characteristics of the race."[27] Like other immigrants, many Japanese Americans retained affection and affinity for their homeland. Although they longed for acceptance in the United States, they continued to hold fast to the traditions and cultures learned as Japanese in Japan. The hope, however, of wanting to be both Japanese and American was violently halted on December 7, 1941.

Much has been written about the incarceration of Japanese Americans during World War II. In her book *Asian Americans: An Interpretive History,* author Sucheng Chan vividly describes the events leading up to and including the period of internment of Japanese Americans. "Compared to the other groups of Asian Americans, the Japanese American wartime experience was traumatic."[28] Right after the United States declared war on Japan, December 7, 1941, more than 40,000 Japanese living on the Pacific Coast—along with their 70,000 American-born children—were moved to relocation camps. The term *relocation camps* refers to the isolated inland centers used to house those of Japanese ancestry from 1941 to 1944.

Government officials and others acting as private advisors told President Roosevelt, "Unlike individuals of German and Italian ancestry, who could be individually recognized and kept under watch, the Occidental eye cannot rapidly distinguish one Japanese resident from another." According to this logic, because of Euro-American failings, it might be necessary to evacuate en masse persons of Japanese ancestry.[29]

On February 19, 1942, President Franklin D. Roosevelt signed Executive Order 9066, authorizing the secretary of war to designate military areas "from which any and all persons may be excluded as deemed necessary or desirable." As a result of this order, local and state governments moved to enforce EO 9066. Los Angeles County fired all clerks of Japanese ancestry, following the California State Board dictate that all descendants of enemy aliens would be barred from civil service positions, but Los Angeles County enforced that regulation only against Japanese Americans.[30]

With no more than a week to sell, store, or dispose of the belongings they had to leave behind, the Japanese sustained great losses of personal property. The powerful Japanese American Citizens' League (JACL) urged everyone to cooperate, and there was little resistance to the mandatory relocation. Japanese living in Hawaii were excluded from relocation due to the potential economic effects and the fact that transporting so many Japanese from Hawaii to the mainland camps would have tied up too many ships needed during the war.

The effects on families living in the camps were tremendous. The *Issei* generation (first generation) lost much of their power, and the strong familial ties were strained as a result of communal living. Families no longer ate meals together; the older youth spent more time with each other and less with their families. Yet traditional Japanese customs were still celebrated. Some of those who lived in the camps have remarked that the relocation camps actually promoted Japanese identification and slowed the American assimilation process.

At the end of the war, August 1945, 44,000 persons of Japanese ancestry were still in camps, fearful of the outside world.

> Those who still owned property found their houses dilapidated and vandalized, their farms, orchards, and vineyards choked with weeds, their personal belongings stolen or destroyed. *Issei* men, now in their sixties, found work as gardeners and janitors; their wives toiled as domestic servants. Despite such harsh circumstances, these old pioneers picked up the broken pieces of their lives and carried on as their children struggled to join postwar mainstream America.[31]

In 1976, more than 30 years after the end of the war, President Gerald Ford rescinded Executive Order 9066.

KOREAN-AMERICAN HISTORY

Nineteenth- and twentieth-century history of Korea is marked with significant periods of occupation. At that time the Meiji government of Japan gained a balance of trade with China regarding Korea, followed by the Sino–Japanese War (1894–1895), a war won by the Japanese. In 1945, Korea was liberated from Japan, and an independent government was established.

As a result of internal conflict created by the partition of North and South Korea at the close of World War II, the United Nations instituted a police action to monitor the North Korean/Chinese push into South Korea. General Douglas MacArthur was in charge of the United Nations forces, and the United States sent many (if not the majority) of troops into Korea during the Korean Conflict, which ended in 1953. Following the conflict, Korea was divided into two countries—Communist-led North Korea and the Republic of South Korea. Divided at the 38th parallel, the separation of the two Koreas is still in place. Families were separated, and reunification efforts were not productive until limited family reunification efforts began in 2000.

There is documentation of Korean political exiles living in the United States as early as 1885, and a small number of Koreans moved to Hawaii to work on the sugar plantations in the early 1900s. The close of the Korean Conflict in 1953 also sent a wave of Korean immigrants to America. In 1970, the Census reported 70,000 Korean residents in the United States. In 1980, there were 357,393, followed by 789,849 in 1990. Today, Koreans represent one of the larger Asian immigrant populations in the United States.

The large numbers of Chinese, Japanese, and Filipinos who immigrated to the United States preceded the Koreans by a century. It was not until the Immigration Act of 1965 that the numbers of Korean Americans grew exponentially. In contrast to the multiple generations of Chinese, Japanese, and Filipino Americans now living in the United States, many Korean-American families still have first-generation heads of households.

Another point of contrast between Korean-American immigration patterns and those of earlier Asian-American immigrants is that Koreans have arrived in the United States in family units. As such, family issues around language, culture, and customs have had an immediate effect on the family unit. In *Asian Americans: Emerging Minorities*, Harry H. L. Kitano writes:

> The following structure is not unusual in the current community: father and mother, born in Korea, following traditional, old-country patterns; eldest daughter, arriving with a Korean high school diploma, being more Korean than American; second daughter finishing high school in America and having more American than Korean ways; and youngest son, thoroughly American. But acculturation is seldom linear and predictable; parents may selectively adopt American ways, and the almost completely Americanized youngster may hold on to some old-country values. The

mixture, referred to as culture conflict, can cause considerable discord within families.[32]

SOUTH ASIAN–AMERICAN HISTORY

In 1980, the Census counted Asian Indians as a census category that included those of Indian and Pakistani background. The term *South Asian* additionally includes Sri Lankans, Bangladeshis, Pakistanis, and other Asians coming from the entire South Asia region. There are large numbers of South Asians living in Fiji where they play an important role in shaping the current political reality of the region. The largest numbers of immigrants from South Asia come from India and Pakistan, which will be the major focus in this chapter. The Asian Indian Census category replaced East Indian in 1980, and has become a significant group within the broader Asian American category. *The South Asian Americans*, written by Karen Leonard, reports, "Asian Indians in the 1990s moved from fourth largest of the Asian American groups to third largest (LEAP 1993), and they stand out among the Asian Americans for their balanced gender ratio."[33] The South Asian region is large, populous, and diverse in many ways—religion, politics, language, and economics are major components of the regional diversity. It is as erroneous to consider all South Asians to be similar as it would be to say the same for all Europeans.

Religion is deeply interwoven into South Asian culture, and many South Asians are Muslim or practice Hinduism, which is a number of diverse religious beliefs and practices grouped together, including Sikhs and Jains. A perpetual conflict between Hindus and Muslims has challenged India for years. Many Muslims left India for Pakistan, but about 13 percent of India's current population is Muslim. Heightened militancy in Kashmir, where Hindu communalism grows, poses a constant threat of war between Pakistan and India.

Language is another of the dividing factors in Indian society. Hindi is India's official national language, and English is a second language, taught in schools. Under a "three-language formula," students are now required to learn Hindi, English, and their mother tongue—usually the state language.[34] There has been some renewed emphasis on the significance of speaking one's local language, but English is still highly valued by the educated and elite.

The early immigrants to the United States came from the province of Punjab. These men had agricultural backgrounds and came to California looking for similar work with better economic conditions. The number of Punjabi immigrants was not as significant as the Chinese, Japanese, and Filipino immigrants who preceded them, and the various laws enacted to bar Asian immigrants had its effect on the Punjabis. The Punjabi immigrants fit into California's regional economies on many levels. They helped develop rice cultivation in Northern California, grew grapes and other crops in central California, and moved to the southern Imperial Valley region to establish cotton growing. Many Punjabis began to move up the agricultural ladder despite legal discrimination and prejudice based on ethnic stereotyping.[35]

These early pioneers, the Punjabi, were mostly Sikh. The remaining 10 to 12 percent were Muslim, although many Americans erroneously referred to them as Hindus. The route of passage to America frequently came by way of Canada. As Canada became more restrictive on its admission requirements, the Punjabi emigrants moved south to the United States. By the 1920s there were Punjabi communities in California, Washington, Texas, Arizona, New Mexico, Utah, and Colorado.[36]

Later events had increased effects on South Asian emigration to the United States. In 1946, the Luce-Celler bill allowed citizenship through naturalization and the use of the Indian quota of 105 immigrants per year set by the 1924 National Origins Quota Act. Then in 1947, both India and Pakistan became independent countries. It was, however, the Immigration and Naturalization Act of 1965 that fueled the greatest migration of Asians, including South Asians.

"South Asians coming to the United States are responding not only to changing U.S. immigration policies but to the global political economy. The structuring of international capitalism, wage differences between countries, political instability in South Asia, family reunification—all these and other factors have produced levels of international migration unprecedented in history. The South Asian countries do not restrict emigration, perhaps because of their continuing problems of unemployment or because of the welcome infusion of foreign-currency remittances. . . . The brain drain is of real concern—it is estimated that one-fourth of the graduates of Indian medical colleges come to the United States annually—but has not led to any significant restrictions on the migration of highly skilled professionals to the United States."[37]

Recent South Asian immigrants have come from all over South Asia, not just India and Pakistan. All the languages spoken on the Indian subcontinent are represented in the United States. In 1980, the "most numerous language groups in the New York area were Gujaratis (34 percent), Hindi (20 percent), and Dravidian speakers (24 percent)"[38] South Asians, for the most part, are doing well in the United States. According to Leonard, those born in India have the highest median household income, family income, and per capita income of any foreign-born group in the 1990 Census. A study of foreign-born professionals shows foreign-born Indians to be the highest paid, with an annual median income of $40,625.[39] A 1991 survey of five Asian-American groups showed that Indians held the most IRAs (individual retirement accounts) and stocks and were the most highly educated.[40] Immigrants born in India also constitute the highest percentage with a bachelor's degree or higher and the highest percentage in managerial and professional fields.[41] In 1980, of the approximately 400,000 Indians in the United States, 11 percent of the men and 8 percent of the women were physicians and another 7 percent of the women were nurses. Leonard reports that one recent estimate put Indian doctors at more than 20,000, or nearly 4 percent of the nation's total, the largest ethnic body of doctors in the United States. Another large professional group is that of Indian computer professionals. Indian engineers are the second largest foreign-born group of engineers, after Chinese, and Indian business students outnumber any other international group.[42]

There is less information available on the smaller numbers of South Asian immigrants from Nepal and the Parsis from India and Pakistan, Sri Lankans, and Afghan refugees. The Bangladeshi are a recent immigrant community, representing both elite professionals as well as younger men and women with less education and economic standing. Most Bangladeshis live in New York, California, and Florida.

CULTURAL GIVING PATTERNS

Specific and sometimes unique traditions of giving and sharing are highlighted in this chapter. All cultures have different constructs of reality, which include beliefs and practices relating to philanthropy. Certain traditions like gift giving, financial assistance, and recognition of key events are expressed uniquely from culture to culture. As an example, the Chinese red egg and ginger banquet celebrates the one-month birthday of an infant. The significance of one month is historical and practical. Infant mortality rates were historically higher, and waiting for a month allowed for this factor. Guests to a red egg and ginger banquet in the United States are treated to a traditional Chinese dinner banquet. Plates of red eggs and ginger are placed at each table to symbolize the health of the child and future fertility of the mother. Guests are expected to give gifts, *laih sih*, wrapped in "lucky" red envelopes to the parents as they greet their guests (this is traditionally cash). A red egg and ginger party is similar to a Western birthday party, but unique in the aspects and traditions surrounding the event. It is not unusual for guests to make contributions to their favorite causes in honor of the baby's birth. In the Bay Area, organizations such as Self Help for the Elderly, On Lok, benevolent associations, and Chinese Hospital in San Francisco are often the beneficiaries of the contributions. The number of guests at the event is symbolic of the stature of the party's hosts.

It is not to suggest that gifts given to family and close friends are philanthropic giving. The authors of *Philanthropy in Communities of Color* found that "What interests students of philanthropy is the giving of goods and services outside the nuclear family without any apparent expectation of economic return."[43] The authors go on to suggest that the study of philanthropic motivation is fundamentally reduced to the question, "Why do individuals give money, goods, and services to others?" Culture and tradition create the differences in response to this question. However, what is the significance of the similarities in philanthropic behavior?

TRADITIONS OF GIVING AND SHARING AMONG CHINESE AMERICANS

An understanding of the evolution of the traditional customs of giving and sharing among Chinese Americans requires knowledge of the kinship system of Chinese Americans. Two primary systems are clans and *hui kuan*.

Clans

Traditional clans in the Chinatowns of the United States are derived from their origins in the lineage communities in southeastern China, home to the majority of early Chinese immigrants. Once in the United States, clanship was associated with surname. Overseas clans served to remind the immigrants of their ties to family and villages in China, but they also organized around type of business or trade. Later generations of Chinese Americans have moved away from the clanship system, choosing not to join the traditional organization serving their clan or surname, forming instead their own nuclear families.

Another type of association developed, similar to clans in function, but structured around the dialect spoken. *Hui kuan* served originally to provide financial aid and general support for recent immigrants. Over time, many of these associations arbitrated and mediated various differences between members and with the outside community. The power of *hui kuan* is evidenced by the Chinese Consolidated Benevolent Association, commonly known as the Chinese Six Companies, in San Francisco, which acted as "an unofficial supragovernment exercising overall community domination inside Chinatown and as the most important voice of the Chinese speaking to American officials."[44]

First-generation Chinese communities in the United States have enjoyed a degree of self-government far beyond that of other ethnic groups. This is partly due to the long period of electoral irrelevance to U.S. politics. Denied naturalization for nearly a century, the Chinese organized an infrastructure for benevolent, protective, and governmental needs.

Traditional Customs Involving Giving and Sharing

Philanthropy in Communities of Color provides a detailed description of traditional customs involving giving and sharing. Those traditions are summarized here.

- *Yeuhng ga* is based on shared responsibility to care for families. This tradition in America is traced to immigrant men sending money back to family and the home village in China.

- *Heung yajh gam* and *chil sinh gam* are similar to *yeuhng ga*, but the monies are designated to build schools in the donor's village in China. This tradition is still practiced today, with the money being used to provide for schools and education for the young.

- *Bong* refers to giving financial and material aid to new immigrants to the United States. Recipients are generally, but not always, members of the donor's family or immediate community.

- *Daaih sang yaht* is a celebration of an elder's 50th birthday and can be celebrated every 10 years following. As in the red egg and ginger celebrations, gifts of *laih sih* are offered to the guest of honor at the dinner banquet. Formal public donations to organizations are often made at these events. *Note*: The 50th birthday is chosen as the first significant milestone for aging, as the word for the number four sounds like *death* in Chinese.)

- *Baai nihn* is practiced during the celebration of the Lunar New Year. It involves the exchange of food while visiting family and friends during the New Year.

- *Jaahk faan* is the custom of giving something back (generally a gift of food) to those who visited to *baai nihn* (see above). Reciprocity is central to the acts of giving and sharing within the Chinese-American community.

Deaths and funerals also include traditional acts of giving and sharing. Immediate and extended family members will often give money to the family of the deceased to help defray funeral costs. Such gifts are unsolicited and are reciprocal. Guests at the funeral receive a coin wrapped in white paper with a piece of wrapped candy as they enter the church or funeral site. White represents death, and the candy is intended to take away the bitterness of the event. It is the responsibility of the family of the deceased to wrap the coins and distribute them to the guests. When leaving the cemetery, guests receive another gift of money (ranging from a quarter to a dollar) wrapped in a traditional red envelope, *laih sih*. The purpose of this gift is to thank the guest for attending the service. Finally, at the banquet following the dinner, guests will often make donations in honor of the deceased to public organizations like the Heart Association, Cancer Society, hospital, health organization, or Salvation Army. Friends and family will often send memorial contributions in honor of the deceased instead of sympathy cards or flowers to the family of the deceased.

Exhibit 2-4 summarizes traditions of sharing and giving practiced by Chinese Americans.

TRADITIONS OF GIVING AND SHARING AMONG FILIPINO AMERICANS

Filipino charitable traditions are based on familial support and the sense of responsibility for those in the extended family. Many years of Spanish rule

EXHIBIT 2-4   CHINESE GIVING—TERMS AND DEFINITIONS

Baai nihn	Translates to paying homage to the year. Term refers to visiting family and friends during the New Year celebration and bringing gifts of food.
Bong	Gifts of financial aid and material support to new immigrants.
Bong sau bob hau	Volunteering time to help someone else.
Chan ji	Money and other gifts given upon arrival at a destination.
Chih sihn gam	A donation or gift of money given to organizations and family associations.
Daaih saang yaht	Celebration of major birthdays (50th and above). *Daaih saang yaht* is never celebrated on the 40th birthday, because saying the number four in Chinese sounds like the word for *death*.
Fui gam; Baahk gam	Gift of money given by extended family to immediate family to defray funeral costs.
Heung yauh gam; Chih-shin gam	Money sent back to hometown or village by those now living in the United States.
Jaahk faan	Custom of giving something back, usually food, to visitors who have come to *baai nihn*.
Jam chah laih sih	Tea ceremony honoring newlyweds when they pay respects to their elders and those of higher status. Bride will pour tea for guests and very generous gifts will be given to the couple. At one time, heirloom jewelry was given. Now gifts of new jewelry of gold and jade are common. Other gifts include watches and new clothes for groom, money for down payment on a house, and furniture for the new house.
Laih sih	Gift of money in red envelope, given on special occasions like New Year, for birth of baby, wedding.
Laih sih (funeral)	White *laih sih* is given when one enters the funeral service; red *laih sih* is given on departure. White is the color of death, and red symbolizes hope and good fortune. These *laih sih* are generally small amounts of money wrapped in the appropriate color envelope and given to all guests at the funeral.
Mun yuht laih si	Specific gift of money in red envelope given to newborn at red egg and ginger party.
Sai chahn	Dinner party given when a traveler returns from a trip.
San nihn laih sih	Specific gift of money in red envelope given to unmarried children by married adults during lunar New Year.
Sinn tohng	Family association; members will contribute annually to support scholarship programs and social activities.
Sung hanhg	Party for someone who is moving away or taking a long trip.
Taam behng	Visiting the sick and bringing food to family and friends; chicken and fruit are most common gifts.
Wui	Rotating credit association; each member makes small monthly payments, and the "pot" is disbursed to a different member each month. Trust plays a major role in *wui*.
Yeung ga	Practice of shared responsibility for maintenance of a family.

Source: Bradford Smith et al., *Philanthropy in Communities of Color* (Indianapolis: Indiana University Press, 2000), pp. 106–120.

and the dominant influence of the Catholic Church have also added to the traditions of giving and sharing among Filipinos. Godparents, as an example, are an important component of the extended family in Filipino culture. *Compadrazgo* is the ritual kinship system that includes a *ninong,* or godfather, *ninang,* or godmother—collectively called *compadres,* or godparents—in the Filipino family structure. *Compadres* will often be successful persons who are expected to provide financial support for their godchild.

Filipino Americans send a large amount of money or remittances back to the Philippines annually. The money is often sent to support family members still living in the Philippines, but also includes money directed to helping a neighborhood or town to build or support hospitals, schools, and other public institutions. One estimate is that $8 billion was remitted by Filipino Americans in 1998.[45] There is no accurate way to arrive at a precise figure, but the total remittances sent to the Philippines make an appreciable difference in the economy of the Philippines. In 1984, U.S. Filipino contract workers alone (based worldwide) sent $625 million back to the Philippines. That amount equaled 11.6 percent of merchandise exports from the Philippines, 2.2 percent of the gross national product.[46] Another 1984 study of physicians emigrating from the Philippines showed that the country gained more in income from the Filipino doctors based in the United States than the projected loss of their income if they had remained in the Philippines.

So strong are familial ties in the Filipino community that external community support is sometimes seen as nonessential. Extended families prefer to live close to one another in the Philippines and in the United States, and they spend much of their free time with each other. Immigrants from a certain town or region of the Philippines will congregate together and provide one another with a support structure. Financial support and temporary housing and other essential needs for the newly arrived is routinely made available to kin arriving in the United States.

Filipino terms expressing charitable acts include:

- *Pasalubong*—gifts of money and goods given on arrival.
- *Tulong*—help or aid given to those in need. This is practiced within the immediate and extended family generally when someone is sick or has a special need. It is not always a gift of money—it can be food or lodging offered to those who have recently arrived from the Philippines.

- *Patimkim*—custom where godparents give gifts of jewelry, clothing, money, or food on the occasion of a baptism or wedding.
- *Pahinaw*—a gift of money for a newborn infant, generally given when the infant visits the godparents.
- *Pabandeha*—reciprocal gift from infant's parents in appreciation for acts of generosity from the godparents.
- *Abuloy*—general religious donations including memorial gifts made in memory of the deceased. Also refers to gifts given to the immediate family of the deceased to defray funeral costs.

These examples demonstrate the highly social nature of giving within the culture. Many Filipino-American groups prefer to hold a special event—a dinner or dance to raise money—rather than to simply give a donation. Reciprocity and recognition are extremely important. This public side of the charitable behavior of Filipino Americans is balanced by the deep loyalty among family, where sharing of resources is expected and freely given.

Because of Spain's control of the Philippines for more than 300 years, the relationship of Filipinos to the Catholic Church is strong. It is estimated that 75 percent of the Filipino Americans living in the greater Los Angeles area are Roman Catholic. Filipino Americans also have an affinity borne from common background with Mexican Americans. Many Filipino names are Spanish in origin, and both cultures embrace the same religious practices of the Catholic Church. There is a similarity in the structure of giving and sharing patterns of Filipino Americans and Mexican Americans. Filipino giving and sharing patterns are summarized in Exhibit 2-5.

TRADITIONS OF GIVING AND SHARING AMONG JAPANESE AMERICANS

The concept of giving and sharing for Japanese Americans can be traced to the influence of the Buddhist and Confucian religions in Japan. Compassion is a core element in Buddhist beliefs, which is expressed in modern Japanese-American philanthropic behavior. The authors of *Philanthropy in Communities of Color* interviewed 40 members of the Japanese community in the San Francisco Bay Area about their philanthropic customs and behavior. Their interviews revealed a strong commitment to family and community as recipients of giving. The intent of giving is generally motivated by the

EXHIBIT 2-5	FILIPINO GIVING—TERMS AND DEFINITIONS
Abuloy	General religious donations; donations to family of someone who has died, typically to defray funeral costs.
Balikbayan	Return to hometown or country.
Barangay	Villages and neighborhoods in the Philippines. Filipinos practice support to those living in their *barangay* or to those who have immigrated from the same *barangay*.
Pabandeha	Reciprocal gift from infant's parents to godparents as appreciation.
Pabuisit	Goodwill money given to visiting infant.
Pahinaw	Custom where godparents throw coins to guests at weddings.
Pakimkim	Custom where godparents give jewelry, clothing, money, or food at baptisms and weddings.
Pasulubong	Gifts of money and goods given on arrival.
Sustento	Allowance or support.
Tulong	Help given to those in need, which is practiced within the family and nuclear community (generally only when someone is in need or sick). Not always a gift of money; can be food or lodging given to relatives who have just arrived from the Philippines.

Source: *Philanthropy in Communities of Color*, pp. 88–104.

desire for harmony, as opposed to giving to help the underprivileged. Another defining aspect for Japanese-American philanthropy can be traced back to the internment of Japanese Americans in World War II. At that time, the first generation of Japanese Americans were wage-earning adults raising the second generation, the first to be born in the United States. Life in the relocation camps redefined roles within the family. No longer did families spend much time together and eat meals together. Rather, group activities and challenges arising from the lack of familial privacy in the camps created gaps between the generations.

The solidarity of the nuclear family was stressed by physical and emotional differences. The older generation struggled to maintain dignity and head-of-household status while the younger generation was preoccupied with education and peer-level activities in an unfamiliar and strained environment. The durability of Japanese-based traditions was tested during this difficult period. Harry H. L. Kitano and Roger Daniels describe the strength of Japanese-bound tradition during incarceration in the relocation camps. "Many of the norms and values that were a part of the Issei culture continued to be carried on by the Nisei. Concepts such as *amae* (the need to be loved), *enryo* (deferential behavior), and *shi-ka-ta-ga-nai* (acceptance, literally 'it can't be helped'), remained familiar."[47]

A sense of duty to care for elders did not diminish. Third-generation Japanese Americans *(Sansei)* still place high value on the need to respect and care for their elders, which ties back to the strong sense of support for kin and community within the Japanese-American population. Again, in *Philanthropy in Communities of Color*, the authors remark, "care of the elderly is not considered charitable activity by Japanese but is more of a duty reflecting Confucian, Buddhist, and other traditional values."[48]

Japanese Americans interviewed also indicated that there is an expectation for social benefit for their giving of time and/or money. The benefits of interaction with others is a significant benefit in volunteering, but there is also a strong need for seeing results of their involvement, or "at least . . . a party after the work is done."[49]

Traditions and customs surrounding special occasions are also honored within the Japanese-American community. The Lunar New Year is a significant holiday for Japanese and, as with other Asian cultures, there are gift-giving traditions associated with this event. Popular traditions include:

- *Nenshimarwari*—the New Year walk-around or visitations to elders and family.
- *Otoshidama*—New Year's gift of money to unmarried children. This gift is presented in a white envelope with a red band on it, all representing good luck, and given in a spirit of generosity.

Traditional gifts of money are made as a gesture of sympathy, or when a person is ill.

- *Omimai* is a gift of money in sympathy. It can also include a monetary gift to one who is ill. Buddhist in origin, this act demonstrates caring for and helping others. *Omimai* today also includes donations made to those who are victims of fire, floods, earthquakes, and other natural disasters.
- *Koden*—gifts of money for the immediate family members of the deceased. This gift is intended to help pay funeral costs or to establish

appropriate memorials honoring the deceased. *Koden* is typically received at the funeral, and the money is given in a special white envelope with yellow and white bands on it. These gifts are immediately recorded at a table set up at the memorial or funeral service, and the exact amount of the gift is recorded along with the name and address of the donor. "Not giving *koden* would result in a loss of face."[50] *Koden* can be given as a contribution to a charitable organization in honor of the deceased, and the gifts can be significant.

> When my mother died, it was the biggest funeral that there had ever been. There were seven Buddhist priests that officiated. There was an incredible amount of *koden* given . . . Dad donated back to the community: $10,000 to JACL, $10,000 to Hamilton Senior Center, $10,000 to Japanese Cultural and Community Center of Northern California, $10,000 to Kimochi, and $10,000 to the church, etc., [plus] . . . something for the living.[51]

In my own experience, a Japanese-American colleague of significant stature in the nonprofit community of San Francisco died a few years ago, and his memorial service was held in a large church. Hundreds of people—family, friends, and professional colleagues—attended, including a former governor and many city and state officials. A table was set up in the back of the church, and I noted that most of the Japanese-American guests were signing a book and leaving cards on the table. Very few non-Japanese seemed to be participating. Of course, this was the table to accept *koden*, and unfortunately, not enough of the non-Japanese were aware of the tradition, so they were not prepared to participate.

- *Orei*—a tangible form of thanks for help given. It has particular meaning for thanking those who attend a funeral. Similar to a Chinese custom, attendees at a funeral are often invited to a banquet immediately following the funeral to thank those who attended. *Orei* can also be expressed more simply, with a canister of tea or a book of stamps.

Additional traditions of giving and sharing revolve around the church, the term used by those interviewed by Smith et al. to refer to their Buddhist temples.

- *Ofuse*—an offering for the church/temple.
- *Gobutuzen*—funeral donation directed to the temple.

- *Goreizen*—family offering of food or incense for the soul of the deceased.

Japanese-American traditions of giving and sharing are summarized in Exhibit 2-6.

EXHIBIT 2-6   JAPANESE GIVING—TERMS AND DEFINITIONS

Boluntary	Voluntary (derivative).
Gobutsuzen	Funeral donation to the temple.
Goreizsen	Family offering in memory of deceased, usually food or incense.
Hodokoshi	Charity.
Kenjinkai	Early prefecture associations in Japan. In the United States, *kenjinkai* provided assistance to newly arrived immigrants in the form of food and lodging, sponsored fundraising activities to help new arrivals get settled in America, and also assisted with weddings and funerals. Also assisted in legal preparation to establish residency.
	Issei continued the practice of sending contributions back to Japan for major disasters there. Following the 1906 and 1989 earthquakes in the San Francisco Bay Area, Japanese nationals gave more money than any other country for 1906 relief efforts and more than $10 million (primarily in individual gifts) for 1989 relief efforts. (*Note*: These gifts were sent for general use, not directed to Japanese Americans.)
Kifu	Donation, endowment.
Koden	Giving money to immediate family of deceased. This is a Buddhist practice of compassion. Monies can be used to help pay for funeral costs or to establish a memorial in the name of the deceased. Gift is generally presented at the funeral or memorial service in a special white envelope with black and white bands. There is a table near the entrance, and a designated person records the name and amount of the gift. *Koden* is a reciprocal practice.
Nenshimarwari	Visiting elders and family at New Year.
Nihonjin Kai	Japanese people association.
Ofuse	Offering at temple.
Ominmai	Gift of money in sympathy, generally when someone is ill. Can be used to pay medical costs or provide general support while one cannot work. Also refers to gifts to those who are victims of natural disasters.
Omiyage	A souvenir or gift given by traveler to host or hostess; can also refer to any gift giving.
Orei	Monetary or material expression of thanks for *koden*.
Otoshidama	Gift of money to children at New Year, presented by an elder to child in white envelope with red band on it.
Senbetsu	Gift given when someone is moving away or going on a trip.

Source: *Philanthropy in Communities of Color*, pp. 121–134.

TRADITIONS OF GIVING AND SHARING AMONG KOREAN AMERICANS

It has been said that there is no country of comparable significance about which so many Westerners know so little. For hundreds of years, the Koreans sought safety in isolation, developing unique customs and a distinctive way of life. But for much of its modern history Korea was violently occupied by Japan, Russia, China, and the United States. Any review of the personality and characteristics of Koreans must be seen in light of these occurrences.

Koreans speak one language—Korean—which is understood throughout the country in spite of regional dialects. The written form of the language utilizes Chinese characters in some formal settings, while at the same time employing the phonetic Korean alphabet. There are also structural similarities between Japanese and Korean in the spoken Korean language. Linguists would classify the Korean language in the same grouping as Japanese. Language is just one of the areas where Koreans have been forced to modify their customs and behavior due to long periods of forced occupation.

It can also be noted that Koreans enjoyed their periods of isolation from the rest of the world. Probably the last 50 years have done more to open Korea to the rest of the world than at any other time in its history. The Immigration Act of 1965 also allowed the opportunity for greater numbers of Koreans to immigrate to the United States. Korean Americans, therefore, are fairly new arrivals compared to those from China, Japan, and the Philippines. Many Korean-American families have first-generation parents, with children becoming acculturated more quickly than the parents.

This brief background gives us some understanding of the traditions of Korean Americans. Like other Asians, loyalty to immediate and extended family is a priority, and this value extends to patterns of giving and sharing. As recently as the late 1960s, Koreans lived in large urban centers like Seoul, Pusan, and Taegu, while a village system continued to flourish in rural Korea. The village structure is family/community centered and self-sufficient.

One of the earliest forms of Korean-American mutual assistance was the formation of membership associations, where dues were assessed and the funds were made available to members in need, as well as to support the ongoing struggle for Korean independence in the period leading up to 1945.

Christianity played an important role in the development of modern Korea, and Koreans were eager to embrace Christianity. Churches have been integral to the development of schools, social services, and political and economic matters in Korea. It was through these churches that a large part of the money to support Korea's independence movement was raised. Second only to the Philippines, Korea is the Asian nation with the largest population of Christians: 25 percent of Koreans profess Christianity. About 70 percent of these Korean Americans are Protestant.

Remittances to Korea to support elderly parents and extended family are referred to as *sang hwal bi*. The actual amount of money remitted to Korea is not documented, but remittance is widely practiced by both first- and second-generation Korean Americans.

Gifts of money and sharing of goods is expressed in other ways in Korean society.

- *Yong don* and *po jo bi*—translates as helping money. In the United States, many older Koreans live with their children, and helping money supplements the basic living needs of the elderly.

- *Chee won bi* and *gi bu kum*—money used on special occasions to help others.

- *Mo kum*—refers to the collecting of money to help on extraordinary occasions like disasters, or it can also refer to pooled collections raised to help those in need.

- *Paek il*—literally translates as 101 days, and refers to the celebration of a newborn. Money and gifts are given to the baby on this occasion.

- *Dol*—Baby's first birthday, another cause for family celebration.

- *Hwan gap jan chi*—60th birthday party. A very significant event. Historically, reaching the age of 60 was quite an achievement, and the event was and is celebrated by family and friends.

- *Ye dan*—gift given from bride's family to groom's family prior to the wedding.

- *Jul gap*—gift of money from groom's parents to newlyweds.

- *Ip sa* or *chui jik*—gifts of money or clothing given to graduate to prepare them for their first job. Money typically used to buy a suit or other suitable item of clothing.

- *Che sa*—the ritual of honoring ancestors on the anniversary of their deaths. It is the son's responsibility to honor the memory of his ancestors, and *che sa* is celebrated for up to five generations.

- *Hun kum*—money given to church or temple.

Finally, there is the tradition of a rotating credit association used extensively in the United States to support Korean Americans in their business ventures. This tradition allows for a Korean-American member of a *kye* to acquire necessary capital to start a small business. During the Los Angeles riots that affected Koreans and African Americans, *kye* provided emergency support to Korean-American merchants who sustained loss of income and inventory.

A summary of Korean-American traditions of giving and sharing is shown in Exhibit 2-7.

EXHIBIT 2-7	KOREAN GIVING—TERMS AND DEFINITIONS
Chee won kum	Interest-free "loans" given to friends and family. Considered to be a social courtesy.
Che sa	Annual tradition of preparing food for ancestor(s) on anniversary of their deaths. Practiced for five generations. This practice demonstrates the filial responsibility of children to their elders.
Chin mok hoe	Social club; a source of *kye* groups. Also includes business associations. "In 1988, when a Korean owned grocery store in New York was boycotted for over a year by members of other ethnic groups, the Korean Greengrocer Association and its members sent money and stock to keep the store going. After the 1992 Los Angeles riot, Korean business associations collected money and other items to help the victims."[52]
Cho pa il	Gifts of money given by Buddhists on Buddha's birthday; used to buy lanterns so that wishes will come true, and to honor ancestors.
Cho ui kum	Money given at funeral, used by immediate family to defray expenses.
Chul san	Support given to family of a newborn (especially to the mother). Can be gifts of money, food, or clothing.
Dol	Baby's first birthday. Immediate family and close friends celebrate, and gifts can include money, clothes, or gold rings. "In times of economic hardship gold rings were considered a means of securing the child's and the family's future financial status."[53]

EXHIBIT 2-7   (CONTINUED)

Dong chang hoe	School alumni association; another source of *kye* groups.
Haam	The traditional box used to present *ye mul* to bride.
Hoi bi	A membership fee paid to social club or school alumni association that is used to support community activities.
Hun kum	Money given to religious organizations.
Hwan gap	Celebration of 60th birthday. A significant celebration involving immediate family, neighbors, church, and friends. Gifts of money are given to the individual, or gifts may be given to organizations in honor of the individual.
Hwan song hui; Song byul hui	Party given to someone who is moving away or taking a long trip.
Hwan young hui	Party given to welcome someone back home.
Ip sa chui jik	Gift given to new graduate. Can be money or clothing suitable for new job.
Jan chi	Korean women helping one another for an event or party.
Jul gap	Gift of money given to groom's family. Generally used to pay for the honeymoon or setting up an apartment.
Kye	"*Kye* is a traditional rotating credit group . . . used extensively by Koreans . . . *Kye* is a way of acquiring enough money to start a business."54
Mo kum	Collecting money to help others.
Paek il	Celebration of baby's first 100 days. Money and other gifts are given to parents for the baby.
Po jo bi; Chee won bi; Gi bu kum	Gifts of money to help others.
Pu ma ssi	Exchange of work. Originated in farm communities in Korea.
Sang hwal bi	Money sent or given by adult children to provide for parents' essential living expenses like rent, food, and utilities.
Ye dan	Gift given from bride's family to groom's family before the wedding.
Ye mul	Personal gift given to the bride from groom's family.
Yong don	Occasional or pocket money sent or given to parents. Similar to an allowance, viewed as supplemental income. Most parents live with their adult children (in Korea, and to some extent, in the United States). The giving of *yong don* is widely practiced in the Korean community.

Source: *Philanthropy in Communities of Color*, pp. 135–145.

TRADITIONS OF GIVING AND SHARING AMONG SOUTH ASIANS

South Asian traditions of giving and sharing mirror the great diversity and remarkable contrasts of Asian Indians. India is made up of 25 states and seven union territories covering a large geographic territory, from the Himalayan foothills to the subtropical region of the south. In addition to English, 18 official languages are recognized. Hindi is spoken by 40 percent of the Indian population. Traditions of giving among South Asians can be traced back through the various religions practiced by South Asians. The breakdown of major religions in India is listed in Exhibit 2-8.[55]

Hindu

There are five basic types of Hinduism in America: Secular Hinduism, Nonsectarian Hinduism, Bhakti or Devotional Hinduism, Reformist Nationalist Neo-Hinduism, and Guru-Internationalist-Missionizing Neo-Hinduism. Hinduism is a complex array of beliefs and practices, based on regional origin. Generally speaking, Asian-American Hindus center their lives on three kinds of practices: personal or family worship in the home (*Puja*); determining crucial times or seasons for important activities (astrology); and celebration of important festivals or holidays.

Important holidays or festivals are celebrated by many Hindus in America:

- Worship of the Goddess Sarasvati is a festival for teachers and students in honor of the great goddess of learning.
- Shiva's Night is a festival for Shaiva Hindus.

EXHIBIT 2-8	MAJOR RELIGIONS OF SOUTH ASIA	
Hindu	83.0%	700,000,000
Muslim	10.9%	92,000,000
Christian	2.4%	20,000,000
Sikh	2.0%	16,000,000
Buddhist	0.7%	6,000,000
Jain	0.5%	4,000,000
Other	0.5%	4,000,000

Source: Reproduced from *World Religions in America, Revised and Expanded*, edited by Jacob Neusner. © 1994, 2000 Westminister John Knox Press. Used by permission of Westminister John Knox Press.

- *Holi* is a lively fertility festival named after the demon-goddess Holika.
- The Ninth Day for Rama celebrates the birth of Lord Rama.
- The Guru's Full-Moon Day honors the particular guru of the Hindu believer.
- The Bracelet-Tying for Protection festival, when brothers commit themselves to protecting their sisters, is symbolized by sisters tying a special bracelet around their brothers' wrists.
- The Fourth Day of Ganesh celebration is when businesspeople, students, and others seek blessings for their work from Lord Ganesh.
- The Nine Nights is celebrated mainly by Bengalis in recognition of the struggle between Lord Rama and the demon Ravana.
- The Tenth Day celebrates the final victory of Lord Rama over Ravana.
- The Festival of Lamps involves the lighting of candles or colored lights to signify the reappearance of the sun and prosperity after the long rainy season.

Muslim

There are 5 million Muslims living in the United States, and Islam is the third largest U.S. religion, expected to rise to second in size by 2010. Members of the Islamic faith live in many parts of the world. It is a misconception to believe that the majority of Muslims come from the Middle East. Although many Arabs are Muslims, most Muslims are not Arabs. The majority of the 1 billion Muslims are Asian and African. Bangladesh, Pakistan, India, Central Asia, and Nigeria have the largest Muslim communities.

Islam is considered to be a way of life for Muslims. Americans, accustomed to the concept of separation of church and state, can find this confusing, especially as Islam does not emphasize a "church" for the preservation and promotion of Islamic beliefs. Muslims believe that Muhammad was the chief prophet of Muslims, much like Moses in Judaism and Jesus in Christianity. Through a series of revelations, Muhammad served as the moral conscience for his community. The Quran, the written interpretation of Islamic law, covers all areas of Islamic life. The five pillars of Islam as identified in the Quran are:

- Profession of Faith (*Shahada*)
- Prayer or Worship (*Salat*)
- Almsgiving (*Zakat*)

- Fasting (*Sawm* or *Siyam*)
- Pilgrimage to Mecca (*Hajî*)

Almsgiving, or *zakat*, refers to individual and community responsibility for others. From its earliest years, charity has been recognized and strongly encouraged in Islam. In fact, financially capable Muslims today are expected to pay an annual 2.5 percent wealth tax to address the needs of the less fortunate. Muslim belief includes a broader community, so Islam emphasizes the need for giving to help others to extend outside of the Muslim community.

South Asian–American Muslims are one part of the community of 5 million Muslims living in the United States. About two-thirds of the American Muslim population are immigrants or descendants of Muslims who came to the United States from another country. The remaining one-third are African-American converts to Islam and a small number of white American converts.

Sikh

Sikhism is only 500 years old. The founder, Guru Nanak (1439–1539), had a revelatory experience and began to travel and teach throughout India, Ceylon, Tibet, and parts of the Arab world. His followers were both Hindu and Muslim, and the name Sikh comes from the Sanskrit word *shishya*, meaning disciple.

Life-cycle events are recognized in Sikhism through naming ceremonies for newborns (*gurdwara*), marriage ceremonies, and funerals, which include cremation. Any kind of funeral monument is forbidden.

Sikhs reject the caste system and practice the principles of equality of gender, race, religion, and social class. Sikh names are gender-neutral, so all Sikh men add the name *Singh* (lion) and women use the additional name *Kaur* (princess). Dropping the last name is an indicator of the emphasis on equality. Another symbol of Sikh's acceptance of universal equality is the *langar*, a communal meal, shared by a congregation. Shared food acts as a social equalizer.

A cornerstone of Sikh faith is the concept of *seva*, the selfless service to the community—not just to the Sikh community, but extended to all others. A respected Sikh theologian, Bhai Gurdas, says, "Service of one's fellows is a sign of divine worship."[56]

PACIFIC ISLANDERS

The 1990 Census counted 365,024 Pacific Islanders, a 41 percent increase over the 1980 count of 259,566. Pacific Islanders include diverse populations who differ in language and culture. They are of Polynesian, Micronesian, and Melanesian backgrounds. The Polynesian group is the largest of the three and includes Hawaiians, Samoans, Tongans, and Tahitians. The second largest group, Micronesians, are primarily Guamanian (Chamorros), but also includes other Mariana Islanders, Marshall Islanders, Palauans, and other groups. The Fijian population is the largest Melanesian group.

- Hawaiians are the largest Pacific Islander group, followed by Samoans and Guamanians.

- Tongans grew more rapidly (146 percent) in the 1980s than the Hawaiians, Samoans, or Guamanians.

- 86 percent of the Pacific Islander population lived in the West in 1990, compared with 56 percent of the Asian and Pacific Islander group as a whole.

- Approximately 75 percent of Pacific Islanders lived in just two states—California and Hawaii.

- Washington was the only other state to have more than 15,000 Pacific Islanders.

- Only 13 percent of Pacific Islanders were foreign born, compared with 63 percent for the total Asian and Pacific Islander population.

- Hawaiians had the highest college completion rate among Pacific Islanders at 12 percent, followed by Guamanians at 10 percent, Samoans at 8 percent, and Tongans at 6 percent.

- The per capita income for Pacific Islanders is below the national average.

ASIAN-AMERICAN GROWTH PATTERNS

In 1970, there were 1.5 million Asian-Pacific Americans, less than 1 percent of the U.S. population. Between 1970 and 1980, the population of Asian Americans doubled, and doubled again from 1980 to 1990. In a 20-year span from 1970 to 1990, the Asian-Pacific–American population quadrupled from 1.5 million to 7.2 million. In 1996, there were 10 million Asian-Pacific

Americans living in the United States, and in 2000 the number grew to 11 million with a projection that 6 percent of the U.S. population will be Asian-Pacific American by 2020.

Factors contributing to the rapid growth of the Asian-American population include the 1965 Immigration Law, which allowed for greater numbers of Asians to immigrate; refugee resettlement efforts for Southeast Asians after 1975; increased efforts to capture a more accurate census count; and the increased birth rate of children born to Asian Americans.

In 1990, Chinese Americans were the largest Asian-American group, followed by Filipinos, Japanese, Asian Indian, Koreans, and Vietnamese. Census forecasts for 2000 predict that the Filipino population will become the largest Asian-American population. At least 17 additional Asian-Pacific American groups are now identified through the U.S. Census.

Asian Americans are a rapidly growing diverse part of America.

- In 1990, the largest proportions of Asian Americans were Chinese (24 percent) and Filipino (20 pesrcent), followed by Japanese with 12 percent of the population.

- The 10 largest Asian groups in America are Chinese, Filipino, Japanese, Asian Indian, Korean, Vietnamese, Laotian, Cambodian, Thai, and Hmong.

- According to the 1990 Census, 54 percent of the Asian population lived in the West, contrasted to 21 percent of the total population.

- Approximately 66 percent of Asians lived in just five states—California, New York, Hawaii, Texas, and Illinois.

- The 1990 Census reported that 66 percent of Asians were born in foreign countries. Among Asian groups, Vietnamese, Laotian, and Cambodian groups had the highest proportion of foreign born, while Japanese had the lowest proportion.

- Asian Americans had a median age of 30 years in 1990, younger than the national median of 33 years. Only 6 percent of Asians were 65 years old and older, compared with 13 percent for the total population.

- The average Asian family had 3.8 persons in 1990, larger than the average of 3.2 persons for all U.S. families. Asian families were larger partly because the percentage of children under 18 years old who lived with both parents was higher than the general population, 81 percent versus 70 percent.

- Among Asian groups, the Hmong had the largest family size, with 6.6 persons, and Japanese the smallest family size with 3.1 persons. Other groups with more than four persons per family were Filipino, Vietnamese, Cambodian, and Laotian.

- Education is highly valued in Asian communities, but the educational attainment of different groups varied widely. The proportion completing high school or higher was 88 percent for Japanese, compared with 31 percent for Hmong.

- At the college level, 38 percent of Asians had graduated with a bachelor's degree or higher by 1990, compared with 20 percent of the total population. Asian Indians had the highest attainment rates, and Cambodians, Laotians, and Hmong had the lowest.

- Asian-American families had higher median family incomes ($41,583) in 1989 than all families ($35,225).

- Japanese had the highest per capita income, followed by Asian Indian and Chinese.

- About 14 percent of Asian Americans lived in poverty in 1989, a rate slightly higher than the 13 percent for the entire nation.

- The Hmong had one of the highest poverty rates followed by Cambodians and Laotians. The lowest poverty rates were for Japanese and Filipinos.

CHAPTER 3

Hispanic/Latino Americans

CUBAN-AMERICAN HISTORY

In 1492 Christopher Columbus landed on the shores of Cuba, the largest and most western island of the Antilean archipelago. The early inhabitants of the island were the Taino and Siboney, tribes of the Arawak federation who existed by hunting, fishing, and farming on this beautiful island. It is estimated that 100,000 Indians inhabited Cuba in the late fifteenth century, but within a few decades of Columbus's discovery, the Taino and Siboney practically ceased to exist, decimated by European-borne diseases and the harsh conditions imposed by the Spaniards.

Spain's primary interest in Cuba, as well as other islands in the archipelago, was gold. Diego Velazquez, a wealthy landowner from Hispaniola (the island that is now the Dominican Republic and Haiti), was sent by Spain to secure the island for gold mining. Gold was not to be the source of wealth found in Cuba—it was Cuba's strategic location. Cuba sits between the Gulf of Mexico and the Caribbean Sea, situated at the crossroads of three major maritime routes: the Straits of Florida, the Windward Passage, and the Yucatan Channel, making it ideal as a resting stop for Spanish conquistadors.

African slaves were imported to work in the fields cultivating tobacco, sugarcane, coffee, and other crops. In the period of 10 months that the English ruled Cuba (1762), more than 10,000 African slaves were introduced into Cuba.[1] The African slaves in Cuba were treated differently than in other Spanish colonies. "The number of 'free colored' people in Cuba was higher than elsewhere, for two reasons. First, white Spanish slave owners customarily freed their many illegitimate children. Second, slaves in Cuba had the right to purchase their freedom or their children's freedom from their owners, an arrangement called *coartacion*. They had to give their owner a down payment and then a fixed sum in installments. The *coartacion* was possible because the Spanish looked upon the Africans not as a people they were born to possess but merely as a commodity, a source of cheap labor."[2] To the Spanish, if one looked white, one was white, even if one's heritage included a person of color. Slavery in Cuba was abolished in 1845 through the Law of Abolition and Repression of the Slave Trade, and all slaves brought to Cuba after 1820 were given their freedom.

Prior to the emancipation of slavery in Cuba were numerous hard-fought struggles to eliminate slavery. In the mid-1800s, an African Cuban, Antonio Maceo, led the fight for freedom for the Cuban slaves. In 1865, the Reformist Party of Cuba demanded that the Spanish parliament abolish slavery, allow for Cuban representation in the parliament, reform the tariff codes, and give equal rights for Cuban-born Caucasians of Spanish blood. At the same time the fate of slaves was being debated, Cuban planters found a new source of cheap labor: Chinese contract workers. Between 1840 and 1870, about 125,000 Chinese became indentured workers in Cuba.[3]

Cuba engaged in two wars for its independence. The Ten Years' War against Spain was a bloody civil war that left Cuba in a state of desperation, and many Cuban growers traded their property titles for stock options in U.S. companies. Some U.S. corporations foreclosed on mortgaged holdings, thereby acquiring a vast amount of Cuban sugar properties. By 1895, less than 20 percent of mill owners in Cuba were Cuban.[4]

When the United States won the Spanish–American War, Puerto Rico, the Philippines, Guam, Wake Island, and Cuba became U.S. territories. Cuba, however, was under U.S. control only until 1902. In 1934, Fulgencio Batista assumed leadership of Cuba. His government was recognized by the United States because he was anticommunist and protected American investments. The gap between the rich and poor widened under his leadership, and citizen unrest prevailed. Fidel Castro led a guerrilla uprising in 1959. The Batista government failed, and Castro assumed power.

Castro and communism nationalized American property, executed or imprisoned Batista supporters, and redistributed land among the peasants. The United States stopped importing sugar and other Cuban products, and embargoed exports to Cuba. Discontent flourished among independent farmers, businesspeople, and corporate employees, resulting in a dramatic increase in the numbers of Cubans immigrating to the United States—

reportedly 700,000 by 1979. Many of these earlier Cuban immigrants were middle class and educated.

The Mariel boatlift of 1980 saw another 100,000 Cubans enter the United States. This "Freedom Flotilla" occurred as a result of Castro's decision to drop the seven-year ban on emigration. "He announced that all Cubans wishing to leave the island should report to the port of Mariel, where Americans could pick them up by boat. 11,000 Cubans showed up . . . Castro then flung open his prisons . . . he allowed Cuban Americans from Miami to load over 125,000 Cubans onto shrimp boats and other vessels."[5] Most of the Mariel boatlift refugees were working-class people. Approximately 1 percent of them had serious criminal records.[6]

The Cuban Adjustment Act, passed in 1966, granted all Cubans seeking asylum in the United States the special status of political refugees, not immigrants. In 1995, the Clinton administration repealed the Cuban Adjustment Act, thereby terminating special treatment as refugees.[7]

Currently, more than one-third of the city of Miami is Cuban. There are Little Havanas all over Florida. The early Cuban immigrants were of middle-class backgrounds, so a strong entrepreneurial spirit thrived in America. It is estimated that in Miami alone there are more than 20,000 independent Cuban business owners and an estimated 40,000 throughout Florida. There are scores of successful Cuban associations and organizations, in addition to the successful Cuban business ventures.

Cubans are patriotic, grateful to the United States for their freedom, and politically conservative. There is a strong sense of nostalgia for Cuba and a high degree of animosity toward Castro. The U.S. invasion of the Bay of Pigs was a fiasco, but Cuban Americans remain steadfast in their determination to overthrow Castro.

DOMINICAN-AMERICAN HISTORY

Immigrants to the United States from the Dominican Republic, El Salvador, Honduras, Nicaragua, and Costa Rica represent a smaller segment of the Hispanic population living in the United States. The patterns of immigration reflect the history of each country with the U.S. government through the last century.

The Dominican Republic and Haiti share the Caribbean island of Hispaniola. Spanish rule was established in 1492 with the arrival of Christopher

Columbus. The native peoples of the island, the Taino, welcomed Columbus warmly, and he was so taken with the beauty of the area and the warmth of the native peoples that he settled in this area, later to become known as the Dominican Republic.

The eastern side of the island was more fertile, so the Spanish colonizers developed plantations in that region. The initial quest for gold was completed by 1543, when the Spanish had mined all the gold in Hispaniola. The remaining parts of the island were pretty much neglected by the Spanish, who eventually ceded the western third of the island to France in 1697. The French renamed the western end of the island Saint-Domingue and imported thousands of African slaves to work the land, as by that time most of the Taino had died from disease or overwork.

By 1795, Spain relinquished the eastern two-thirds of the island to France, and nine years later, the African slaves revolted against France and declared the western region of the island an independent nation called Haiti. The Spanish colonists were not pleased with the chain of events. They reestablished Spanish rule for the rest of the island in 1808. Under the leadership of Juan Pablo Duarte, Santo Domingo rebelled against the Haitians, and in 1844, the Spanish-speaking half of Hispaniola proclaimed its independence, becoming the Dominican Republic.

Decades of internal strife followed in the Dominican Republic, leading up to the prolonged and violent dictatorship of Rafael Leonidas Trujillo Molina from 1930 until 1961. Atrocities of war were inflicted on many, and the kidnapping and murder of Jesus de Galindez, a professor from Columbia University who exposed Trujillo's atrocities, was one of a chain of events that led to an aborted invasion of the Dominican Republic by exiles in 1959. In 1961, Trujillo was assassinated, leaving the country in economic and civil disarray.

Before 1960, few Dominicans resided in the United States. The civil war in 1960 caused many Dominicans to immigrate to the United States. The economic recession of the 1980s brought many more Dominicans, a total of 250,000 in that decade alone. At that time, Dominicans were the second largest national group of immigrants from the Western Hemisphere with Mexico as the largest.[8]

By 1990, the U.S. Census reported 506,000 Dominican Americans, with more than half of that number living in the greater New York area. Washington Heights in Manhattan has the largest Dominican-American

population in the country. A sizable number of undocumented Dominicans reside in the United States. "No reliable data has been published, but
many researchers believe that there may be as many as 300,000 undocumented Dominicans in the United States."[9]

Many Americans of Dominican descent are of mixed African and Spanish heritage, and they have encountered some of the same prejudice and
discrimination endured by African Americans. Contrary to the myth that
the majority of Dominican Americans come from the poorest numbers of
Dominican Republic society, Dominican Americans are more highly educated than those who remain on the island. Many of the Dominicans
moving to America are professionals, and the majority of Dominican
Americans are not on welfare, receiving food stamps, or collecting workers' compensation. Most Dominican Americans work as laborers at the blue-
collar level. A large number of Dominican women are employed in the
garment industry as seamstresses in New York City. Signs of upward economic mobility in the Dominican-American community are visible. An
increasing number of small businesses owned by Dominicans are flourish-
ing in New York.

SALVADORAN-AMERICAN HISTORY

Like other countries in the region, El Salvador has Spanish colonialism in
its history. Pedro de Alvarado was the Spanish conquistador who landed on
the shores of El Salvador in 1524. The native inhabitants of the country were
the Pipil, an industrious people closely related to the Aztec. Under Spanish rule, cultivation of cacao, indigo, and coffee were the major sources of
commerce. The Spanish granted 14 families, known as *los catorce grandes*, the
power to control the agricultural development of the country. Native peoples were the major source of the workforce.

In 1856, El Salvador proclaimed itself a sovereign nation, and its early
governments were essentially oligarchies controlled by *los catorce grandes*.
The government was determined to develop a strong economy by supply-
ing international markets with Salvadoran coffee. The exploitation of native and *mestizo* workers was extensive, and they were prohibited from
owning land to farm on their own. By the early 1900s, El Salvador was one
of the most prosperous Central American countries, but discontent was
growing among the exploited poor.[10]

La Matanza, meaning "The Slaughter," of 1932 marks one of the low points in El Salvador's history. Coffee prices fell during the Depression, causing pay cuts for the already poorly paid workers in the country's coffee industry. A series of leadership struggles yielded the formation of the Farabundo Marti National Liberation Front (FMLN), a communist rebel force, an active part of El Salvador's struggles for 50 years. Civil war erupted in 1980, led by the military against the FMLN and its followers. U.S. economic aid was sent to El Salvador in support of the government, despite concern that the government was guilty of many human rights violations. In 1989, Alfredo Cristiani, a wealthy coffee grower, was elected president of El Salvador. Under United Nations supervision, the new government and the FMLN signed a peace accord, which called for redistribution of land, downsizing of the military, and a civilian-controlled police force.

The 1990 Census reported 565,000 Salvadorans living in the United States. There are additional hundreds of thousands of undocumented and uncounted Salvadorans. And in 1990 about one out of every six Salvadoran Americans was born in the United States. In the 1980s, at the height of the civil war in El Salvador, 214,000 Salvadorans immigrated legally.

In the 1990s, with the civil war behind them, Salvadorans continued to face economic hardships. "The only way for many families to survive has been to send members north to work in the United States. These newer arrivals, and the immigrants who came before them, send payments of approximately $1 billion (known as 'remittances') back home annually, which makes them the largest source of foreign exchange revenue in El Salvador."[11]

According to a study released in 1997, Los Angeles has the largest Salvadoran population outside of El Salvador. Washington, D.C., and Houston follow.

MEXICAN-AMERICAN HISTORY

Mexican culture derives from the ruins of Aztec civilization and from centuries of Spanish contact with indigenous people, including the Spanish colonial frontier pushing northward, placing a distinctive imprint on the southwestern United States. Mexicans play an important role in U.S. society; the influences of their Indian and Spanish ancestors and the deep influence of the Catholic Church continue to be defining benchmarks for the Mexican population of the United States, one of the fastest-growing populations in the country. The outline of the history of Mexicans in the United States is taken from *Mexicanos: A History of Mexicans in the United States* by Manuel G. Gonzales.

Spaniards and Native Americans

Spaniards can be traced back to the Paleolithic period (35,000 B.C.–10,000 B.C.) through archaeological evidence found on the Iberian Peninsula. It is believed that the Romans were the most influential peoples to settle in this region. Brief occupations by French and Germans followed the decline of the Roman Empire. The impact of African culture on Spain began with the arrival of the Moors in 711. The Moors settled Moorish Spain and remained there for 750 years. During this period of time, a Jewish community grew and prospered, particularly in Granada, Barcelona, Cordoba, and Toledo. The productive coexistence of Moors and Jews was interrupted by a fanatical Islamic sect, which eventually led to a resistance movement and the subsequent arrival of Christians. Pope Urban II launched the first crusade to regain Jerusalem, resulting in the emergence of Catholicism as the primary religion of the people.

Under the rule of King Ferdinand and Queen Isabella, the Moors and the Jews were expelled from the country, and Spain embarked on expanding its influence in the world. Christopher Columbus sailed to the New World under the Spanish flag. Details of Columbus's discoveries in the Western Hemisphere are well known and outlined in other sections of this book. "Although Europeans often saw the Americas as 'virgin' territory, at the time of contact, according to current estimates, the two continents were occupied by almost one hundred million inhabitants."[12]

The tribes of Mesoamerica provide the key to understanding the Mexican Indian legacy. Centuries of pre-Columbian civilization preceded the European explorers to the Americas. The affluent Olmec society allowed for the development of a writing system, a calendar, and a polytheistic religion. The Christian era followed somewhere between 300 and 900 A.D. Mexican culture thrived during the era that saw Oaxaca and the Valley of Mexico (Mexico City today) grow into the largest metropolis in Mesoamerica. "The greatest civilization of the classical period, indeed the most advanced of all New World societies, was the Mayan."[13] The Mayans tracked stars, developed the concept of zero, and were able to perform simple brain surgeries.

Mayan astronomers were able to trace the path of Venus with an error of only 14 seconds a year. Like the Greeks in the Old World, the Mayans were unable to overcome political differences, and by the time the Europeans arrived in Mexico, the Mayan culture was well into decline.

The decline of the urban civilization created a migration north to the Yucatan peninsula. The Aztecs trace their origins to the northern deserts of Mexico—a term derived from *Mexica*, which is what they called themselves. The Aztec empire was vast, and when the Spaniards arrived in 1519, they found 6 million inhabitants living throughout southern Mexico. The Spanish conquest created massive destruction and few Aztec relics survived. The conquest of Mexico by Spain was followed by Mexican rebellion, only to be defeated again by the Spaniards in 1521. The Mexicans were supported in their rebellion by their Indian allies. Today both Mexicans and Mexican Americans exalt their Indian roots.[14]

The Spanish Frontier

Spain controlled Mexico for 300 years and, during that time, moved to expand its acquisitions by moving in all directions to seek gold and glory for Spain. The Spanish move to the northeast took place along the Caribbean shores of North America, including Cuba and the area now known as Florida. A concurrent move was made to find the riches of the American Southwest. An expedition in 1540 by Vasquez de Coronado led him to the Sonoran desert, into the area now called Arizona. Moving east, he came across a significant population of Pueblo Indians living in about 90 towns. Coronado was led by the Indians to believe that the riches he sought were farther north, and he ventured as far north as Kansas, only to discover no riches.

The Spanish continued to explore the areas north of Mexico, and wherever the Spanish went they set up missions. Missionary work was delegated to the clergy, who were expected to convert the native peoples to Catholicism. The two most active monastic orders were the Franciscans and the Jesuits.

Another distinguishing feature on the Spanish frontier of North America was the *presidio*, or garrison. The function of these forts was to provide protection against foreign intruders and to pacify native populations. The attitude of the Spanish to the neighboring Pueblo peoples was relatively peaceful. "Fearful of the Apache and other hostile tribes, the Pueblos, for their part, were often willing to cooperate with whites."[15] The prevailing view, however, was that the Pueblos were an inferior people. A combination of unrelenting missionary efforts to convert the Pueblo people, a prolonged drought, and increased labor demands led to the Pueblo Revolt of 1680, where Pueblo villagers were successful in driving the Spanish south.

Meanwhile, the French were appearing as a real threat to the Spanish in North America, and the colonization of Texas became imperative, as the French were establishing themselves in Louisiana, the Mississippi delta, and westward to Texas. The Spaniards moved east into Texas with partially successful efforts in the last half of the eighteenth century. Shortly thereafter, with permission from the Spanish crown, the Spaniards moved into Alta California, an area of immense promise. Spanish missions were established throughout California in the late eighteenth and early nineteenth centuries.

The Mexican Far North

The Mexican period of Southwest history was brief, lasting from 1821, when Mexico achieved independence from Spain, until 1848, when the young republic lost its northern territories to the United States with the signing of the Treaty of Guadalupe Hidalgo. In the early 1830s, Anglo settlers in Texas became increasingly antagonistic toward the Mexican government and the Mexican people living in Texas, and a move for Texas independence gained ground. The Texans suffered a terrible defeat at the Alamo, but Santa Anna's victory had not come without cost. The delay gave Sam Houston time to amass troops and, spurred by the cry, "Remember the Alamo!" Houston's men defeated the Mexican forces, giving Texas, the Lone Star Republic, independent status for a decade. Discrimination, abuse, racial violence, and other forms of mistreatment marked treatment of Tejanos, Spanish Southwestern persons living in Texas, under the Lone Star Republic.

President James L. Polk presided over the period of the Mexican War and American expansion. Polk was elected on the promise that he would "reoccupy" Oregon and "reannex" Texas.[16] After Texas was annexed, the relationship between Mexico and the United States deteriorated further. The Treaty of Guadalupe Hidalgo was signed in 1848.

The Great Migration

Manuel Gonzales writes that the dominant theme of Mexican-American history in the twentieth century is immigration. With the exception of the 1930s, every decade saw a significant influx of Mexican immigrants into the United States. Statistics on actual numbers of immigrants are highly unreliable, but it is generally accepted that more than 1 million Mexicans entered the United States between 1900 and 1930, joining the half million already in residence.

Many of the immigrants settled in the Southwest and California. Eventually, Mexicans made their way as far north as Alaska. By the mid-1990s, an estimated 20,000 Mexicans would settle in Juneau, Alaska, working mainly in hotels and restaurants, and a sizable community was to be found on Kodiak Island, working in the salmon canneries. The other major migration occurred east of the Rockies, through the Great Plains and into the Great Lakes region, as Mexican laborers followed the sugar beet crop. The first Mexican migrants were foreign-born, but by the 1920s they were gradually replaced by the native-born, recruited mainly from enlistment centers in Texas. Gonzales notes, "Mexican migration to the Midwest was not haphazard; each sequence of the journey was well planned by the migrants and involved consultation with family members or friends and especially with those who had already made the extended trip north."[17]

Mexicans immigrating to the United States did not sever their ties with Mexico. Close family bonds and other sentimental reasons kept the attachment strong. Moreover, the geographic proximity to Mexico made it relatively easy to return home.

The Depression

The Depression affected most Americans, and Mexican Americans were not excepted from economic hardship. Perhaps the Mexicans most impacted were the Hispanics of northern New Mexico and southern Colorado. Isolated in an impoverished area, many of the rural Mexican villagers were forced to abandon rural life for the cities. Denver's population tripled during the 1930s.

Mexican Americans living in the urban centers of Los Angeles, Chicago, Dallas, and Kansas City found life to be difficult. Schools were often segregated, living conditions were often not much better than conditions in

Mexico, and sanitation was deficient. The problems of living in the barrio were numerous. As might be expected, the collapse of the economy increased racial tensions, primarily in the Southwest. The "Mexican Problem" was a popular topic in the national press throughout this period of U.S. history. Congress moved to restrict Mexican entry into the United States. Congressional opponents agreed that Mexicans were racially inferior, but countered with the argument that Mexican labor was indispensable. Not surprisingly, the economic argument won, but public sentiment was so strong that Congress was forced to pass legislation in 1929 making illegal entry a criminal offense.

During the Second World War, the Mexican-American population saw momentous changes. Middle-class Mexican-American communities grew significantly, and the population now reflected the children of immigrants, rather than immigrants alone. Studies show that a significant number of middle-class Mexican Americans attempted to ameliorate working and living conditions for the Mexican community at large, with some success.

The Chicano Movement

Gonzales writes of this period in U.S. history:

> The decade comprising the mid-sixties to the mid-seventies was a period of extraordinary ferment in the Mexican communities of the United States. Immigration from Mexico, for example, increased markedly . . . The most momentous changes though, were political and psychological. . . . Following the lead of the African-American community . . . many Mexicans, now calling themselves Chicanos or Chicanas, embarked on their own campaign to improve socioeconomic conditions and win full recognition of their rights as U.S. citizens . . . The leaders of the Chicano Generation stressed pride in their ethnic roots while de-emphasizing assimilation into the American mainstream.[18]

The Chicano movement consisted of hundreds of organizations focusing on a variety of issues. The key organization of the movement was the United Farm Workers (UFW), led by two extraordinary people: Cesar Chavez and Dolores Huerta. The strike against local grape growers in the central California community of Delano, north of Bakersfield, was initiated in 1965 by the Agricultural Workers Organizing Committee (AWOC), a Filipino union led by Larry Itliong. Chavez was asked to join the strike, and soon became the leader of the entire operation. Cesar Chavez believed and practiced a nonviolent philosophy. Although he is widely associated with his labor efforts, Chavez was a motivating factor in the civil rights and human rights movement beyond the Mexican-American community.

HISTORY OF PUERTO RICANS IN THE UNITED STATES

Puerto Rico, 1,000 miles southeast of Miami, is 100 miles long and 35 miles wide. Residents of Puerto Rico are American citizens, as Puerto Rico is a trust territory of the United States.

The Arawaks, the indigenous inhabitants of the island, named it Borinquen, meaning "the land of the brave lord." It is said that Columbus christened the Arawaks, *Taino*, meaning "peace," because it was the first word they said when they laid eyes on him.[19] In 1493, Columbus claimed the island in the name of Queen Isabella and King Ferdinand, and named it San Juan Bautista, but he did not stay. In 1508, Juan Ponce de Leon of Spain explored the island in search of gold. When he first saw the bay at San Juan, he exclaimed, "Ay que puerto rico!" ("Oh, what a rich port!"), which is how the island came to be known as Puerto Rico.[20] Ponce de Leon stayed on the island and became its first governor.

The Taino welcomed the Spaniards, but soon found themselves stripped of their lands and subjected to slavery. They rebelled in 1511 and as a result, 6,000 Taino were shot on the spot. Needing laborers to keep the economy of the country running, Ponce de Leon requested a shipload of African slaves in 1513.

By the seventeenth century, tobacco and ginger were the main crops developed on the island, and Puerto Rico was thriving "on the backs of the Taino and African slaves."[21] African slavery was abolished in Puerto Rico in 1873. By then, the Africans had established firm roots and did not choose to leave the island. Intermarriage was common among the three groups— the Taino, Africans, and Spanish—which accounts for the racial diversity found in Puerto Rico today.

On April 25, 1898, the United States declared war on Spain to liberate Cuba from Spanish rule. The war did not last long, and Spain surrendered. The Treaty of Paris was then signed on December 10, 1898, and Cuba, Puerto Rico, Wake Island, Guam, and the Philippines became U.S. possessions. In 1900, the United States declared Puerto Rico a U.S. territory, and an American was appointed by the president to be the governor of Puerto Rico. The subsequent Foraker Act stated that Puerto Ricans were neither American citizens nor citizens of an independent nation. With the impending threat of World War I, on March 17, 1917, President Woodrow Wilson, under immense pressure from the islanders, signed the Jones Act, thereby granting citizenship to all Puerto Ricans. Among the obligations of U.S. citizenship was eligibility for the draft, and during World War I, almost 20,000 Puerto Ricans served in the U.S. armed forces.[22]

Puerto Rico's population doubled to 2 million by the 1920s, the standard of living on the island declined, and unemployment rose, while jobs on the U.S. mainland were plentiful. A steady migration of Puerto Ricans to urban centers, particularly the New York area, occurred from the 1940s until the 1960s. By the 1950s, Puerto Ricans lived in all states, but 80 percent settled in New York and surrounding areas.

The issue of statehood for Puerto Rico has been debated for more than 100 years. In 1978, President Jimmy Carter called for a referendum on the issue of statehood, but that referendum never took place. In 1989, President Bush announced to Congress that he favored statehood for Puerto Rico. No progress to speak of was made until November 14, 1993, when the people of Puerto Rico voted to retain their commonwealth status. The vote was close—48 percent supported the commonwealth; 46 percent favored statehood; and 4 percent chose independence. If Puerto Rico ever becomes a state, it would be about twentyfourth in population, meaning that it would send two senators to the Senate and seven representatives to the House.

One third of all mainland Puerto Ricans live in poverty. Yet large numbers of Puerto Ricans are white-collar employees, and in 1993, more than 53 percent of the mainlanders 25 or older had finished high school. There is a high concentration of economically underprivileged Puerto Ricans in New York, but Puerto Ricans in other regions of the country do much better.[23]

The challenges facing Puerto Ricans living on the mainland include discrimination, language barriers, differences in cultural values, the welfare system, and education.[24] James Olson in *The Ethnic Dimension in American History* writes, "The immigrants brought a uniquely syncretic heritage with them. Because of their Hispanic culture, they place great value on the uniqueness of human nature, seeing a special quality to life regardless of race, religion, or class. Compassion and empathy, for them, were the most important parts of human character."[25] In Puerto Rico, race is not an issue; generations of whites, blacks, mestizos, and mulattoes have co-existed with reasonable comfort. This was not the case on the mainland, where Puerto Ricans discovered racial divides between white Puerto Ricans and black Puerto Ricans among other factors causing separation.

Most Puerto Ricans came to the mainland as Spanish speakers, and many chose to continue to speak Spanish not English. Educational success in U.S. schools was limited and far below the national average. Some Puerto Rican groups concentrated on education as the path out of poverty, and in 1961, the organization ASPIRA was established to help young Puerto Ricans attend college. (ASPIRA takes its name from the Spanish verb "aspira," to aspire.) ASPIRA was the first Puerto Rican agency in New York City to be funded by outside (nonfederal) monies.[26] Initial funding for ASPIRA came from foundations, including the Rockefeller Brothers Fund, Field Foundation, Taconic Foundation, Nathan Hefheimer Foundation, and the New York Foundation.

The Civil Rights Act of 1964 and the Voting Rights Act of 1965 were enacted to protect the civil rights of blacks and other minorities. The Economic Opportunity Act of 1965 inaugurated an ambitious antipoverty campaign. Puerto Rican community organizations in New York City took this legislation as an opportunity to further their drive to "exploit and develop the particular strengths of the Puerto Rican community in fighting poverty and, at the same time, to attack some of the major barriers to the group's emergence as an effective actor in the city's affairs."[27]

The antipoverty programs had a major effect on the role of Puerto Rican nonprofit organizations. These organizations provided funding for social services and supported self-sufficiency. However, the bureaucracy surrounding the antipoverty programs created more emphasis on paid work, thereby deemphasizing volunteer efforts. And the dependence on government funding created a guarded reaction to the incumbent political power structure.[28]

Currently, the Puerto Rican community in the United States stills lags behind other Hispanic groups on key socioeconomic indicators. The decline of manufacturing as a source of employment displaced many Puerto Ricans from the job market. There is a growing effort among Puerto Rican nonprofits to strengthen coalition building and to diversify funding opportunities from foundations and corporations.

TRADITIONS OF GIVING AND SHARING AMONG HISPANICS/LATINOS

Mexicans

The traditions of giving and sharing within the Mexican community are centered around the family, or *familia*. In his book *The Buried Mirror*, Carlos Fuentes called the Mexican family "the hearth, the sustaining warmth . . . and the security net in times of trouble."[29]

Those interviewed by Smith et al. for *Philanthropy in Communities of Color* about the importance of traditions and customs, both immigrants and those whose families had been here for many generations, agreed that *familia* is essential to understanding giving among Mexicans.

Familia extends beyond the immediate family to include aunts and uncles, grandparents, cousins, other relatives, and often includes those who are not related biologically, but are from within the neighborhood or community. "Among Mexicans in the United States, the concept of *familia* is often extended to include all Mexicans or all Hispanics. No matter how inclusive one's *familia,* the primary obligation of the *familia* is the same: to give aid and support to *familial* members throughout life."[30] Examples of support through one's *familia* include housing for family members. The close-knit Mexican family expects to provide housing for not only one's children and parents, but also for other family members until they are established in the United States. In addition to housing, extended family members will share food, money, services, and jobs with their relatives in Mexico as well as the United States. Remittances are widely used within the Mexican community, with Mexicans living in the United States or other places outside of Mexico sending or bringing money and gifts home to Mexico.[31]

Traditions involving giving within the Mexican community can be grouped into celebrations, illness and death, and religious giving.[32]

Celebrations

- *Compadrazgo* refers to fictive kinship, those not biologically related to the individual, but sharing the bonds of closeness with the family.
- *Padrinos* are godparents. They are required to play a significant role in the life of their *ahijado*, or godchild.

- *Compadres* are co-parents and are expected to provide for the religious and educational aspects of their *ahijado's* development.
- The sacraments of baptism, first communion, confirmation, and marriage are significant events in the lives of Mexican Catholics. In addition to the religious ceremony, parties are often held to commemorate the event.
- *Bolos* are coins of various amounts given to children attending family celebrations. It is generally expected that the *padrino* and father of the child will give *bolos*.
- *Quinceanera* marks the fifteenth birthday for Mexican girls. A *quinceanera* is a blend of a coming-out party and a confirmation—a "wedding without the bride."

Religious Customs

Many Mexicans are Catholic, and the church is a key element in the Mexican community for religious instruction, education, and socialization.

Mexican children learn to make donations from their allowances to the church at a very early age. A person interviewed by Bradford Smith and his co-authors said this about giving to the church:

> Growing, you always gave to the church. My father made sure the whole family put money into the basket. Now it is only my children who put money in. My wife's family still puts in 15 to 20 percent of their income for repairs to the church, etc. My family went to church because of guilt, they "had to." My wife's family because of gratitude and duty. In poor families all the kids will go to parochial school. In my family church was the only place you gave consistently and at holidays. Hispanics will give much of their extra money to the church even if they hardly ever go to church.[33]

Giving to Organizations

Mexican Americans are generous in their gifts of money and goods to those in need in Mexico. Much of the monetary giving is through remittances, but Mexican Americans also respond generously to natural disasters like floods and earthquakes.

Giving also occurs through organizations located in Mexico, such as orphanages, youth-serving organizations, and community centers in various urban centers.

Gifts of oneself—time, volunteering—are considered to be as valuable a contribution as one of money or goods in the Mexican community. "You should try to give love and help. You should be able to feel good about giving. You should try to do it every day."[34]

GUATEMALANS AND SALVADORANS

Guatemalans practice many of the same giving customs as Mexicans. For Guatemalans the family is central to their lives, and *familia* is a strong concept among the Guatemalans.

There is an expectation of mutual support at the time of death to help pay for funerals. A gift equal to a month's pay, money *para sivirle* [to serve you], would not be unusual.

Guatemalans living on the West Coast report using ham radios to communicate with family and friends in times of need. If someone dies and needs money to send back to Guatemala, someone will go on the radio and ask for money.[35]

Salvadorans living in the United States are consistent in their efforts to provide financial support for family members living in El Salvador. Families are close-knit, and children will give money to their parents for much of their lives. Caring for the elderly is seen as a gift of love and respect, not an obligation.

Religious Giving

Santos are religious icons, images of saints, especially those of a town or church's patron saint. Gifts and donations are frequently made in honor of *santos*.

Celebrations

- *Despiedida* (parties) are held for family members who are preparing to move elsewhere. Guests will often offer gifts of money to support the sojourner.

- *Ofrendas* are altars built by some families to accept gifts of food. These are religious and spiritual celebrations.

HISPANIC/LATINO DEMOGRAPHICS

One out of nine people in the United States is of Hispanic origin. According to a March 2000 Census brief, the Hispanic population in the United States was 35.3 million, or 12.5 percent of the total population. In 2000, Mexicans were 58.5 percent of all Hispanics. People of Puerto Rican origin accounted for 9.6 percent of the total Hispanic population, while people of Cuban origin, Central and South American origin, and other Hispanics each accounted for 3.5 percent, 4.8 percent, and 3.8 percent, respectively. Exhibit 3-1 shows the distribution of Hispanic population in 1990.

The 1990 Census briefs reported the following:

- Hispanic Latinos are the second largest minority group and the fastest-growing subgroup in the United States.

- The Hispanic population grew by 53 percent between 1980 and 1990.

EXHIBIT 3-1   HISPANIC/LATINO POPULATION IN THE UNITED STATES

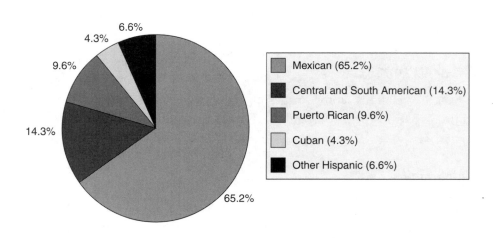

Mexican (65.2%)

Central and South American (14.3%)

Puerto Rican (9.6%)

Cuban (4.3%)

Other Hispanic (6.6%)

Source: U.S. Census, 1990.

- The Mexican population nearly doubled between 1970 and 1980.

- Both the Cuban and Puerto Rican populations grew at least four times as fast as the rest of the nation.

- In 1990, nearly 9 out of every 10 Hispanics lived in just 10 states. The four states with the largest proportion of Hispanics were California, Texas, New York, and Florida.

- The remaining states with significant proportions of Hispanics are Illinois, New Jersey, Arizona, New Mexico, Colorado, and Massachusetts.

- Central Americans represented about 6 percent of the total Hispanic population. Of the Central Americans, about 43 percent were Salvadoran, 20 percent were Guatemalan, and about 15 percent were Nicaraguan.

- South Americans represented nearly 5 percent of the Hispanic population. Of the South Americans, 37 percent were Colombian, 19 percent were Ecuadorian, and 17 percent were Peruvian.

- In 1990, nearly 7 out of every 10 Hispanics were younger than 35 years old compared with just 5 out of every 10 non-Hispanics.

- In 1990, about half of the Hispanic population had at least a high school diploma compared to 44 percent in 1980 and 32.1 percent in 1970.

- About 44 percent of Mexicans, 53 percent of Puerto Ricans, and 57 percent of Cubans had a high school diploma or higher.

- Nearly 75 percent of the Hispanic population were native-born and naturalized citizens, compared with about 97 percent of the non-Hispanic population.

- About 67 percent of Mexicans were born in the United States.

- About 21 percent of Central Americans and 25 percent of South Americans were born here.

- All persons born in Puerto Rico are U.S. citizens.

- About half of the Hispanic foreign born arrived in the United States between 1980 and 1990.

- About 20 percent of the Central American foreign born arrived between 1970 and 1979, and about 70 percent arrived between 1980 and 1990. Central Americans represented the largest proportion of newly arrived Hispanic immigrants during the 1980s.

- About 46 percent of the Cuban foreign born arrived between 1960 and 1969. Many Cuban refugees arrived in the United States following the Cuban missile crisis in the early 1960s.

- In 1990, about 78 percent of Hispanics spoke a language other than English at home. Spanish was spoken by nearly all of the Hispanic non–English speakers.

CHAPTER 4

Native Americans

HISTORY OF NATIVE AMERICANS IN THE UNITED STATES

The history of Native Americans goes back at least 20,000 to 40,000 years ago to the Paleo-Indians, those who came via the Bering Land Bridge, who were the ancestors of the current Native Americans. Much has been said about extending the timing of the arrival of the first population back to 100,000 years. A problem with determining the earliest dates is that these are evidenced by stone tools, and the possible earliest examples of such tools are not much different from stone that might have been altered by natural causes rather than man. As these examples are not found with evidence of big game hunting (an obvious example of human behavior), it is hard to say if they were tools. Gordon R. Willey's *An Introduction to American Archaeology, Volume One: North and Middle America* provides a detailed review of archaeological perspective on the long history of Native Americans.

Evidence of sophisticated Native American physical structures remain, and the area known as Chaco Canyon is still maintained by southwestern Pueblo Native Americans of New Mexico 3,000 years later. During the time of Julius Caesar, there developed a community known as Woodland cultures, popularly referred to as Moundbuilders, living on the Ohio River Valley and extending to the upper Mississippi and Great Lakes subareas. These Indians constructed phenomenal sculptures from earth of animals, serpents, even burial sites for decorative and habitation purposes. As the Woodland culture went into decline, another community developed west of the Mississippi valley in the general vicinity of modern-day St. Louis, Missouri. This community, known as Cahokia, also built huge earthen mounds, the largest of which was 100 feet high with a base larger than the Great Pyramid of Egypt. The inhabitants did not have a written language so we do not know exactly who they were, what language they spoke, or what they called their village. The focal point of Cahokia is a huge mound, but the site is filled with many other mounds. Cahokia was itself a walled city, surrounded by a palisade fence with bastions on it.

The most powerful of the northeastern Native Americans, the League of the Iroquois, lived in the Pennsylvania and upper New York area, from the Adirondacks to the Great Lakes. The League itself is not a tribe. A tribe is a grouping of people that has certain social characteristics. The League was made up many tribes, including the Mohawks (people of the flint), Oneidas (people of the stone), Onondaga (people of the mountain), Cayugas (people at the landing), and Senecas (great hill people). Dekaniwidah, speaking to the vision of Hiawatha, the Mohawk chief, said this to the Iroquois: "We bind ourselves together by taking hold of each other's hands so firmly and forming a circle so strong that if a tree should fall upon it it could not shake nor break it, so that our people and grandchildren shall remain in the circle in security, peace and happiness." All Iroquois land was held and worked in common. Hunting was done together, and the catch was divided equally throughout the village. A French Jesuit priest wrote in the 1650s: "No poor-houses are needed among them, because they are neither mendicants nor paupers. . . . Their kindness, humanity and courtesy not only make them liberal with what they have, but cause them to possess hardly anything except in common."[1]

Native American, or American Indian, is the name for those earliest inhabitants of the United States. Columbus miscalculated the size of the world and thought he had arrived in India, hence the name *Indian*. The term *Native American* addresses the fact that this population first inhabited the Americas. Anthropologists believe that North American Indians migrated some 25,000 years ago from Asia via the Bering Straits, down through Alaska. The migration continued south, in search of warmer climates, over a period of thousands of years into North, Central, and South America. It is believed that there were as many as 75 million people in the Americas at the time of Columbus's arrival. An estimated 25 million were living in North America.

The history of European arrival in the Western Hemisphere dates back to the sixteenth century. Native Americans were then long established residents of the Americas. Early relations between European settlers and Native

Americans were, for the most part, mutually beneficial. By the early seventeenth century, various European countries were establishing permanent settlements in North America. Jamestown was settled by the British in 1607, and France settled Quebec in 1608. Spain established a settlement in Santa Fe in 1610, New Amsterdam was settled by the Dutch in 1626, and the north Pacific coast was claimed by Russia in the 1740s. As more European settlements were established, the Native American population began to decline. European-borne diseases caused rampant death among Native Americans. In the 1600s, smallpox, cholera, and measles, unknown to the Indians, just about decimated some tribes, sometimes within weeks. In the nineteenth century, smallpox, measles, cholera, and tuberculosis were the cause of death for thousands of Indians living in the western part of the United States.

Disease was but one cause of the death of so many Native Americans. Casualties of war—intertribal and external—was also a significant factor in the decline in population. During the Revolutionary War, the majority of Indians sided with the British, who had positioned themselves as defenders of Indian lands against the land-hungry Americans. Factions of the Oneida and Tuscarores sided with the Americans, while most of the Six Nations (Iroquois) supported the British. This split weakened the alliances between tribes. After the war, with their homelands destroyed, Native nations moved to reservations in New York and Canada.

The Treaty of Paris signed at the close of the war ceded the entire Northwest Territory to America from England, disregarding completely the tribal people who were living there, and made no provisions for those Indian nations who had supported the British during the war.

Following the Revolutionary War, the U.S. government became more focused on the acquisition of land. "Recognizing that the U.S. was not strong enough militarily to take Indian land by force and that peace with Indian nations was a matter of national security, Congress expressed an enduring, if often violated, commitment to treat Indians fairly and to respect their property rights."[2] From this legislation, the Bureau of Indian Affairs (BIA) eventually emerged. Superintendents were appointed and territories were created to manage Indian relationships. From all appearances, however, the loyalties of the BIA were with the white citizens of the territories, not the Indians.

Battles over land continued well into the nineteenth century. When Andrew Jackson was president, the U.S. government forcibly removed tribes to west of the Mississippi River. The Indian Removal Act was designed to force Native Americans from their homelands to designated sections of land west of the Mississippi. These designated areas were called *reservations*; hence the non-Indian term used to describe the living communities of Native Americans. About 100,000 Native Americans were relocated, and missionaries and government officials proceeded to move ahead to "educate" and "civilize" the relocated Native Americans.

Examples of forced relocation of Indian peoples continued throughout the nineteenth century. Native Americans were once again forced to move when California, Oregon, Arizona, and New Mexico became states and the transcontinental railroad was completed. The Apaches and Pueblo peoples were subjected to the harsh rule of the Spanish governors in the Southwest. In Texas, laws were passed denying Indians all rights, "leading to a battle between the Texas Rangers and Comanches, Kiowas and Apaches for several decades until the Indians were defeated. The Spanish, Mexicans, and Texans in turn almost completely exterminated Texas Indians."[3] These events, along with the discovery of gold in California, created a major influx of pioneers moving west, and Indians once again found themselves being moved out of their homelands. Unlike the white settlers and other immigrants, Native Americans tie the concept of home directly to the land. Where many of us are comfortable with home being a transitory entity, the land is inextricably bound to Native Americans, and home and land are synonymous. The repeated removal of Indians from one place to another violated a deeply held religious and cultural tenet of Native American being.

General Allotment Act (Dawes Act)

It was the general sentiment of the federal government in the late nineteenth century that Native Americans should be assimilated into white civilization, embrace agrarian values, and become individual land owners. Through the General Allotment Act, land was parceled out to individual Native Americans in 160-acre parcels to heads of households. Remaining lands were put up for public sales by the U.S. government. All lands were held in federal trusteeship for 25 years. Because individuals (single persons under 18 and orphans) received only 80 acres, on death of the head of household the estate transfer allowed for acreage to be transferred at the single individual/orphan allotment. This clause of the Dawes Act created a massive loss of Indian property, whereby estates were partitioned in accord with state or territorial inheritance law, which maximized the number of heirs to an allotment and minimized the acreage each heir received.

Indian Reorganization Act (IRA)

Weakened by the effects of military defeat and the land allocation system developed in the Dawes Act, the BIA continued on a course to further attempt assimilation of Native Americans. In 1901, BIA field agents were instructed to curtail certain Indian customs and to see that the identified customs were modified or discontinued. These customs included the wearing of long hair by males, face painting by both sexes, wearing Indian dress, and dances and feasts.

"It was assumed that it was necessary to force Indian people into giving up their heritage. It did not occur to the reformers of that time that there was anything about Indian culture that should be encouraged. By the early twentieth century, it was obvious that allotment, education, and coercion had failed to turn Native Americans into prosperous Christian farmers; rather, the results were enclaves of poverty stricken, landless people surrounded by growing numbers of whites."[4]

By the 1920s, concern was growing about the mishandling of Indian affairs. John Collier, a founder of the American Indian Defense Association, became an advocate of native rights to freedom of religion. He was a staunch supporter for land rights of the Pueblo people of the Southwest. In 1926, a government-authorized report, "The Problem of Indian Administration," was released. This report (also known as the Meriam Report, after Lewis Meriam, who led the study) was very critical of the BIA and its programs. In 1933, President Franklin D. Roosevelt appointed John Collier as Indian Affairs commissioner. Under Collier's watch, many of the recommendations of the Meriam Report were instituted, and in 1934 the Indian Reorganization Act (IRA) repealed the 47-year-old land allotment system and "forbade further allotments of Indian land in severalty and the sale to whites of unallotted or heirship lands." The IRA was only partially successful. "Efforts at tribal reorganization failed because Collier and his coworkers had basic misconceptions about Indian peoples and how they functioned."[5]

Termination

The reforms of the 1930s were followed by two decades of backlash. A congressional study in 1943 determined that ending the "special relationship between Indians and the federal government would best solve the 'Indian problem.'" In 1947, the BIA began to identify Indian groups that they believed were able to manage without the benefit of the federal trust. More than 100 tribal groups were singled out as ready for termination. In spite of substantial Indian opposition, House Concurrent Resolution 108 was adopted in 1953. It called for the termination of federal relationships with tribes as soon as possible. Between 1954 and 1964, Congress terminated California rancherias, the Poncas of Nebraska, Peoria, Ottawa, and Wyandot tribes in Oklahoma, the Klamath Tribe of Oregon, 61 tribes and bands in western Oregon, Catawbas of South Carolina, the Alabama Counchattas of Texas, Southern Paiutes, Utes of the Nintahs, Ourays of Utah, and the Menominee of Wisconsin.

Urbanization of Native Americans

In the early 1950s, the federal government launched a massive effort to voluntarily relocate Native Americans to urban centers, believing that they would benefit from job and educational opportunities available in cities. This effort had the support of the BIA, and incentives like free one-way bus tickets, temporary subsidized housing, and free clothing were offered to interested Native Americans. It became apparent, however, that many Indians were discouraged by urban life, and by 1953, almost a third had returned to reservations.

By the end of the 1950s, Indian resistance and national public sentiment caused the federal government to abandon its termination policies. Congress restored federal recognition to a number of terminated tribes in the 1950s and 1960s. "Indians witnessed a historic shift from assimilationist goals and policies toward a policy in which the federal government recognized and respected cultural differences, encouraged self determination, and financially aided tribes in achieving this goal."[6]

Self-Determination

The Kennedy and Johnson administrations propelled a move toward Native American self-determination that has extended through current administrations. In 1966, President Lyndon B. Johnson appointed Robert Bennett, an Oneida, as the first Indian Commissioner of Indian Affairs. In 1969, President Richard M. Nixon appointed Louis Bruce, a Sioux–Mohawk, to head the BIA, only the third Indian to do so. Commissioner Bruce proceeded to fill a majority of positions with Native Americans. Three points identify President Nixon's policy on Native Americans: No tribe would be terminated without its consent; tribal governments would be encouraged to take over federally funded programs for their benefit; and tribes would be helped to become economically self-sufficient. This policy, known as *self-determination*, is the official policy of the government today.

In 1971, the Alaska Native Land Claims Settlement Act granted natives legal title to approximately 44 million acres. In return, all native claims in Alaska were extinguished. During the Ford administration, the Havasupais won their peaceful struggle to retain trust title to a portion of their ancient homeland along the south rim of the Grand Canyon. In 1975, the Indian Self-Determination and Education Assistance Act was passed. This act was significant in that it "contained language repudiating termination policy, committing the federal government to a relationship with Indians and obliging it to foster Indian involvement and participation in directing education and service programs."[7]

During the Carter administration, Congress enacted the American Indian Religious Freedom Act (AIRFA), which assured Native Americans that their religious beliefs and practices and cultural preferences were secure from interference. In later years, Supreme Court rulings limited the Native religious practices that the government promised to protect.

In the 1960s, Native Americans sought to reverse 150 years of "repressive and vacillating federal policies" and moved to reestablish Indian reservations as independent and economically sufficient communities. During the 1970s, Indians went to federal and state courts to claim land and protect their treaty rights. The American Indian Movement was established in 1968; in a display to encourage public action, American Indians occupied Alcatraz in 1969, took over the BIA building in 1972, and occupied the town of Wounded Knee, South Dakota, in 1973.

The issue of water rights was raised in the 1970s, and Native American activists demanded that water rights be protected. Congress and the courts recognized the government's obligation to protect the land and its resources into the future, and in the 1980s the Supreme Court reaffirmed three sources of sovereignty within the constitutional system—the federal and state governments and American Indian tribal governments. By the late 1980s the Supreme Court turned sharply away from the recognition of tribal rights, signaling that the Court would no longer be the ultimate protector of "essential tribal interests in difficult cases."[8] In spite of government vacillation and opposition, Native Americans continue to build models of successful sovereignty in Indian country. More and more Native Americans communities are working with state governments and private businesses to build solid economic projects to benefit Indian country.

TRADITIONS OF GIVING AND SHARING AMONG NATIVE AMERICANS

Clara Sue Kidwell's "True Indian Giving: Age-old Traditions of Sharing Communally Still Influence Modern American Indian Generosity" was published in *Foundation News and Commentary* in 1990. It is reprinted here:

> Even as Christopher Columbus set foot on the Americas, the generosity of the natives was obvious. "No request of anything from them is ever refused, but they rather invite acceptance of what they possess, and manifest such a generosity that they would give away their own hearts," the explorer wrote in his journal.
>
> The apparent generosity of the Indians reflected attitudes about wealth that contrasted sharply with capitalist-based European values. Even now, 500 years after the opening of the New World, age-old traditions still play a vital role in Indian community life despite the loss of lands and lifestyle imposed by the white man.
>
> Tribalism is a way of life based on mutual obligation and responsibility among members of extended family groups, to share a sense of common origin. Tribal societies are characterized by relatively small populations, subsistence economies, and highly structured social systems that regulate the exchange of material goods.
>
> Tribalism instills a strong sense of the distinctive identity of one's group, whether it is the immediate or extended family. Loyalty to this group precedes any larger racial or ethnic loyalty; in fact, under the tribal system, extended family relationships and kinship obligations are the most important social factors in any individual's life.
>
> High value has always been placed on egalitarianism—the idea that each individual is valuable to the community for what he or she can produce

and contribute. Men as hunters produced food; women produced the children who sustained the tribal identity; children became more important when they reached sexual maturity and proved their ability to be productive.

As the individual was necessary to the tribe, so the tribal group was necessary to the survival of the individual. Reciprocity—the exchange of goods and services according to carefully prescribed norms—became the cornerstone of community life, and giving was looked upon not as altruism but as a vital mechanism for the distribution of resources within a group.

While the term *Indian giver* has taken on pejorative connotations in modern parlance, the original definition of an Indian gift—one for which a reciprocal gift was expected, according to the Oxford English Dictionary—was a shining example of the importance of generosity and sharing. As one Navajo explained to author John Ladd in the mid-1950s, "The good man is honest and tells the truth to the people, and has a lot of money and livestock. And he's helping some people, poor people—so he's a good man."

Suspicion Toward Wealth

On the plains, the chief of a group was generally the poorest man in the village, because he assumed the responsibility for the needs of community members who could not provide for themselves, particularly widows and orphans with no male relatives to hunt for them. A person who accumulated many material possessions rapidly or mysteriously was viewed with suspicion. Was the person using witchcraft—manipulating spiritual powers—for personal gain? For example, a successful gambler might be suspected not of cheating by the ordinary means but of exploiting devious spiritual powers.

Ultimately, however, value was not associated with material goods but with intangibles: songs, names, and the power associated with visions and medicine bundles. As a Crow man told anthropologist Robert Lowie, "All who had visions . . . were well-to-do; I was to be poor, so I had no visions."

Sometimes spiritual sanction could lead to wealth, usually for an orphan with no family to rely on. Pawnees tell of an orphan named Small, who lived by his wits and the generosity of those who could give him scraps of food. One day he started out to hunt ducks, but fell asleep by the river. He awoke to find himself in the great duck lodge under the river, where a council was in progress. Several of the ducks wanted to kill Small right away because he had been hunting them; others pointed out that he could not kill them unless they gave themselves to be killed. The ducks spared Small and, because he was an orphan, they decided to give him gambling power and let him return to his village. Subsequently, he became quite a rich gambler.

In Europe, on the other hand, wealth was measured in inherited private property, which invariably meant land and the ability to control it and its products. Even the rights of the peasants working the soil were determined by the owner. Money—derived from control of the land or from trading its products—was passed on to heirs.

Disbursing the Estate

Indian societies often destroyed or disbursed personal property upon the death of the owner. According to Choctaw burial custom, for example, the corpse was placed on a scaffold—sometimes with the body of the person's favorite horse placed underneath the planks—and allowed to decay. When most of the flesh was gone, the bones were cleaned and bundled to be interred, and the family of the deceased hosted a great feast for the community. Upon the death of a Crow, the family distributed all possessions to other members of the tribe. When a Blackfoot died, the spouse rubbed his or her head with white earth and sat before the tepee in mourning as a sign for others to come and take away the possessions of the deceased.

Other tribes put possessions in the grave in the manner of the ancient Egyptians, so that the deceased could take them to the next world. The Mimbres, a people who lived in what is now southern New Mexico in the late eleventh century, buried their dead with fine pottery vessels, after making a hole in the bottom of each to release the spirits of the pots. That ensured that the pots would not be used by anyone else, and would therefore accompany the deceased to their new homes. Interestingly, these pots and other possessions were the same ones the dead had used in everyday life; grave goods were not specially made.

Tradition of the Give-Away

Another custom mitigating against the accumulation of Indian wealth is the give-away. Although it takes many forms across North America, each serves to honor individuals and validate their status. As a form of reciprocity, the give-away assures the giver of social recognition and acknowledges the receiver as a person of worth. It emphasizes the American Indian precept that status depends on accumulated property—not to hold but to give away.

The potlatch, the much-noted custom of the Northwest coast tribes, best illustrates the idea of distributing possessions in order to secure an individual's position in society. The host group invites to the potlatch others with whom it has a social relationship. Guests receive large quantities of goods. The principal dynamic of the event is competing with, even shaming, one's ostensible peers. Status is asserted by distributing so much wealth that guests are left feeling that they cannot match the display; or they are challenged to try to match it by hosting their own potlatches.

Before the arrival of the Europeans, food, blankets woven of cedar bark, and dentalium shell necklaces were the usual items distributed at potlatches. With the introduction of European goods, the potlatch became more elaborate. The account of Daniel Cranmer's potlatch on Canada's Village Island in 1921 gives the flavor of the occasion:

"I started giving out property. First the canoes. Two pool tables were given to two chiefs. It hurt them . . . the bracelets, gaslights, violins; guitars were given to the more important people. Then 24 canoes, some of them big ones, and four gas boats. . . . Then I gave button blankets, shawls and common blankets. . . . There were also basins, maybe a thousand of them, glasses, washtubs, teapots and cups given to the women in the order of their positions. I gave furniture: boxes, trunks, sewing machines, gramophones, bedsteads and bureaus . . . everyone admits that that was the biggest yet."

Modern Modifications

The potlatch continues in a form modified by a wage-based money economy. At Neah Bay, Washington, a Makah community, a 1971 potlatch honored and validated the status of a young woman on her sixteenth birthday. She and her grandmother, who held a basket in her lap, sat in the middle of the community hall, and people filed past to offer congratulations and put money—usually a dollar bill—into the basket. The young woman's family served a meal and, in turn, distributed gifts to the guests.

Another, more formal, tradition reflects the potlatch theme. Here the entire community, rather than one family, hosts the event. The give-away consists of an individual giving money (usually a dollar) to honor a person's accomplishment or to console someone who has experienced a loss. In the latter case, the donor would stand and announce, "I give one dollar to wipe away the tears of [the recipient]."

In contemporary Plains Indian communities, the give-away remains the norm. A person with a recent significant accomplishment will make gifts to honor the community that had fostered and supported him or her and to reinforce tribal identity. The items generally include star quilts, modern expressions of the value of women's work.

Forced Breakdown

European colonization of America devastated Indian tribes. For one thing, the introduction of trade goods during the colonial period changed the value system in Indian communities by introducing new means of exchange. Later, tribal societies began to break down under pressure from the U.S. government to form them into the image of late nineteenth century agrarian societies. With the passage of the Dawes Act in 1887, much Indian reservation land was allotted to individuals, destroying communal land-holding patterns and forcing the European system of private property on the tribes. The guiding values of reciprocity and exchange were badly damaged.

Over the last century, traditional American Indian values have been hard-pressed to withstand outside forces. Kinship ties and tribal identity, two fundamentals of Indian life, have been seriously weakened. Many Indian languages and customs have perished. Yet giving remains an essential part of life in Indian communities; it is a matter not of altruism but of mutual responsibility and honor. Wrote M. Scott Momaday in *The Names*:

"I see the crooked ravines which succeed to the sky, a whirlwind tracing a red, slanting line across the middle distance, and there in the roiling dust a knoll, a gourd dance and give-away, and Mammedaty moves among the people, answers to his name; low thunder rolls upon the drum. A boy leads a horse into the circle, the horse whipping its haunches around, rattling its blue hooves on the hard earth, rolling its eyes and blowing. There are eagle feathers fixed with ribbons in the braided mane, a bright red blanket on the back of the black, beautiful hunting horse. The boy's arms are taut with the living weight, the wild will and resistance of the horse, swinging the horse round in a tight circle, to the center of the circle where Mammedaty stands waiting to take the reins and walk, with dignity, with the whole life of the hunting horse, away. It is good and honorable to be made such a gift—the gift of this horse, this hunting horse—and honorable to be the boy, the intermediary in whose hands the gift is passed . . . Oh my grandfather, take hold of this horse. It is good that you should be given this horse to hold in your hands, that you should lead it away from this holy circle, that such a thing should happen in your name.[9]

NATIVE-AMERICAN DEMOGRAPHICS

According to the U.S. Census Bureau, the American Indian, Eskimo, and Aleut population has grown more rapidly than the country's population as a whole in the 1990s, 16.0 percent versus 9.7 percent between 1990 and 1999 (see Exhibit 4-1). Not all Native Americans live on reservations. Not all people who believe they are Native Americans are recognized as such by the state and federal governments, (i.e., Lumbee Indians in southeastern North Carolina have state recognition, but not federal). Are they Native Americans? They have no reservation today and have never had one. Are they Native Americans? They believe themselves to be.

- Census population projections predict that the Native-American population will grow to 3.1 million by 2020. This means that the Native Americans as a population group will grow faster over the next two decades than either whites or African Americans, but more slowly than Hispanics or Asians and Pacific Islanders.

- In 1997, about half of the nation's Native American households were located outside metropolitan areas.

- The metropolitan areas with the largest Native American population in 1996 were Los Angeles–Riverside–Orange County, California; Phoenix–Mesa, Arizona; New York–northern New Jersey–Long Island, New York–New Jersey–Connecticut–Pennsylvania; Tulsa, Oklahoma; San Francisco Bay Area, California; Oklahoma City, Oklahoma; Seattle–Tacoma–Bremerton, Washington; Albuquerque, New Mexico; Flagstaff, Arizona; Utah; Minneapolis–St. Paul, Minnesota–Wisconsin.

- The 10 states with the largest Native American populations in 1998 were California, Oklahoma, Arizona, New Mexico, Washington, Alaska, North Carolina, Texas, New York, and Michigan.

- Arizona added 42,000 more Native Americans to its population between 1990 and 1998 than any other state. Next were New Mexico, Texas, California, Florida, and North Carolina.

EXHIBIT 4-1 25 LARGEST INDIAN TRIBES IN THE UNITED STATES

Rank	Tribe	Total	Percent	State(s)
1.	Cherokee	369,035	19.0	Alabama, Georgia, Missouri, North Carolina, Oklahoma, Oregon, Tennessee
2.	Navajo	225,298	11.6	Arizona, New Mexico, Utah
3.	Sioux	107,321	5.5	Minnesota, Montana, North Dakota, South Dakota
4.	Chippewa	105,988	5.5	Michigan, Minnesota, Montana, North Dakota, Nebraska, Wisconsin
5.	Choctaw	86,231	4.5	Alabama, Louisiana, Mississippi, Oklahoma
6.	Pueblo	55,330	2.9	New Mexico
7.	Apache	53,330	2.8	Arizona, New Mexico, Oklahoma
8.	Iroquois	52,557	2.7	New York
9.	Lumbee	50,888	2.6	California, North Carolina
10.	Creek	45,872	2.4	Florida, Oklahoma
11.	Blackfoot	37,992	2.0	Montana
12.	Canadian and Latin American	27,179	1.4	Florida, Minnesota, Montana, Washington, Wisconsin
13.	Chickasaw	21,522	1.1	Oklahoma
14.	Tohono O'Odham	16,876	0.9	Arizona
15.	Potawatomi	16,719	0.9	Michigan
16.	Seminole	15,564	0.8	Florida, Oklahoma
17.	Pima	15,074	0.8	Arizona
18.	Tlingit	14,417	0.7	Alaska
19.	Alaskan Athabaskan	14,198	0.7	Alaska
20.	Cheyenne	11,809	0.6	Montana, Oklahoma
21.	Comanche	11,437	0.6	Oklahoma
22.	Paiute	11,369	0.6	Arizona, California, Nevada, Oregon, Utah
23.	Osage	10,430	0.5	Oklahoma
24.	Puget Sound Salish	10,384	0.5	Washington
25.	Yaqui	9,838	0.5	Arizona
	Total	**1,937,391**	**100.0**	

Source: U.S. Census, August 1995.

- Florida's Native-American population increased 56 percent between 1990 and 1998, the largest increase among all states. Nevada, at 48 percent, was next.

- In 1996, 134,000 Native Americans were enrolled in colleges and universities. Nearly 60 percent of these students were women.

- The number of U.S. businesses owned by Native Americans increased 93 percent between 1987 and 1992, from 52,980 to 102,271. The rate of increase for all U.S. firms was 26 percent (13.7 million in 1987 to 17.3 million in 1992).

- Receipts for Native-American–owned businesses increased 115 percent from 1987 to 1992, from $3.7 billion to $8.1 billion. Receipts from all U.S. businesses during the same period grew by 67 percent, from $2 trillion to $3.3 trillion.[10]

- Two-thirds of the Native-American householders living on reservations own their own homes.

- In 1990, more than half of all Alaska Natives were Eskimos, about 36 percent were American Indians, and 12 percent were Aleuts.

Native-American philanthropy is evolving from handouts to self-help and self-governance.[11]

- Generosity and sharing are of great importance within the Native American tribal culture.

- "Native Americans are unique among minorities in that they desire to maintain the integrity of their culture's social, cultural, governmental, religious, and economic systems, and they have thousands of federal laws that govern their tribal lives."[12]

- "The foundation for the Indian way of life is sharing and community participation. Caring and redistribution of wealth grow from this foundation."[13]

- There are similarities in philanthropic practices among Native Americans, but individual tribal customs vary extensively.

CHAPTER 5

Diverse Fundraising and Philanthropy Today

AFRICAN-AMERICAN PHILANTHROPY

Samuel N. Gough, Jr.

As the black church grew, so too did its philanthropic outreach. In *A Study on Financing African-American Churches National Survey on Church Giving, A Research Report,* Dr. Walter V. Collier states in his introduction:

> Historically Black churches have operated with a strong sense of self-determination and faith since the dark days of slavery. Black Baptist and Methodist churches long ago created economic ministries, called "mutual aid societies." Black churches have served as a refuge and a place where destitute African-Americans have sought food, clothing, housing as well as spiritual strengthening. Dr. Andrew Billingsley's [a noted sociologist] work confirmed the continuation of these traditions, as reflected in the current spectrum of community outreach programs supported by Black churches. Dr. Billingsley's study identified several areas of church and program operation that are tantamount to effective outreach ministry. Chief among them are: progressive ministerial leadership, strong community support, and an adequate funding base.[1]

Collier notes, "African Americans have supported their own religious institutions since the founding of Black congregations in the South during the 1770s. The subject of giving to the Black Church, however, has remained obscured in the general church literature and only briefly addressed by African-American church scholars."[2] He presents statistics on the ecclesiastical characteristics of the Black churches in the study. In the sample, the following variables were considered—interdenominational differences, member demographics, attitudes toward giving to the church, how congregations evaluate their houses of worship, estimated size of member donations, and reasons for giving.

Some of Collier's findings are presented here:

- "African Americans alone earned more than $324 billion in 1995. If they were a country, they would have ranked fifteenth, just behind Russia and ahead of India.

- There is untapped wealth in this community, as well as in the Latino and Asian American communities.

- As with the nation as a whole, the majority of giving in the African-American community is to the church. The factor that most influences giving to the church is family income.

- The largest donor group is people 42 to 53 years of age. The second largest is 30 to 41 years old. The third is age 54 to 65.

- 52 percent of these prospects are married; 24 percent are single; 13 percent are divorced.

- 29 percent of these givers have some college, and another 21 percent have a bachelor's degree.

- In terms of household income, 53 percent of these donors to churches earn between $20,000 and $60,000.

- 41 percent of them made annual, outright gifts to their churches in the range of $500 to $2,500; 23 percent of them gave $2,500 to $4,500.

- If we look at a typical profile of a major African-American donor to the church, that person would be female (61 percent), 48 years old, with an associate's or a bachelor's degree (58 percent) and a family income in the $50,000 range. Since women tend to outlive men, the older she gets the more likely it will be that she is single, divorced, or widowed with no children or with grown children, planning for retirement.

- In the next 10 years, groups now considered minorities will populate the majority of the largest states in this country, and they will increasingly control significant portions of this country's wealth."[3]

In 1990, while an assistant program officer in the Human Rights and Social Justice Program at The Ford Foundation, Emmett D. Carson wrote

Working Papers: Black Volunteers as Givers and Fundraisers. The paper provides a brief overview of the origins of black philanthropy, an examination of the socioeconomic profile of black volunteers and givers, a description of what motivates blacks to volunteer and the kinds of organizations that they are likely to support, a look at some organizations that routinely involve volunteers as givers and as fundraisers, and areas suggested for future research.

Working Papers shows that research data suggest that blacks are more likely to engage in volunteer activities under the auspices of a black organization because such organizations are more likely to solicit their support. The paper concludes that black organizations may serve as important models for nonprofit organizations that are concerned with developing volunteers who also are active givers and fundraisers. The report further notes that 46.6 percent of all donors give to their own church, and a typical donor to all causes is a married (80.9 percent) woman (64.2 percent), 35 to 45 years of age (69.5 percent), whose family income is in the over-$40,000 level (87.6 percent). Her religious beliefs are something other than Protestant or Catholic.[4]

In June 1999, the Council on Foundations published *Cultures of Caring: Philanthropy in Diverse American Communities.* Dr. Joanne Scanlan writes in the introduction, "The public, the media, and grant making organizations often view 'minority' population groups (with the possible exception of Asians) as recipients of charity—not as donors. This view is little more than stereotyping."[5] *Cultures of Caring* focuses on four groups—African Americans, Asians, Latinos, and Native Americans—their attitudes on giving, how they select the organizations they support, how they think about setting up endowments, and how they feel about establishing foundations, setting up funds in community foundations, and contributing to existing charities.

Scanlan points out that education and income levels are increasing among the four groups. In her summary, she makes eight "Recommendations for Expanding Diverse Philanthropy," summarized as follows:

- "Increase awareness of the general population in diverse communities about the value and need to support charities with donations.

- Bring more diverse people into institutional philanthropy so that more people become familiar with the art of philanthropy as practiced by foundations and corporate grant makers.

- Encourage greater diversity among the ranks of professional advisors to the wealthy.

- Help donors retain confidence in their giving by linking them with other donors.

- Strengthen the organizations that affluent donors already favor with gifts and contributions of time, so that they can take on the building of permanent endowments.

- Increase the number of skilled development people from diverse communities.

- Recognize that the process to establish a private foundation or to build an endowment in a charitable organization is extremely complicated and time consuming.

- Act locally."[6]

In the *Cultures of Caring* chapter "Reflections on Endowment Building in the African-American Community," Mary-Frances Winters sets the stage for African-American philanthropy.

Perhaps for their very survival, African Americans have been compelled to share and give back from the moment they arrived on the shores of this country. When they have money to give, they give; when there was no money to give, a generous heart, a strong back or a keen mind were offered freely. As a value, "giving back" is firmly rooted in black history.

Today, armed with growing capacity, the descendants of slaves now generate philanthropy that benefits the many families who continue to struggle economically, just as their forefathers and mothers before them. Within the African-American community, philanthropy is just as much about time and other voluntary action as it is about money. Many black donors would not, in fact, describe their behavior as philanthropic, and some are uncomfortable with the term. Development officers and board members report that their educational efforts begin with defining the word philanthropy.

Yet, how philanthropy is defined and conducted within the African-American community is in transition. African-American communities are moving from a survival model to one of community self-sufficiency and economic empowerment. Black philanthropy has gained much momentum in the past decade alone. Black celebrities and sports figures have gained wide notice for their generosity. In addition to individuals, black organizations such as churches and fraternal organizations are beginning to examine more sophisticated investment strategies, which are also tied to philanthropic enterprises. Individuals are moving from unstructured, unplanned patterns of giving to a more deliberate thought process. Organizations are moving from a survival mentality to one looking to long-term sustenance.[7]

Ms. Winters identifies three categories of givers who emerge from the research and three categories of organizations that provide points of entry for African-American philanthropy. She concludes with the following summary of recommendations:

- "Build capacity of nonprofit organizations to develop endowments;
- Provide broad-based educational initiatives, perhaps starting in black churches, on philanthropy and endowment-building;
- Use traditional and well-established organizations to develop comprehensive, visible educational programs on philanthropy;
- Develop a wide-net promotional campaign that covers the elements of philanthropy;
- Support training and education for development specialists;
- Develop a comprehensive database of affluent African Americans for use by nonprofits;
- Select several large African-American organizations such as the NAACP, Urban League, or United Negro College Fund to partner in a matching grant program for endowment;
- Focus efforts toward historically black colleges; and
- Respect the importance of time—of life stages—and consider that the leap to endowment may be premature for some individuals and organizations."[8]

In early 2000, Alice Green Burnette, former assistant secretary for institutional advancement at the Smithsonian Institution, wrote a report on African-American fundraising, *The Privilege to Ask: A Handbook for African-American Fund Raising Professionals*. Her work was produced under the auspices of The Institute of Church Administration and Management, Interdenominational Theological Center in Atlanta, Georgia, with grant support from Lilly Endowment, Incorporated, and The Ford Foundation. She had three research goals:

- "Increase the number of African-American fundraising professionals
- Improve their preparedness and productivity

- Strengthen and expand the financial base of the institutions and organizations they serve."[9]

Burnette's focus was on the people who raise funds. However, she recognized that it was important to make note of other factors.

> The traditions of philanthropy in the African-American community and, especially, those fostered by the Black church, must be better understood, better communicated, and better developed in terms of reliance on contemporary techniques, all with the objective of reaping long-term benefits for both Black churches and the broader African-American community.
>
> Because increasing the level of support from Black donors is a crucial goal to reach, the changing demographics of the African-American community, and the level of financial resources within that community must be analyzed. This analysis can suggest how to redirect a larger portion of those resources for philanthropic purposes within the community. Such a redirection would have the additional benefit of heightening the level of confidence—the precursor of increased financial support—of the majority individuals, as well as foundations and corporations.[10]

Burnette interviewed four categories of people—presidents of black institutions and organizations, black fundraising professionals, black corporate giving and foundation executives, and trustees of black institutions and organizations.

In "Philanthropy in the United States," she states: "there are four points which African-American fundraisers must understand as they devise ways to enlist/entice the support of prospective *Black* [sic] or *white* donors:

- Wealthy people give out of their own interests and self-interest;
- Increasingly, and especially with regard to the newly rich, traditionally practiced philanthropy is being replaced by social investment expectations;
- The neediest organizations and institutions focus on their 'needs' rather than on their potential to contribute to society and as a result, do not present themselves as capable of meeting social investment expectations; and
- Major donors talk to each other."[11]

A number of African Americans at various economic levels have made significant endowment gifts. Examples include gifts from Drs. William

"Bill" and Camille Cosby to Spelman College; Willie E. Gary, Esq., to Shaw University; Oprah Winfrey to Morehouse College; Jean Fairfax, who created a $1 million endowment for African-American causes, and Earl G. Graves, who gave $1 million to Morgan State University. Also on that list are Matel Dawson, a Ford Motor Company employee, who gave more than $810,200 to various charities and established a $100,000 endowed scholarship at Louisiana State University, and Oseola McCarty, a laundress, who established a scholarship fund with $150,000 that she donated to the University of Southern Mississippi. Gifts to establish endowments are usually made when individuals have reached the highest level of motivational needs.

A common factor in all the examples listed is that these donors were motivated to give and that they had professional help with satisfying their philanthropic intent. Institutions/organizations seeking major gifts understand the need to have someone who works on their behalf with potential donors. What should not be forgotten is that people generally give as a result of being asked to give by the right person, for the right reason.

The Ford Foundation, in 1968, initiated the first formal, foundation support of efforts to strengthen the fundraising abilities of individuals who worked on behalf of institutions that served black populations. These were the people who would direct the development programs at their respective institutions.

Fourteen men from 10 historically black colleges and universities were selected to participate in a program designed to increase their capabilities to serve as development officers at their respective institutions. These men plus two other individuals were the charter members of the Association of Fund Raising Officers In Negro Colleges, later renamed the Association of Fund Raising Officers, Incorporated (AFRO, Inc.). The association was founded in 1970 "as a clearinghouse for information of interest to the Membership. It shall be a professional association of persons involved in institutional development (alumni affairs, fund raising, public relations, and government relations). It shall serve as a forum for the airing of problems and the suggestion of solutions on matters of mutual interest and concern."[12]

One year later, 10 more people, men and women, went through the Ford Foundation program. After that, a three-year grant was made by the Foundation to Howard University to administer a program that trained 21 people in the principles and techniques of fundraising.

Several years later, the Ford Foundation made two more grants of $250,000 each—one to AFRO, Inc., and the other to the Council for Advancement and Support of Education (CASE)—both of which enhanced the development knowledge and skills of people who worked or desired to work in educational institutional development. The individuals who completed these programs were well trained in understanding black philanthropy, particularly donors to institutions of higher learning. The people who were formally trained in these programs were among the leading development officers in the nation.

Howard University was among the first historically black colleges and universities (HBCU) to devote substantial resources to a development program that focused on alumni and other friends of the university, corporations, foundations, labor, and other organizations. There had been a history of raising funds from alumni, dating back to the 1950s. The focus was to urge alumni to contribute to funds for scholarship.

In 1972, Howard University began the quiet phase of a $100 million, major gift campaign that was the largest fundraising effort ever attempted by an HBCU. The staff that managed that campaign had a dual challenge: to learn many of the principles and practices of fund raising and to adapt what they learned to potential donors to a black university.

In 1968, Howard University reported raising $270,000 from alumni as the culmination of a two-year campaign in celebration of its hundredth year. That was 10 times larger than the amount ever raised in a single year from alumni. (At that time, the only organized fundraising efforts were directed at alumni.) That success led to the subsequent major gift campaign.

This campaign was publicly announced on March 1, 1976, at the university's Charter Day celebration. It was announced that more than $19 million had been raised in gifts, grants, and pledges. A feasibility study was conducted, and the campaign was crafted with the aid of an external, professional fundraising firm. That firm continued to work with the university throughout the quiet phase of the campaign and for a year or so following the public announcement. A diverse, international group of highly respected, influential, affluent donors was needed to reach that ambitious goal. These individuals were identified and recruited to form the International Sponsors Council. They gave of their own resources and helped to open the doors to other centers of wealth.

The campaign was extended for 17 years from 1972 until the goal was reached in 1989, exceeding the original goal by $1,273,000. Twenty-five percent of the $101,273,000 was raised in the final three years. Ten percent was from mature or irrevocably committed planned gifts.

It might be worth noting some of the lessons from that campaign:

- Requests for gifts and grants for academically based scholarships and need-based financial aid had an appeal for many donors.

- Of the 11 schools and colleges at the university, graduates of the College of Medicine gave the most money. Several donors to the college established named funds.

- There was no direct correlation made between the size of a donor's gift and his or her direct involvement with the university following graduation. Some major donors had maintained close contact over the years; others had not. However, most major donors had recent positive contacts with the university.

- Generally, donors appreciated public recognition for their generosity.

- Often, the size of a gift or grant was determined by the size of a gift or grant from the donor's peer.

- Planned gifts became increasingly more understood by donors and important to the attainment of the campaign goal.

- Faculty and staff members made significant contributions. These gifts were used to demonstrate the commitment that Howard University employees had to the university.

In 1997, Rodney Jackson, president and CEO of The National Center for Black Philanthropy, located in Washington, D.C., convened the First National Conference on Black Philanthropy in Philadelphia, Pennsylvania, with this mission:

> The corporation is organized . . . to educate the public about the importance of black philanthropy; to promote full participation by African Americans in all aspects of philanthropy; to conduct research into the contributions of black philanthropy to the social well-being of all Americans; and to strengthen and support institutions involved in black philanthropy.[13]

The First National Conference and the subsequent conference two years later in Oakland, California, brought together more than 600 people, who participated in scores of sessions over four days that were under four tracks—Individual Donors, Grant Makers, Fund Raisers, and Faith-Based Organizations. In the intervening years, regional conferences were held around the country. The National Conferences were the largest gatherings of people brought together on the basis of their mutual interest in black philanthropy. Individuals representing donors and funders exchanged information and ideas about the current status and the future of philanthropy as it pertained to people of African descent. Specific recommendations resulted from each National Conference, and follow-up on the implementation of those recommendations began shortly thereafter. The National Center for Black Philanthropy published the proceedings from both National Conferences.

There are several ongoing efforts by organizations to encourage black philanthropy at all levels. For example:

- At the Second National Conference on Black Philanthropy, Mr. Jackson introduced 3/4 = 1 percent. Attendees were asked to complete pledge cards indicating that they would commit 1 percent of their annual incomes to a nonprofit organization of their choice on March 4 each year. There was no recommendation as to which nonprofit organization they should make their pledge to, but a return portion of the pledge card was to be detached and sent to the National Center for Black Philanthropy so that the center could determine the success of this effort.

- The College Fund/UNCF, founded in 1944, is a collaboration of private colleges and universities that have banded together primarily to raise funds. Through The College Fund/UNCF solicitations are made on behalf of the member institutions. The funds collected are distributed on the basis of a predetermined formula to the member institutions.

- The United Black Fund (UBF) of Washington, D.C., was started by Dr. Calvin Rolark in 1969 as a federation of black charities, in response to the fact that black charities were not receiving a fair share of charitable dollars from local United Ways. It was the first black charitable federation to receive funds from the Combined Federal Campaign. As a result, UBF entered into a working agreement with the United Way of the National Capital Area to share the funds jointly collected.

- Since 1972, the National Black United Fund (NBUF) has initiated and supported programs that encourage the philanthropy of African Americans. Through its 22-affiliate organizations, it works to strengthen communities and promote wealth building in the African-American community. A major source of support comes from contributions made through workplace giving. NBUF operates as a national community foundation by allowing donors to pool and channel their gifts through it to assist a range of charitable endeavors. Also, it offers donors an opportunity to establish donor-designated funds.

- The Twenty-First Century Foundation is an independent, endowed black foundation created to advance the welfare of the black community through fundraising and grant making. Its vision is to develop effective giving programs with an emphasis on building endowments to support black nonprofit organizations and to be a forum for black donors to apply innovative approaches to significant issues that affect the black community. It, too, offers donors an opportunity to establish donor-designated funds

- The Association of Black Charities of Maryland (ABC-MD) was founded in 1985, to represent and to respond to issues of special significance to the African-American communities in the State of Maryland, as well as to foster coordinated leadership on issues concerning the community. It has allowed African Americans in the state to select their own challenges, priorities, and solutions. Its program focus is to:
  - Achieve self-sufficiency
  - Direct attention to how major issues affect the black community
  - Raise the profile on programs and services that effect positive change
  - Mentor the next generation of leaders

In recent years, several large, nonprofit institutions have sought to enlist significant numbers of African Americans as donors and as volunteers. Many major universities started this trend with the establishment of black alumni organizations. Efforts to increase the diverse base of volunteer and donor support recognize that within the first 25 years of the twenty-first century, current minorities will become the majority in many urban areas.

The origins of black philanthropy go back to Africa (see Exhibit 5-1). In this country, that tradition was borne of the need to survive in a dangerous and hostile environment. Even in cases where the conditions were less life threatening, African Americans had to establish institutions, organiza-

EXHIBIT 5-1   AFRICAN-AMERICAN PHILANTHROPY TIMELINE

Period	Events			
1700	Mutual aid societies, social services, education	Fraternal Order of Prince Hall Masons (1775)	African Union Society (1781)	African Society of Mutual Aid & Charity (1796)	
1800	By 1800, several hundred organizations existed to provide charitable assistance to the black community	Anti-slave efforts	Black churches emerge: AME, Baptist	Post–Civil War activities— Blacks hold elected offices	
1860	Role of church continues to be strong	Individual philanthropists emerge, Thomy Lafon, New Orleans	Tuskegee Institute formed	Other black colleges emerge— Bethune-Cookman, Spelman, Morehouse, etc.	
1900	Black sororities and fraternities formed for college-educated blacks	Boule formed (1904), NAACP formed (1908)	Urban League founded (1910)	Marcus Garvey Back to Africa movement (1914)	National Council of Negro Women founded (1935)
1940	United Negro College Fund (1943)	Links (1946)			
1950	United Negro Appeal (1955)				
1960	Civil rights movement	Financial support for civil rights movement is single greatest manifestation of philanthropic behavior in United States		Black businesses emerge— Johnson Publishing, Black Enterprise, Essence	United Black Fund (Washington, 1969)

EXHIBIT 5-1   (CONTINUED)

Period	Events				
1970	21 Century Foundation formed (1971)	National Black United Fund established (1974)	United Black Fund of American established (1977)		
1980	Entertainers, sports figures, and others of wealth begin to give large gifts	Scholars and researchers begin serious study of African-American philanthropy	Community foundations extend outreach to African Americans	Mega church movement emerges	Number of black-owned businesses increase
1990	First National Conference on Black Philanthropy (1997)				

Source: Mary-Frances Winters, "Reflections on Endowment Building in the African-American Community," *Cultures of Caring* (Washington, DC: Council on Foundations, 1999).

tions, and systems that provided for their education, welfare, care, and spiritual development. The church, by far, has been the keystone on which philanthropy has been built. Fraternal orders and mutual aid societies were created around the needs of the community.

African Americans have supported, and continue to support, the institutions and organizations that seek to ameliorate problems in their community, which will enhance the quality of their lives. The scope of their support spans a range of nonprofit institutions and organizations; however, most often their support has been focused on the institutions and organizations that meet the needs that most affect them.

As with the population in general, African Americans see religion, education, and health organizations as prime targets for their philanthropy. However, they usually give to those institutions/organizations in which they have some active involvement in their destiny.

This involvement may be in the form of serving as volunteers in some capacity, as well as being advisory committee and board members. The greater the involvement, often, the larger the gifts, based on their ability to give.

A summary of African–American philanthropy is provided by Bradford Smith et al. in *Philanthropy in Communities of Color:*

- "The African–American church is the focal point of much charitable giving in the black community.
- Direct giving to individuals is more valued in the African–American community than giving to nonprofit organizations.
- Donating time, skills, and knowledge is often seen as more desirable than donating money.
- Definitions of family that include relatives, friends, neighbors, and strangers are important to understand African–American giving patterns.
- African Americans who do well are expected to give back their skills, money, and knowledge to the community."[14]

RECENT RESEARCH ON ASIAN-AMERICAN GIVING PATTERNS

The Council on Foundations' 1999 report, *Cultures of Caring: Philanthropy in Diverse American Communities,* examines the philanthropic potential in four groups, including Asian Americans. Highlights of Asian-American charitable giving are excerpted here.

Highlights of Asian-American Philanthropy

Asian-American ethnic groups share some common values; and Asian donors are heavily influenced by the values of family, hard work, the need for respect, and "saving face."

Asian Americans tend to:

- Support programs that strengthen the family
- Support programs that improve education for youth
- Support health care and long-term care for the elderly
- Consider philanthropy as a repayment for community debts
- Support programs that facilitate employer/employee efforts for the poor

Cultures of Caring interviewees indicate that philanthropic activities begin to occur within the third to fifth generations and are generally influenced by Neo-Confucian ethics—a value system that links a reverential attitude toward human life with respect to others and a sense of social responsibility. Asian Americans tend to support the elderly and their housing needs, as well as health services, education (particularly scholarships), religion, and political causes.

The growth of foundations in the Chinese-American community is linked to successes in the fields of technology and real estate. Philanthropic traditions of giving and helping in the Chinese-American community can be traced to Confucian tenets, which stress benevolence, wisdom, universal order, and peace and service to others; and Chinese family associations are an important source of charitable giving.

Although many differences exist among Asian groups, the values and behaviors of East Asians are generally rooted in the religious teachings of Buddhism, Confucianism, and Taoism. Compared with mainstream America, giving practices among Asian Americans are generally considered more focused, ethnic specific, ritualistic, and institutionalized. Total giving in the Asian-American community is highly correlated with socioeconomic conditions, age, and attitudes toward volunteering and family support. Much of the research on Asian giving focuses on Chinese, Japanese, Filipino, and Korean Americans.

As socioeconomic status and age increase in the Asian-American community, so does overall giving. In addition, although self-identity is not significantly related to Asian-American giving, it plays a role in the existence of many Asian nonprofits.[15]

Jessica Chao's article "Asian-American Philanthropy: Expanding Circles of Participation" in *Cultures of Caring* explores various practices of Asian-American philanthropy from the donor's perspective, as derived from information gathered from 39 major donors and 50 other individuals. Her findings are summarized below.

"Asian-American philanthropic practices vary widely:

- No single form of Asian-American philanthropy exists. Within the Asian-American community, philanthropy is as richly diverse as the population itself, reflecting the specific social adaptation techniques of various ethnic groups, from a variety of economic strata and from various levels of acculturation and Americanization.
- Each wave of Asian immigrants, whether Chinese, Filipino, Japanese, Korean, or South Asian, adapts to its new environment by sharing

goods, time, and money to survive, to create community and to invest in and adopt a new community of participation.

- Among Asian Americans, informal giving is related to close family and social circles. These circles of family and friends seem to expand as financial means increase and as the perception of needs transitions from survival and emergency issues to broader "quality of community life" issues.

- The variety of indigenous forms of giving money and volunteering time through mutual aid associations and other essentially immigrant self-help strategies exist simultaneously and in parallel with other forms of giving, including Asian-American alumni and professional associations, volunteer language and cultural schools, and elite philanthropy to major mainstream institutions.

- The practice of sending remittances to support family, schools, and projects that improve the living, health, and community conditions in the "home" country permeate Asian-American immigrant generations. Annual remittances are estimated to be in billions of dollars.

- The most frequent answer to the question about why Asian Americans have given time or money is that giving is done out of a sense of duty and obligation to one's family, community, and society. All of the donors interviewed cited family influence as a major, if not the only, reason whey they feel obligated to give.

- Donor characteristics depend on generation and country of origin: Although Asian-American ethnic groups exhibit more similarities than dissimilarities, a few variations exist among the groups: Japanese Americans have a more focused interest in civil rights, civil liberties, and political representation issues—even outside the Japanese-American community. Filipino Americans focus a great deal of their giving to the Philippines. Chinese-American donors are particularly diverse in their interests, but cultural heritage is a strong interest.

- Second- and third-generation donors are more likely to give to social justice and civil rights causes and to have a stronger sense of philanthropy as a tool for civic and political participation. As a result, pan-Asian and collective, united, or federated fundraising efforts are potentially appealing to them.

- More often than not, the major donor class created its wealth in this country. Entrepreneurial wealth has tended to come from high-technology industries and financial services, especially investment banking and venture capital. There is a great deal of trade and business with Asia. Professional affluence is most often from law, medicine, and financial services.

"Many factors determine giving preferences:

- Philanthropic preferences tend to follow business and social behavior. In general, the more Americanized Asian Americans are likely to give to formal nonprofits, to U.S. entities, and to pan-Asian charities. In contrast, the more foreign-oriented tend to give more informally to family, friends, and mutual aid associations; to charitable causes in their home country and to ethnic-specific causes.
- Financial contributions in other than nominal amounts almost always follow significant contributions of time through volunteering on boards, advisory councils, and event committees.
- Passion for a cause or constituency—such as the elderly, youth, or victims—respect and confidence in the leadership of the nonprofit, and identification with the social and business peer group represented by the board are all critical in decisions about committing significant time and money to an organization.
- Education and scholarships, nursing homes and services for the elderly, youth services, immigration services, cultural institutions and cultural heritage programs, and social justice and civil rights causes receive the most frequent, if not the largest, gifts.

"In recent years, foreign-born entrepreneurs and wealthy families from Korea, India, and the Chinese emigrant population have used donations as a means to invest in U.S. nonprofits. They are often significantly wealthier than their American-born counterparts. Like their mainstream counterparts, most of the donors interviewed prefer supporting immediate needs and direct services rather than endowments or service organizations.

"The first donation to a formal nonprofit outside the ethnic community is often to the United Way or to an alma mater. As donors became more familiar with nonprofits, however, the United Way and alma maters do not always remain the highest priority for giving.

"Successful fundraising efforts require a "personal" touch:

"The most effective fundraising appeal is the personal "ask" from a well-respected friend or business associate or a family member. The prestige of the person asking for funds has direct impact on the likelihood of a positive response. The personal connection to and participation in a particular nonprofit is a strong indicator of the likelihood that a financial contribution will be made, especially when larger gifts are requested.

"Among Asian-American donors, there is an accepted "tit-for-tat" practice among social and business peers. Requests to favored charities are generally reciprocated with donations to the peer's favorite causes. Visible acknowledgement of contributions and gifts tailored to different levels of giving is important to most of the Chinese, Japanese, and Filipino Americans interviewed.

"Family gifts are a popular fundraising tool for universities and museums. Gifts named in memory of a deceased family member also hold special appeal. Filipino-American donors enjoy events and social gatherings, particularly dinner dances and entertainment. Many fundraisers and donors mentioned that this is the most effective way to introduce a Filipino American to a charity. Second- and third-generation Japanese Americans, and often Chinese Americans, enjoy golf tournaments and ethnic holiday celebrations. Personal invitations are important for acceptance to these fundraising events.

"Appeals for endowments, foundations, community funds, and united funds require special thought: Most million-dollar-plus gifts from Asian Americans are for capital projects—some also endowment maintenance for the capital project. Endowment gifts were almost always given to institutions from which the donor of the donor's family benefited—an alma mater or hospital, for example—or an institution that the donor participated in on a regular basis, such as a cultural institution. They were never the first contribution to an institution. The most frequent contribution to an endowment was to the alma mater in response to an ongoing, publicized capital campaign.

"When asked whether they would consider giving endowment gifts to Asian-American organizations, many of those interviewed mentioned that issues of permanence, track record, history, and strength of leadership would be important facts to consider in such a decision. Most of the Asian Americans interviewed preferred not to have a foundation but instead chose to create their own private foundation because of the fear of losing control to an unfamiliar entity.

"Among donors, the appeal of Asian-American federated or community funds, and united fundraising organizations varied. For smaller donors ($10,000 or less in annual contributions), particularly American-born professionals, pooling funds collectively can be attractive. Such funds offer a way of "paying at the office," aid in deciphering among many charities, and are attractive in their coalescing role. For several major donors with specific passions, the united, collective, or federated fund concept was not as compelling. They fear potential bureaucracy and losing control, and prefer instead to make their own decisions on charities."[16]

Giving patterns among Asian Americans is summarized in *Philanthropy in Communities of Color,* by Bradford Smith et al.

Filipino Americans

- "Much of Filipino giving is characterized by reciprocal obligation.
- The sharing of food, both in times of need and at ceremonial occasions, is very important to Filipinos.
- A system of ritual god-parenthood is used to help pay for specific celebrations and to expand the support network of one's family.
- Filipinos send and take a large amount of money, material goods, and food to relatives living in the Philippines.
- Regional organizations, based on town or district of origin in the Philippines, are popular with Filipinos in the United States.
- Filipinos are very religious (Catholic) but give little to the church."[17]

Chinese Americans

- "Clans and mutual benefit associations are important centers of Chinese philanthropy.
- Money is given more easily than time, but time given has a higher value.
- Chinese give to mainstream charitable organizations as well as to Chinese organizations.
- There is a strong sense of reciprocity in Chinese sharing and helping.
- Chinese often make donations to charitable organizations as part of ceremonial events such as births, weddings, and funerals.
- Confucian and Buddhist traditions have some influence on Chinese philanthropy."[18]

Japanese Americans

- "Confucianism and Buddhism are significant influences in Japanese giving behavior.
- For Japanese, time and money are given with equal readiness due to a strong sense of payback, or of doing one's share toward community survival.
- Japanese donate to both Japanese and dominant-culture organizations.
- Japanese mutual aid associations, originally established for economic survival and political advocacy, have become more social, focusing less on giving assistance and more on preserving the culture.
- *Koden,* consisting of monies given to defray funeral costs, is probably the most common Japanese giving practice. Some of these monies are then donated back to the community."[19]

Korean Americans

- "Much Korean sharing and helping takes place within the extended family.
- First-generation Koreans give primarily to Korean ethnic organizations and Korean Protestant churches.
- Giving practices in the Korean community are strongly influenced by social relationships.
- Koreans are not generally expected to participate in giving traditions until they are married.
- Koreans sometimes give indirectly by buying something not really needed from a relative or friend.
- Protestant and, to a lesser extent, Buddhist churches are a focal point in Korean giving practices."[20]

HISPANICS/LATINOS AND FUNDRAISING

If a fundamental principle of fundraising is to know the donor's interests, then giving habits are important. Hispanic giving traditions are primarily informal, including financial support for newly arrived family members, remittances sent to one's native country, or even a godparent's financial support for a godchild's education. There is also a pattern of more formal charitable giving by Hispanics. The Hispanic Federation's annual survey of Hispanic New Yorker giving in 1999 asked those surveyed if they gave to a charity in 1998. Of these who responded to the survey, 63 percent said yes and 37 percent said no. This survey of New Yorkers was fairly constant with the Roper Report (1999) national data. The Roper Center reported 57 percent of Hispanics giving in 1998 (see Exhibit 5-2).

The organization or charity of choice for Hispanic giving is overwhelmingly the church. Regardless of income, education, age, immigration status, ethnicity, gender, or language preference, churches were the number-one recipients—48 percent gave to the church, followed by 20 percent giving to a nonprofit or community group, and 16 percent to "charitable causes." Forty percent said they gave $20 or more to an organization outside the church.

Hispanic giving to nonreligious institutions and charitable causes increases with the level of education attained. Only 12 percent of Latinos with an eighth-grade education gave to a nonprofit organization, compared to 37

EXHIBIT 5-2   PERCENT MAKING A CONTRIBUTION BY INCOME

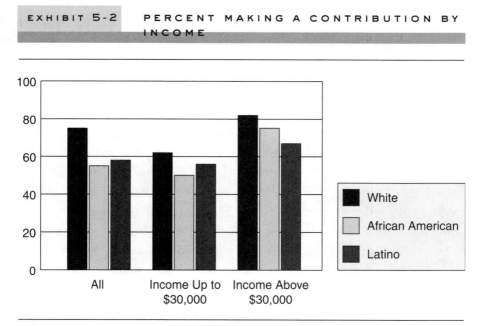

Source: Roper Center for Public Opinion Research, 1999. Report to the W. K. Kellogg Foundation by the Roper Center at the University of Connecticut, February 1999. Reprinted with permission.

percent of those with a college degree. There is also a correlation between income and giving, which is consistent with education leading to higher income potential.

Surveys of Hispanic donors give us some insight to the types of appeals currently being used to raise money in the Hispanic/Latino community. Of those interviewed by the Hispanic Federation, 24 percent replied that they gave in response to a direct mail solicitation. Puerto Ricans received mail more often than Dominicans or other Hispanics—31 percent, 16 percent, and 23 percent, respectively. There is another side to this data. Even though mail solicitation was the most common way for Hispanics to learn about a charity, 40 percent did not receive any requests. Furthermore, only 34 percent of those surveyed gave more than $100 to charity in 1998.

Although direct mail can to be a useful educational tool for Hispanic donors, the personal approach is a significant factor in Hispanic giving. The more respected (in the eyes of the donor) the "asker," the higher probability for a larger gift. This is no different from "mainstream" fundraising. The difference is one of relationships. Just as we develop good matches for peer-level solicitation in existing major gifts programs, we should do the same in cultivating diverse new donors. The medium of mail and media will continue to drive a stream of irregular and smaller gifts, but greater success will come from the cultivation of respected individuals in the Hispanic community who will help create new donor relationships.

A few words about identifying Hispanic leaders to develop organizational fundraising capacity—many boards wrestle with the "need" to diversify the board membership. Those trustee and nominating committees who challenge themselves to consider the underlying needs for diversity are a step ahead of the game. It is like peeling an onion. A layer certainly could be the desire for racial/ethnic or another type of diversity, but the next layer could be a need for an individual with passion for the work of the organization. Yet another layer might be affinity and recognition within the particular community—in this case, Hispanic. It is this last layer that appears to be overlooked the most, and could very well be a key to unlocking the support of the community for one's organization. We are accustomed to marketing our causes, but are we building relationships based on respect and relevance, within specific communities?

That leads to the question of favored causes. Education and job training rate high with Latino donors (31 percent); 23 percent indicated they would give to major disaster relief; and 19 percent would give to health/AIDS causes. In my own professional experience in working for a disaster relief organization, I can reflect on the generosity of Hispanic donors in the wake of major disasters, particularly in Central America. The conversion of these disaster gifts to repeat donations is difficult, however. I would characterize those difficulties as follows:

- There is a lack of understanding of local need versus disaster relief.

- Mainstream organizations have limited visibility in the community, or, put another way, organizational relevance is tied to disaster relief in the native country only.

- Respected spokespersons in the community have not been asked to support the organizations' overall work.

- Appeals are typically limited to mail and phone with media support.

How, then, do we change this cycle? I offer a few possibilities:

- Increase collaboration between organizations seen as central to Hispanic causes and those organizations with broader, nonethnic specific missions.

- Continue to use mail, phone, and/or media to promote and educate, but follow up with local neighborhood gatherings designed to engage dialog and forge new relationships. People will support what they help create.

- Recognize the generosity of Hispanic donors in their communities. A simple cake and coffee reception in a neighborhood church or community meeting place could be well received. Recognition, however, needs to be sensitive to the level of the gift and the donor's desire.

In addition to non–Hispanic-based organizations fundraising in the Hispanic community is Hispanic fundraising within and outside of its community. The first example is the Hispanic Scholarship Fund (HSF).[21] The mission of HSF is to double the rate of Hispanics earning a college education to 18 percent by the year 2006. The rapid growth of the Hispanic population in the United States makes these groups the fastest-growing segment, and projections indicate that Hispanics will be the largest minority in the United States by 2050. This is a young population—nearly 40 percent of all Hispanics are under the age of 19.

HSF is responding to the educational gap in Hispanic education. This gap is becoming wider as the population grows:

- Hispanics have higher dropout rates (29.5 percent) compared to less than 8 percent for non-Hispanic whites.
- Hispanics have lower college attendance—36 percent of Hispanics attend college, compared to 45 percent for non-Hispanic whites.
- Only 10.3 percent of all Hispanic adults have a bachelor's degree, compared with 24.6 percent for non-Hispanic whites.

In 1999, HSF awarded more than $9.3 million in scholarships, an increase of 165 percent over the prior year. More than 4,200 students were recipients of the scholarships. These are admirable statistics, but clearly not enough to achieve the goal of doubling the current rate of Hispanic students earning college degrees.

HSF experiences generous support from the corporate community. More than 50 percent of HSF's funds are from direct corporate contributions—particularly stunning when less than 5 percent of total giving in the United States is reported to come from corporate sources.[22]

The fundraising strategy makes sense. Corporations stand to benefit from an educated workforce. The growing Hispanic population is a major source of future employees. In fact, HSF reports that more than 100 of the nation's Fortune 1000 companies invest in HSF.

Another successful fundraising strategy used by HSF is special events. Volunteer Hispanic employee committees in events around the country raise more than 27 percent. Not only do the events provide revenue for the organization, they add visibility and build support from employees who, one person at a time, take a step closer to creating an individual relationship with the organization.

The next example of Hispanic-based fundraising comes from southern California—the Hispanic Legacy Fund in Ventura, California. Ventura County has a large Latino population, and in 1996, with the support of the Ventura Community Foundation, the Hispanic Legacy Fund had raised $356,772 from businesses, foundations, and individuals in response to a cause identified as "Destino 2000: The Hispanic Legacy Fund." Its mission: "To make our world a better place for Latinos in Ventura County." In addition to raising money for the cause, Destino 2000 raised community understanding, particularly among non-Latinos, of the issues facing the community.

A well-known rancher and Hispanic leader chairs the Destino 2000 campaign. He is appreciative of the non-Hispanic generosity flowing from major corporations and foundations, but stresses that success requires support from all levels of the Hispanic community, regardless of the dollar amount. "We have to encourage philanthropy in our community. We have to get mastery back in our hands."[23]

Fundraising for Destino 2000 is fairly diversified. Corporate and foundation support is primarily from non-Hispanic sources, but there is mutual understanding of the need for individual support from members of the Hispanic community.

Three key traditions exist in Hispanic giving—family, church, and mutual assistance.[24]

- Hispanic/Latino philanthropy includes the tradition of voluntary associations, like *mutualista* societies created to provide support to individual Latinos in need.

- A traditional giving relationship exists between Latinos and the Catholic Church.

- Hispanics tend to support relatives abroad before contributing to non-religious institutions.

- Hispanic giving occurs informally, among family and friends and the church, where the personal connections are essential, while other factors like charitable tax deductions are less important.

- A strong sense of cultural heritage affects Hispanic giving. It is manifested in the desire to preserve traditions, a sense of family responsibility, remittances to country of origin, and a preference for giving to groups that assist their ethnic communities.[25]

- Almost 52 percent of Hispanics polled for the 1999 Roper Report indicated that they contributed to their church, while African Americans reported 42 percent and whites reported 41 percent.

- Hispanics place importance on being asked to give by a trusted person or a personal friend.

- An appeal via letter was noted in the Roper Report as at least somewhat important by 25 percent of those interviewed.

Alternatively, Henry Ramos in "Latino Philanthropy: Expanding U.S. Models of Giving and Civic Participation," written for *Cultures of Caring*, offers these considerations for expanding Latino philanthropy:

- "The number of Latinos achieving professional career status is increasing, and so is the number of Latinos who are participating in high-end, organized philanthropy. Currently, however, the number of Latinos engaged in organized philanthropy is relatively small when compared with the potential pool of such donors nationwide.

- Although Latino donors prefer to support Latino constituencies in need and Latino community causes, they generally give as much—and sometimes more—to mainstream organizations.

- Latino donors report a surprising dearth of effective, targeted outreach efforts by nonprofits in general, and by more established mainstream institutions especially, to solicit their involvement and financial support.

- Increasing numbers of Latino donors are supporting community innovations designed to help both Latinos *and* the larger society, including, for example: emerging Latino-focused community grantmaking institutions; effective community-based citizenship promotion efforts; and mixed-use community development, childcare, and arts projects.

- Few Latino donors, no matter how forward looking, support endowment for Latino or mainstream causes. These donors prefer instead to address the more immediate needs of the Latino constituencies they care most about.

- Latino donors appear most concerned about the needs of Latino children, youth, and families—undeniably among this nation's most needy populations.

- Due to growing national concern over issues such as immigration and bilingualism, Latino donors are increasingly committed to supporting more self-help–oriented philanthropic vehicles designed to protect the Latino interests that are currently subject to challenge.

- Latino donors have shown a strong interest in supporting cultural arts activities, particularly those that celebrate and expose more broadly Latino art forms and traditions.

- In contrast to reasons for giving for many mainstream philanthropists, tax and other institutional incentives are not the principal driving forces for giving within the Latino community. Familial and culturally based factors, such as a sense of responsibility to one's relatives and kin, seem to drive these donors' giving.

- Like mainstream philanthropists, Latino donors seem to respond most favorably to appeals from respected leaders and peers in their community or profession for support or organizations or causes with which they have personal experience—either as a beneficiary or a volunteer.

- Large-scale Latino donors (who are typically few in number and relentlessly cultivated for financial support in their communities) believe strongly that special efforts are needed to train and prepare larger numbers of Latinos—both at the higher and the lower ends of the socioeconomic spectrum—to participate more extensively in giving to U.S. philanthropic institutions. Culturally appropriate education, outreach and incentive programs will be required to achieve this.

- Finally, Latino donors believe strongly that if opportunities for Latino leadership and participation in organized philanthropy are to be increased, mainstream grantmaking institutions must do a better job of incorporating Latinos within their staffs, governing boards, and advisory bodies."[26]

The authors of *Philanthropy in Communities of Color* offer the following summary on Hispanic/Latino traditions of giving.

Mexican Americans

- "The family and extended family serve as an extensive and complex framework for sharing and helping.

- A system of ritual god-parenthood is used to help pay for specific celebration and to expand the support network of one's family.

- Money, goods, and clothing are often taken or sent back to Mexico to be distributed in one's hometown.

- The church is an important center of philanthropic activity.

- Housing is frequently shared with relatives and friends.

- Little giving or volunteering is directed toward non-Mexican, non-church organizations."[27]

Guatemalan Americans

- "Guatemalan giving occurs primarily within the extended family.
- Guatemalans send a large amount of money and goods to relatives, friends, and local communities in the home country.
- Many respondents spoke of people returning to Guatemala for family gatherings, religious holidays, festivals, and pilgrimages.
- Churches, primarily Catholic, are focal points of giving within the Guatemalan community.
- Guatemalans in the Bay Area make use of volunteers in "radio clubs" to send messages back and forth to Guatemala via ham radios.
- Many Guatemalans provide food and lodging to new immigrants.
- Little giving or volunteering is directed at charitable organizations outside the Guatemalan community. Guatemalans have a generally low opinion of mainstream American philanthropic institutions and practices."[28]

Salvadoran Americans

- "Most Salvadoran giving takes place within the extended family and ethnic community.
- Salvadorans send and bring large amounts of money and goods to family and friends in El Salvador.
- Salvadorans prefer to give directly to individuals and tend to distrust large charitable organizations.
- Salvadorans rarely relinquish the care of elderly parents to government or nonprofit organizations.
- Salvadorans commonly provide shelter to other Salvadorans for little or no money.
- Some Salvadorans give to and volunteer for mainstream nonprofit organizations."[29]

NATIVE AMERICANS AND FUNDRAISING

Communities of Native Americans are commonly referred to as *tribes*. Native Americans lived in groupings that varied in their size and level of social complexity. These groups are known as *band, tribe, chiefdom,* and *state* or *nation,* going from least complex to most. Not every Indian belongs to a tribe or has a chief. Chiefs lead chiefdoms, but bands and tribes have different and less complex forms of leadership. Governors lead members of the Native American Pueblo communities in Arizona and New Mexico.

The relative level of social complexity found among various individual groups really influenced how the Native Americans dealt with European contact and what happened later (less complex groups were dispersed, wiped out). The more complex groups like the League of the Iroquois with their chiefdoms could band together and fight more successfully.

Native American Perspectives on Racial and Ethnic Identity Labels

American Indian and Native American are the most common racial and ethnic labels used to identify the general population of indigenous peoples in the United States. The article "What We Want to be Called" by Michael Yellow Bird printed in *The American Indian Quarterly* reports on the state of this ongoing debate.[30] The author maintains that there is no clear consensus on which label is more preferable, and cites some recent discussions on university campuses as to which racial labels most appropriately describe the students, their organizations, and the academic Native studies programs they attend. At Northern Arizona University, First Nations students debated whether to call their Native studies program "American Indian" or "Native American" studies. Cornell University reports increased discussions among students about what to call their "American Indian" studies program. In 1998, First Nations students at the University of Kansas changed the name of their student organization from Native American Student Association (NASA) to the First Nations Student Association (FNSA). This change was prompted by students' desire to counter imposed racial labels and to promote notions of inclusiveness, sovereignty, accuracy, and identity empowerment among First Nations students.[31]

Yellow Bird writes, "Historically, and even in contemporary times, Indigenous Peoples in the United States and Canada have not regarded themselves as one monolithic racial society. While Indigenous Peoples have, in the past and the present, found common ground in their experiences and dealings with European American colonizers, they have also often viewed one another as diverse peoples, distinguishable according to language, behavior, dress, geography, foods, technologies, creation stories, and numerous other characteristics."[32] Indigenous peoples in the United States represent more than 550 distinct tribes, including 223 Alaska Native Villages. A survey conducted in 1995 by the Bureau of Labor Statistics, U.S. Department of Labor, found that indigenous peoples preferred a variety of different racial identity labels: 49.8 percent preferred "American Indian"; 37.5 percent preferred "Native American"; 5.7 percent had no preference; 3.7 percent preferred some other term; and 3.5 percent preferred "Alaska Native."[33]

Many words are often used to demean groups of people.[34] "In the United States several derogatory labels are used to demean Indigenous Peoples and have become institutionally oppressive to these groups through past and present use. Three more common labels are *savages*, *redskins*, and *squaw* (a gender-specific label used to refer to Indigenous women)."[35] Yellow Bird further identifies cross-cultural references that further impact Indigenous People's identity. The Spanish term *Indio* (Indian) is used as a term of abuse in Latin America, and to be "Indian" is to be associated with the lowest social rung of society. Similarly, in some Mexican-American communities in the United States, Indian is used to refer to a person of lower social class who is from a "backwards, inferior culture."[36]

Giving Among Native Americans

There is little research on the giving patterns of Native Americans, but Mindy Berry, in "Native American Philanthropy: Expanding Social Participation and Self-Determination," part of the Council on Foundations' *Cultures of Caring* series, conducted more than 100 interviews with Native Americans, and she shares those findings in her work. Her paper includes Native American donor models, and is summarized as follows.[37]

The most common forms of giving among Native Americans are ranked:

- Informal personal giving
- Public charities (tribal foundations, nontribal funds, and service associations
- Tribal giving programs (enterprise, governmental, intertribal consortia)
- Workplace giving programs

- Community foundation funds
- Private foundations

The most common interests of Native donors are:

- Education (scholarships for schools, memorials, internships, etc.)
- Cultural preservation
- Economic development
- Youth
- Elderly services
- Arts
- Health care
- Rehabilitation services (e.g., drug and alcohol addiction counseling)
- Environmental or natural resources
- Emergencies and disasters

The most common giving styles among Native donors:

- Prefer to make anonymous, need-based gifts
- Respond to personal appeals through family or community relations
- Prefer individuals and groups they know well
- Like to participate in decision-making by serving on a board, committee, or council and in events
- Follow a give-and-receive model: When one gives, it will come back, maybe not immediately, but sometime in the future—a mutual exchange relationship

There are differences in giving traits for reservation-based Native donors and nonreservation-based donors:

- Reservation-based Native donors prefer:
  - Tribally sponsored charitable activities such as the United Way, Special Olympics, or Native organizations
  - Assorted needs of tribal members, children, and elders
  - Educational scholarships
  - Local sports activities (for their children)

- Nonreservation-based Native donors prefer:
  - Historical and cultural projects
  - Local university
  - Human services
  - The arts (museum or artist training)
  - Emergency help for those in need
  - Church and related activities

Berry notes that tribal based foundations are growing, with variations in size, variety, and structure. Most were:

- 501 C-3 organizations
- Community based
- Single constituency oriented
- Established within the 1990s
- Focused on tribal or community issues
- Increasingly more reliant on tribal and private funds, as opposed to state and federal government sources

There are 30 tribal colleges in the United States, and most have some form of institutional grant-making vehicles for scholarships and technical assistance. Eighteen have gaming on their reservations, and fewer than five received a share of the gaming profits. The Menominee of Wisconsin, one of the more successful tribes, contributed more than $2 million to establish a tribal college, the College of the Menominee Nation.

According to Berry, as of August 1998, at least 16 community foundations, with 33 individual funds, held Native-initiated or controlled, advised, or focused funds:

- "In Montana, a tribe was invited to establish an advised fund as part of a community foundation outreach initiative.
- In New Mexico, a local Native American artist set up an advised fund and was encouraged to do so not only for tax purposes, but also for ease in administering charitable contributions.
- A fund in Minnesota evolved from a broader mission of diversity. This fund, controlled and advised by a committee of Native American community leaders, focuses on cultural preservation, education, chil-

dren, and elders. It makes grants up to $3,500 and provides technical assistance up to $1,500.

- In the Duluth–Superior area of Minnesota, the Anishabe Fund was established within the community foundation to foster cultural awareness of the Anishabe/Ojibwe artistic, spiritual, and domestic traditions. The fund provides grants between $300 and $1,000 for qualifying projects."[38]

These are the most effective fundraising messages among Native Americans:

- Convey respect for people's dignity and cultural traditions.
- Stress the importance of developing relationships with others.
- Foster partnership opportunities.
- Focus on empowerment in Native communities, as opposed to continued dependence on inferiority.
- Respond to injustices toward and urgent needs of Native people.

The most effective solicitation methods:

- Soliciting tribal vendors
- Using earned income from educational and advocacy materials
- Accessing the Internet for funding opportunities and posting their own Web sites
- Raising money from tribal employees, their financial advisors and legal counsel, and companies that employ tribal members
- Establishing workplace giving programs such as Earth Share, Navajo Way, Change for a Dollar, and others

Recent accounts of Native American giving indicate that philanthropy within the Native American community is increasing. Native Americans in Philanthropy reports that Native grant-makers increased from 3 to 32 between 1973 and 1996. Berry reports that Native tribes and related organizations involved in grant-making have increased by 50 percent or more. "Native American giving, which is very much reflective of their communal orientation—particularly in tribal settings—is expressed not only in more formal exchanges but also in less formal assignments of time, goods and spiritual activities."[39]

CHAPTER 6

Challenges and Opportunities of Diversity in Philanthropy Today

RECOGNITION

In fundraising language, recognition has become synonymous with acknowledgment or thank-you systems. Donors are generally thanked in some way after they have made a contribution. A broader definition of recognition taken from *The American Heritage Dictionary of the English Language*, Fourth Edition, reads, "An awareness that something perceived has been perceived before." Recognizing those who support our charitable efforts must obviously be an ongoing component of donor cultivation. Appropriate forms of recognition for diverse communities is critical and essential in the philanthropic exchange. A universal trait is the desire to be recognized.

> Among the tribes of northern Natal in South Africa, the most common greeting—the equivalent of "hello" in English—is the expression of *sawu bona*. Literally it means, "I see you." If you are a member of the tribe you might reply by saying *sikhona*, which translates into English as "I am here." The order of the exchange is significant. It means that until you see me I do not exist; when you do see me, you bring me into existence. The meaning implicit in the perennial wisdom of this tribe is part of what is called *ubuntu*, a frame of mind or world-view characteristic of sub-Sahara African peoples. *Ubuntu* is the key word used to shorten a phrase in the Zulu language that translates "a person is a person because of other people."[1]

Within the philanthropic context, *recognition* is usually the term used to note that an act of generosity has occurred. The notion that a "person is a person because of other people" applies aptly to the appreciation of diversity in others, for it is when we recognize each other that we bring into being the uniqueness of the individual.

Those who are involved in the acquisition of financial donations from individuals may want to consider this broader interpretation of recognition. Why is it that we choose to "recognize" after the donation has been made? Should we utilize a more comprehensive form of recognition that begins with acknowledging the individual before the gift is secured?

Within diverse populations, there are a variety of ways in which donors would like to be thanked, just as is the case among the general population of donors. Lord Chesterfield is credited with saying, "In order to please people, you must please them in their own way." And, in order to please them in their own way, we must know what those preferences are.

Traditional second- and third-generation Chinese Americans may desire very specific forms of recognition for their financial generosity. Public recognition among their peers is imperative. It would not be unusual for a well-known donor from this profile to offer such details as appropriate comments to be made by the speaker, or the right present to give in thanks for the individual's contributions. This type of expectation contrasts with other Asian Americans, who may not identify strongly with a peer group and for whom public recognition is not desirable. The same contrast in expectations extends to the Filipino-American community, where the more traditional Filipinos will expect highly visible and public acknowledgment for their generosity, whereas less traditional Filipinos may want exactly the opposite.

Persons from Native American cultures may not understand the exchange of gifts and recognition. Giving in the Native culture does not occur because there is an expectation of reciprocity or thanks. Giving is simply a way of life. Native American appreciation flows from respect for the land and is inextricably interwoven with the individual. Land is sacred, and the land gives life to the being.

Latino and Hispanic preferences for recognition vary between individual groups. Acceptable and appropriate recognition for a Puerto Rican will not be the same for a Cuban American. Mexican Americans and Central Americans with strong ties to the Catholic Church may prefer acknowledgment in the presence of the church, which is so central to their communities. A typically American form of thanking a donor is the thank-you letter, sent to the majority of donors. Imagine the value of a thank-you letter sent (in English) to a person for whom English is a second language. Imagine the impact of a thank-you letter sent to an Asian American prominent in the community, and for whom there is no public acknowledgment of the donor's generosity. Imagine a form thank-you letter sent to any donor that is regarded as mass-produced and impersonal. Where is "I see you" and "I am here" in these exchanges?

How do we create effective ways of recognizing individuals as individuals? The standard thank-you letter is not going to be replaced, nor should it be, as it is necessary and appropriate as gift confirmation. The text, tone, and signature on the letter are all elements that can offer more personalization to all donors, not just those who are viewed as "diverse." Using phrases or words that reflect the donor's background will demonstrate appreciation for the individual. The style of language and tone of the letter also show recognition of the person. A letter, after all, should be written with the receiver in mind, not the sender. And, finally, who signs the letter? How many times have we sent an acknowledgment letter without considering the effect of the signer to the receiver? Understandably, a prominent person within the organization signs most thank-you letters, but what is the connection to the donor? One of the most powerful words in any thank-you letter is *you*. The tone of the letter needs to be directed to the donor as an individual, in some way personalizing the exchange. A phrase of thanks in the donor's language, a quote from a prominent person known to the donor, an analogy to traditions of generosity within the donor's diverse community, could be sensitive and effective additions to thank-you letters.

Donor recognition in a public venue requires some consideration, also. Do we hold our recognition events in the community of the donor, or based on organization considerations? For example, many nonprofits use their annual meeting to honor and pay tribute to selected volunteers and/or donors. Are these events held in neighborhoods or facilities where the donors live, work, and worship? The section of this book that covers the traditions of giving and sharing describes many forms of exchange that are both historical and valued among diverse individuals. Finding appropriate ways to weave those practices into all aspects of the philanthropic exchange can only enhance the importance of appreciating each donor as an individual.

We can learn much from giving and recognition within the Native American community where giving is inextricably tied to a profound sense of the universe. Dagmar Thorpe writes that, "despite the highest statistics of poverty in the nation on a per capita basis, [reservation-based Indians] are . . . among the most generous people in America."[2]

James Joseph, former president of the Council on Foundations, observes in his book, *Remaking America*, "Paramount among these values is the tradition of sharing. Giving is not charity but honoring the community . . . a matter not only of altruism but of mutual responsibility. Gift-giving is a unifying cultural trait in which both the giver and the receiver are honored and their equal status validated."[3]

And, in *The Honor of Giving: Philanthropy in Native America*, Ronald Austin Wells quotes Black Elk, "You have noticed that everything an Indian does is in a circle, and that is because the Power of the world always works in circles, and everything tries to be round . . . The sky is round, and I have heard that the earth is round like a ball, and so are the stars. The wind, in its greatest power, whirls. Birds make their nests in circles, for theirs is the same religion as ours . . . Even the seasons form a circle in the changing, and always come back again to where they were. The life of a man is a circle from childhood to childhood, and so it is in everything where power moves."[4]

The gift moves in a circle.

EXAMPLES OF FUNDRAISING IN DIVERSE COMMUNITIES

San Francisco Public Library

Several years ago, the San Francisco Public Library launched a capital campaign to build a new main library. The existing main library needed to be replaced with a larger, seismically sound structure. After years of waiting, a bond measure was placed before San Francisco voters to construct a new home for the main library. The proposition won, and the capital campaign for private funds to finance the nonconstruction costs of the campaign commenced. Private donations were needed for interior design, book acquisition, and equipment.

This was one of the city's major capital campaign efforts, and it involved the expected cast of high-level community and civic leaders in the initial stages of the campaign. The new library wasn't the only capital campaign in town: the opera and symphony were also raising capital funds, as were numerous hospitals and schools, and all of these worthy and necessary ventures were expecting support from community leaders. A successful and well-known fundraising firm was engaged to manage the campaign, and the library foundation board rolled up their sleeves to raise $30 million.

Author and board member of the library Peter Booth Wiley writes that significant community leaders were recruited to lead the campaign, which was originally structured as a conventional capital campaign "following the traditional idea of a fundraising pyramid, they went first after the small number of donors at the top of the pyramid who were expected to make the largest donations. . . . The results were disappointing."[5] The campaign lacked excitement. "The inspiration for turning the Library Foundation's commitment to a community-based approach into a funding reality came from Steve Coulter, a vice-president at Pacific Bell, in the form of a proposal that the library be presented as a series of collections and services rather than a main building with many branches throughout the city."[6] This proposal went forth into the communities, and out of the library's need to raise a lot of money from a much broader base grew the notion of "affinity groups." These self-identified groups included Chinese Americans, gays and lesbians, African Americans, Filipinos, Latinos, as well as representatives of children's services, adult literacy, art, music, and the physically impaired. All of these groups worked to develop programs and raise capital for the "Main Campaign." This effort resulted in an unprecedented community-based fundraising effort that was highly successful; it also resulted in a new main library that reflected San Francisco, as the affinity groups' efforts were acknowledged with designated space and/or services specific to each group. There is an endowed Gay and Lesbian center, and multilingual children's books in 39 languages. It is a library for the illiterate and the newcomer. Organization for the public campaign came from within communities. The campaign was heralded as a celebration of San Francisco's diversity. "There was an additional payoff: the excitement and notoriety generated by the foundation's new strategy pulled in many large donors who were originally skeptical. Remarkably, the foundation soared right past its goal of $30 million. . . . In one six-month period in 1993 the foundation grew from 600 donors to over 17,000."[7] The successes of the affinity groups surfaced new leaders and new donors.

Performing Arts in Harlem

Another example of successful fundraising in diverse communities comes from the performing arts community in New York City, where nonprofit arts organizations were pursuing culturally specific approaches designed to increase audience size and diversity, as well as increased financial support for productions. As background, a study of black charitable behavior in 1985 (Joint Center of Political Studies, reported by Giving USA) found that African Americans gave more of their income to churches and other religious organizations compared to an overall church contribution. Emmett Carson, CEO of the Minneapolis Community Foundation, has noted that the black church has long provided for much of the spiritual, social, and economic needs of the African-American community, so it is not unreasonable to assume that the church serves as a conduit for channeling charitable contributions within the African-American community.

This performing arts organization in New York City took this study seriously, and to attract African-American audiences and individual donors, the organization set up a series of short performances in an intimate Harlem studio space, and followed each with a cake and coffee reception, modeled after those found in local black churches. Marketing for the performances focused on posting flyers on bulletin boards of neighborhood black churches. All of the performances were sold out, and a stream of $25 donations was made at the end of each performance/reception. The development staff followed up with newsletters and requests for repeat donations. In all, there was a quadrupling of $25 gifts within the first year.[8]

CORPORATE GRANT-MAKING TO RACIAL ETHNIC COMMUNITIES

In 1999, corporations and their foundations contributed $8.97 billion, or 5.1 percent of total charitable giving in the United States, according to *Giving USA 1999*. The National Committee for Responsive Philanthropy's report, *Grants: Corporate Grantmaking for Racial and Ethnic Communities*, is an exhaustive compilation of the racial/ethnic corporate grant-making of 124 surveyed companies based on giving in 1995 (see Exhibits 6-1 through 6-4). The surveyed companies reported giving $1.3 billion in 1995 (17 percent of U.S. corporate giving). Listed among the reasons for surveying racial/ethnic corporate grant-making are:

EXHIBIT 6-1	TOP FIVE CORPORATE DONORS— AFRICAN-AMERICAN CAUSES

	Company/Foundation	Total
1.	Coca-Cola	$2,705,400
2.	Exxon	2,696,467
3.	Ford Motor Company	2,690,675
4.	General Motors	2,555,729
5.	Prudential Insurance	2,273,703

Source: *Grants: Corporate Grantmaking for Racial and Ethnic Communities,* National Committee for Responsive Philanthropy, 2000. Moyer Bell Limited: Rhode Island. NCRP. All rights reserved. Reprinted by permission.

EXHIBIT 6-2	TOP FIVE CORPORATE DONORS— ASIAN-AMERICAN CAUSES

	Company/Foundation	Total
1.	AIG/Starr Foundation	$1,571,410
2.	St. Paul Companies	510,700
3.	Bank of America	205,500
4.	Gannett Company	840,400 [sic]
5.	Chevron	183,211

Source: *Grants: Corporate Grantmaking for Racial and Ethnic Communities,* National Committee for Responsive Philanthropy, 2000. Moyer Bell Limited: Rhode Island. NCRP. All rights reserved. Reprinted by permission.

EXHIBIT 6-3	TOP FIVE CORPORATE DONORS— NATIVE-AMERICAN CAUSES

	Company/Foundation	Total
1.	Coca-Cola	$465,000
2.	General Mills	329,000
3.	St. Paul Companies	316,430
4.	Intel	230,000
5.	ARCO	225,900

Source: *Grants: Corporate Grantmaking for Racial and Ethnic Communities,* National Committee for Responsive Philanthropy, 2000. Moyer Bell Limited: Rhode Island. NCRP. All rights reserved. Reprinted by permission.

EXHIBIT 6-4   TOP FIVE CORPORATE DONORS—
                    HISPANIC/LATINO CAUSES

	Company/Foundation	Total
1.	Levi Strauss	$2,501,000
2.	Bank of America	1,187,200
3.	Citibank/Citicorp	834,194
4.	Dayton Hudson	793,030
5.	Coca-Cola	720,000

Source: Grants: Corporate Grantmaking for Racial and Ethnic Communities,
National Committee for Responsive Philanthropy, 2000. Moyer Bell Limited:
Rhode Island. NCRP. All rights reserved. Reprinted by permission.

- African Americans, Asian-Pacific Americans, Hispanics/Latinos, and Native Americans are the fastest-growing segment of the U.S. population.

- Together these communities are the fastest-growing economic power in the United States. Within 10 years, these four communities will have more purchasing power than any single European nation.

- The Conference Board estimates that less than half of corporate contributions are actually reported by corporations. If so, corporate funding is the fastest-growing area within the philanthropic sector.

Characteristics of the companies surveyed include:

- Reported revenues were nearly $2 trillion in 1995.

- Seventy-five of the surveyed companies are on *Fortune*'s list of the Global Five Hundred, the 500 largest companies in the world.

- Twenty-nine are on *Fortune*'s list of the 50 most profitable corporations in the world.

- Forty-seven were on the *Chronicle of Philanthropy*'s 1998 largest corporate donors list.

Education was the top interest area for corporate grant-making for racial/ethnic communities, with racial/ethnic scholarship programs receiving the largest share of this funding (see Exhibit 6-5). Racial/ethnic majority colleges received substantial support from the surveyed companies, $6.8 million. Culture-specific scholarship programs, like the National Hispanic Scholarship Fund, received $6.8 million. Overall, 87 percent of education funding

EXHIBIT 6-5	TOP FIVE MAJOR INTEREST DONORS	
	Donor	**Total Given**
Arts and Culture	AIG/Starr Foundation	$1,509,000
	St. Paul Companies	1,085,738
	Dayton Hudson	1,009,095
	Coca-Cola	720,000
	Times Mirror Company	485,000
Education	Exxon	4,630,647
	Coca-Cola	4,468,400
	Hewlett-Packard	3,314,621
	General Mills	3,097,058
	AIG/Starr Foundation	3,025,410
Health	AIG/Starr Foundation	1,665,000
	Aetna, Inc.	1,522,650
	Levi Strauss	1,185,400
	Chevron	1,023,500
	Metropolitan Life Insurance	878,340
Human Services	AIG/Starr Foundation	1,811,000
	General Mills	1,766,633
	Anheuser-Busch Companies	1,727,099
	Chicago Tribune Company	1,710,044
	Dayton Hudson	1,255,517
Public Benefit	Metropolitan Life Insurance	2,397,000
	Bank of America	1,942,866
	Levi Strauss	1,928,015
	St. Paul Companies	1,831,421
	Bankers Trust	1,377,500

Source: Grants: Corporate Grantmaking for Racial and Ethnic Communities, National Committee for Responsive Philanthropy, 2000. Moyer Bell Limited: Rhode Island. NCRP. All rights reserved. Reprinted by permission.

benefited African Americans or "Racial/Ethnic General." One-third of all funding for African Americans was awarded for higher education, while just 6.8 percent of Asian-Pacific American funding was for higher education.

Exhibits 6-6 through 6-9 on racial/ethnic grant-making are based on the NCRP report. The introduction states, "Surveyed companies gave grants to 6,351 organizations. Who are these organizations? How big are they? Who is responsible for them?

- "58 percent of the surveyed grantees were local organizations, but 16 percent were hospitals, colleges, or units of local government; 14 percent were national organizations, and 13 percent were chapters or

EXHIBIT 6-6   TOP TEN FUNDED METRO AREAS FOR AFRICAN AMERICANS

	Number of Grants	Total $ Given	Top Funders	Top Funding Areas
1. New York Area	589	$16,189,147	Prudential Insurance Exxon AIG/Starr Foundation	Higher education Community centers Economic development
2. Washington, DC	255	$5,325,490	Citibank/Citicorp Ford Motor Company Aetna, Inc.	Higher education Primary and secondary education Medical care Public policy R&D
3. Atlanta	221	$4,769,456	Coca-Cola AIG/Starr Foundation Bristol-Myers Squibb	Higher education Neighborhood improvement Primary and secondary education
4. Detroit	226	$4,411,597	Chrysler Corporation General Motors Ford Motor Company	Community centers Higher education Historical and cultural preservation
5. Minneapolis/St. Paul	148	$3,302,875	St. Paul Companies General Mills Honeywell	Primary and secondary education Youth Business

6. Chicago	272	$2,806,171	Chicago Tribune Amoco Sara Lee	Medical care Higher education Primary and secondary education
7. St. Louis	103	$2,286,729	Anheuser-Busch May Dept. Stores Toyota Motor Sales	Hunger and homelessness Youth development Primary and secondary education
8. San Francisco/Oakland/San Jose	73	$1,990,866	Chevron Clorox Transamerica	Medical care Primary and secondary education Youth
9. Raleigh/Durham/Chapel Hill	37	$1,642,505	Glaxo Wellcome General Electric RJR Nabisco	Higher education Medical care Primary and secondary education
10. Baltimore	136	$1,502,825	General Motors Chrysler Corporation Hewlett-Packard	Civil rights Higher education Primary and secondary education

Source: *Grants: Corporate Grantmaking for Racial and Ethnic Communities*, National Committee for Responsive Philanthropy, 2000. Moyer Bell Limited: Rhode Island. NCRP. All rights reserved. Reprinted by permission.

EXHIBIT 6-7   TOP TEN FUNDED METRO AREAS FOR HISPANICS/LATINOS

	Number of Grants	Total $ Given	Top Funders	Top Funding Areas
1. Los Angeles	199	$2,623,186	ARCO Anheuser-Busch Cos. Levi Strauss	Civil rights Higher education Primary and secondary education
2. Chicago	166	$2,120,350	Chicago Tribune Co. Amoco Bank of America	Services for the disabled Medical care Community development
3. New York/Northern New Jersey	183	$2,057,570	Bankers Trust Chase Manhattan Coca-Cola	Higher education Community centers and services Neighborhood improvement
4. Washington, DC	107	$1,671,400	RJR Nabisco Levi Strauss General Motors Corp.	Civil rights Medical care Primary and secondary education
5. San Francisco/Oakland/San Jose	137	$1,497,295	Levi Strauss Bank of America Citibank/Citicorp	Higher education Medical care Civil rights Primary and secondary education

City				
6. Miami	55	$1,225,907	Citibank/Citicorp AIG/Starr Foundation Coca-Cola	Primary and secondary education Higher education Civil rights
7. San Antonio	65	$1,151,212	Levi Strauss Coca-Cola General Motors Corp.	Higher education Primary and secondary education General medical care Medical care for women
8. El Paso	72	$1,049,503	Levi Strauss General Electric Exxon	Higher education Medical care Community education
9. Minneapolis/St. Paul	43	$932,205	St. Paul Companies General Mills Dayton Hudson	Job skills education Higher education Historical and cultural preservation
10. Dallas/Fort Worth	36	$767,000	Coors Brewing Procter & Gamble Levi Strauss	Job skills education Medical care Immigrant/refugee services

Source: Grants: Corporate Grantmaking for Racial and Ethnic Communities, National Committee for Responsive Philanthropy, 2000. Moyer Bell Limited: Rhode Island. NCRP. All rights reserved. Reprinted by permission.

EXHIBIT 6-8   TOP TEN FUNDED METRO AREAS FOR NATIVE AMERICANS

	Number of Grants	Total $ Given	Top Funders	Top Funding Areas
1. Minneapolis/St. Paul	68	$1,162,260	St. Paul Companies General Mills Dayton Hudson	Primary and secondary education Job/career/life skills education Job development and placement
2. New York/Northern New Jersey	24	$584,000	Coca-Cola Merrill Lynch & Co. Chase Manhattan	Historical and cultural preservation Higher education Public policy R&D
3. Denver	29	$398,405	Intel 3M Company General Electric	Higher education Primary and secondary education Civil rights and race relations
4. Albuquerque	13	$241,300	Hitachi America Levi Strauss Coca-Cola	Family and children services Higher education Primary and secondary education
5. Phoenix	11	$214,500	McDonald's Hitachi America Honeywell	Medical and physical health care Higher education Primary and secondary education

6. Anchorage	25	$164,400	ARCO	Hunger and homelessness
			Exxon	Higher education
			Unocal	Medical and physical health care
7. Washington, DC	5	$113,000	Coca-Cola	Historical and cultural preservation
			Exxon	Civil rights and race relations
			Sara Lee	Medical and physical health care
8. Tulsa	8	$95,000	Coca-Cola	Higher education
			Whirlpool	Historical and cultural preservation
			Amoco	Medical and physical health care
9. Rapid City	5	$85,000	Metropolitan Life Ins.	Medical and physical health care
			ARCO	Higher education
			AIG/Starr Foundation	Primary and secondary education
10. San Francisco/Oakland/San Jose	5	$66,500	Intel	Higher education
			Wells Fargo & Co.	Housing
			Dayton Hudson	Performing arts
				Medical and physical health care

Source: Grants: Corporate Grantmaking for Racial and Ethnic Communities, National Committee for Responsive Philanthropy, 2000. Moyer Bell Limited: Rhode Island. NCRP.

EXHIBIT 6-9 TOP TEN FUNDED METRO AREAS FOR ASIAN-PACIFIC AMERICANS

	Number of Grants	Total $ Given	Top Funders	Top Funding Areas
1. New York/Northern New Jersey	69	$1,676,956	AIG Starr Foundation JP Morgan & Company Merrill Lynch & Company	Historical and cultural preservation Medical care, visual arts Primary and secondary education
2. Minneapolis/St. Paul	54	$915,700	St. Paul Companies General Mills Pillsbury Company	Arts and culture Community centers and services Community education, higher education
3. San Francisco/Oakland/San Jose	86	$792,306	AIG Starr Foundation Chevron Levi Strauss	Higher education, medical care Community development Visual arts
4. Honolulu	68	$444,990	Gannett Company Bank of America Chevron	Primary and secondary education Arts and culture Higher education
5. Boston	18	$395,000	AIG Starr Foundation Boston Globe Polaroid	Visual arts Civil rights Primary and secondary education

6. Los Angeles	37	$336,031	ARCO	Civil rights
			JP Morgan & Company	Community development
			Hitachi America	Historical and cultural preservation
7. Chicago	18	$97,000	Sara Lee	Community centers and services
			Chicago Tribune Co.	Civil rights, medical care
			McDonald's	Family and children services
8. Orange County/Anaheim	4	$73,500	Baxter Intl. Allegiance	Medical care
			Dayton Hudson	Historical and cultural preservation
			Bank of America	Community development
9. Washington, DC	9	$43,000	Avon Products	Civil rights
			General Electric	Historical and cultural preservation
			Exxon	Higher education
10. Houston	5	$23,400	McDonald's	Youth development programs and services
			Compaq Computer	Historical and cultural preservation
			Exxon	Civil rights

Source: Grants: Corporate Grantmaking for Racial and Ethnic Communities, National Committee for Responsive Philanthropy, 2000. Moyer Bell Limited: Rhode Island. NCRP. All rights reserved. Reprinted by permission.

national headquarters of the 400 most popular recipients in the U.S., the *Chronicle of Philanthropy*'s "Philanthropy 400."[9]

- African Americans, Asian-Pacific Americans, Hispanics/Latinos, or Native Americans control just 40 percent of these recipients; the rest are controlled by non-Hispanic whites or a combination of racial/ethnic communities and non-Hispanic whites.

- More than three-fourths of the survey recipients are regular nonprofits; 13 percent are units of state, country, or municipal government (including units of tribal government); and 10 percent are religion-affiliated schools, and churches/synagogues."[10]

The NCRP report recommends the following for giving to racial/ethnic groups (see Exhibit 6-10):

African Americans

1. "Increase overall corporate grant-making for African Americans.

2. Increase funding to organizations benefiting African-American women.

3. Increase funding for other special population groups within the African-American community.

4. Increase funding to organizations in southeastern states that benefit African Americans.

5. Increase giving to African-American colleges and support organizations."[11]

Asian-Pacific Americans

1. "More corporations should make grants for Asian-Pacific Americans (APAs).

2. Increase the amount to APA-controlled organizations.

3. Increase the average APA grant size.

4. Increase funding for education.

5. Increase overall giving."[12]

Hispanics/Latinos

1. "More corporations should award grants to Hispanic/Latino causes and charities.

2. Increase the amount to Hispanic/Latino-controlled organizations.

3. Increase the Hispanic/Latino average grant size.

4. Increase funding for national Hispanic/Latino organizations.

5. Increase overall corporate support."[13]

Native Americans

1. "More corporations should award grants to Native American causes and charities.

2. Increase the amount to Native American–controlled organizations.

3. Increase the Native American average grant size.

4. Increase funding for Native American health and human services.

5. Increase overall corporate support."[14]

REMITTANCES

A widely shared form of providing financial support to family members and neighbors is the transaction of remittances—gifts of money and/or goods from migrated family members back to those in the home country. Charitable giving is generally defined as financial support for those not related to the donor—therefore, remittances delivered to immediate family are not philanthropic in a definitional sense. Those gifts or remittances offered to a broader community outside of the family unit do bear review in the context of philanthropic giving.

Although they usually earn lower wages, collectively immigrants manage to send substantial sums of money to their countries of origin. Many of these home countries receive more from their migrated citizens than they do in official development assistance. The International Monetary Fund (IMF) estimates that immigrants sent about $70 billion a year to their countries of origin in the 1990s, whereas official development assistance in the same time period amounted to an estimated $58 billion. If it is calculated that each migrant helps five or six people at home, between 200 and 240 million people around the world depend on the support of friends or family members working abroad.[15]

In Egypt, for example, financial transfers were the leading source of external revenue in the 1980s, bringing in as much money as tourism receipts

EXHIBIT 6-10 RACIAL/ETHNIC GIVING BY SPECIFIC INTEREST AREAS

Type of Recipient	Total Racial/Ethnic Funding	African Americans	Asian Americans	Hispanic/Latinos	Native Americans
Arts and Culture	$9,812,947	$3,358,301	$1,962,522	$1,027,400	$600,000
	907 grants	309 grants	80 grants	162 grants	28 grants
	87 donors	69 donors	34 donors	50 donors	15 donors
Children/Youth	$12,517,231	$4,383,442	$144,170	$795,447	$297,530
	1,015 grants	309 grants	25 grants	112 grants	22 grants
	101 donors	75 donors	16 donors	42 donors	17 donors
Colleges and Support Organizations	$46,249,164	$20,366,064	$148,180	$3,436,417	$979,105
	1,832 grants	685 grants	17 grants	202 grants	76 grants
	111 donors	100 donors	14 donors	68 donors	45 donors
Communications Programs and Organizations	$1,231,560	$131,916	$114,700	$25,000	$112,430
	72 grants	14 grants	8 grants	2 grants	9 grants
	35 donors	10 donors	4 donors	2 donors	5 donors
Community Education and Job Preparation Organizations	$9,061,067	$2,016,383	$58,000	$2,067,428	$217,230
	446 grants	107 grants	8 grants	135 grants	14 grants
	91 donors	43 donors	6 donors	55 donors	8 donors
Government Services	$3,078,156	$1,248,384	$22,500	$245,710	$153,000
	182 grants	43 grants	4 grants	24 grants	13 grants
	57 donors	20 donors	4 donors	14 donors	9 donors
Health Facilities and Programs	$13,157,671	$4,504,292	$445,000	$1,437,183	$215,000
	649 grants	204 grants	32 grants	84 grants	16 grants
	94 donors	60 donors	20 donors	335 donors	13 donors

Category					
Neighborhood and Community Improvement Organizations	$31,500 5 grants 4 donors	$1,784,950 128 grants 27 donors	$113,000 21 grants 13 donors	$4,087,160 299 grants 53 donors	$11,993,386 870 grants 73 donors
Other Recipients	$23,000 3 grants 3 donors	$59,400 13 grants 9 donors	$96,500 8 grants 5 donors	$386,063 47 grants 27 donors	$1,201,453 141 grants 49 donors
Philanthropy and Volunteer Service Organizations	$128,500 6 grants 6 donors	$589,995 37 grants 24 donors	$342,750 9 grants 9 donors	$830,982 79 grants 39 donors	$2,975,176 202 grants 70 donors
Primary, Secondary Schools and Support Organizations	$273,130 19 grants 14 donors	$2,021,945 140 grants 53 donors	$248,750 31 grants 21 donors	$6,070,055 384 grants 87 donors	$21,612,718 1,187 grants 105 donors
Public Policy Organizations	$132,000 14 grants 13 donors	$2,463,155 162 grants 57 donors	$585,265 45 grants 26 donors	$2,395,400 173 grants 72 donors	$8,011,950 540 grants 95 donors
Services for Special Populations	$94,500 6 grants 2 donors	$1,501,635 156 grants 41 donors	$189,000 32 grants 15 donors	$1,528,780 195 grants 57 donors	$8,610,949 939 grants 103 donors
Social Service Agencies	$335,900 26 grants 13 donors	$2,368,400 253 grants 66 donors	$654,151 68 grants 28 donors	$7,930,146 547 grants 88 donors	$18,409,392 1,425 grants 103 donors
Trade Associations and NPO Support Organizations	$224,450 18 grants 12 donors	$939,039 76 grants 39 donors	$152,205 16 grants 11 donors	$2,258,760 123 grants 52 donors	$11,603,688 498 grants 86 donors

Source: Grants: Corporate Grantmaking for Racial and Ethnic Communities, National Committee for Responsive Philanthropy, 2000. Moyer Bell Limited: Rhode Island. NCRP. All rights reserved. Reprinted by permission.

and tolls paid on the Suez Canal. In Yemen, remittances from migrants amount to 150 percent of export revenue, while the sums sent to Haiti account for 6 percent of the gross national product. It is important to note that the numbers of remitted dollars are based on official transactions—money sent through banks or post offices, as well as "institutional" transfers like retirement benefits, sent to immigrants' home countries through governmental agreements. It is extremely difficult to accurately assess the amount of remittances sent through informal networks such as migrant visitors returning "home" with envelopes of cash given by other migrants for delivery to residents of the country of origin.

Some immigrants achieve high levels of income relative to others in both the home country and in their current country of residence. Many immigrants in the United States, however, earn lower wages. For migrants from Mexico, many Central American countries, the Philippines, and southeast Asian countries their lower U.S. wages far exceed the earning ability of those in the home country. From a philanthropic perspective, we should look at the impact of the remittances on the economic structures in the home countries, as well as the level of "sacrificial giving" undertaken by the migrant participant.

Consider these reflections on remittances as productive investments, as discussed in "Consequences of Migration and Remittances for Mexican Transnational Communities" in *Economic Geography*:

> As purposeful decision makers, the recipients of remittances . . . from overseas sojourners make choices among investing in productive activities, saving for [the] future . . . or spending on immediate necessities. . . . Decisions at odds with the expressed wishes of the overseas donor are to be expected, and how remittances are used will be influenced by the . . . behaviors of the donors. Long absences might contribute to a growth of independence by the recipient, while shorter-term sojourns should reinforce the strength of the donor's influence on remittances expenditures and investment decision making.
>
> The donor's need to be certain of the implementation of his or her investment wishes will in turn affect return intentions. Communal and familial mores will in turn affect return investments. The heightened status acquired through the symbolic demonstration of affluence—redistribution of wealth via gifts, . . . donating extravagantly to community projects, to the church, to relatives—also influences remittances dispensation.[16]

The expectations or benefits flowing from remittance giving can be related to fundraising practices in the United States. Donor intent, recognition, frequency of giving, and donors as investors are also key to migradollar (remittance) behavior. Further study of the relationship of remittance practice and philanthropic giving would give a much fuller opportunity for the nonprofit sector to more fully understand the untapped opportunities for a fuller and more beneficial philanthropic sector.

Here are a few additional highlights on remittance giving:

- *Migradollars* is a colloquial term used by migrants and scholars to describe the transnational flows of U.S. currency.

- Until recently, the most commonly held assessment of remittances was that they brought a host of negative influences to the recipients, they increased dependent relations, and they were obstacles to development and progress in the Third World communities. Recent research finds fault with these conventional wisdoms which prematurely dismiss remittances' positive influences on the lives of rural people in Mexico, Latin America, and the Caribbean.

- Anthropologists have coined the term *cultural capital* to represent the full complement of people's cultural practices. Migrants accumulate cultural capital from two sources: their home society and the cultural realm they are visiting or to which they are emigrating.

- Migration researchers refer to cash carried personally by couriers or by returnees as *pocket transfers*, to differentiate personal shipments of remittances from more regular transfers via money orders, cashiers' checks, or electronically transferred funds. Pocket transfer funds can be substantial, but are difficult to measure.

CHAPTER 7

Interviews: Influences on Giving

T hirty-five individuals were invited to participate in interviews directed at individual giving patterns established in childhood; racial/ethnic/religious customs; and current philanthropic practices. The majority of the 13 persons who participated are professionals in the philanthropic sector. The interviewees were given the opportunity to respond electronically (via e-mail), and their responses are taken directly from those written responses. An attempt was made to assure racial/ethnic, geographic, age, gender, and religious diversity. Due to the limited number of participants, these interviews are not statistically valid. Readers interested in participating in the ongoing survey may contact the author at jgpdiversity@pacbell.net for an electronic version of the interview.

Questions fell into three categories each with multiple questions:

- Family giving patterns
- Cultural giving patterns
- Personal giving patterns

Respondents were given the opportunity to identify the culture(s) they identified with, and no limit was placed on the number of possible identifications.

SUMMARY OF INTERVIEWS

Although the number of respondents was limited, certain questions elicited similar responses across racial/ethnic lines.

- The majority of respondents learned about giving or philanthropy as children from their families.
- Almost all of the respondents could specifically identify ways that nonprofit organizations are a part of their culture.
- Most felt that philanthropy is encouraged in their culture, with emphasis on the unique forms of philanthropy practiced yet not always recognized as philanthropic.

Respondents generally do not limit their giving to organizations with an impact on their culture.

- "My involvement in philanthropy and voluntarism is cross-cultural; therefore, it does have an impact cross-culturally." (African-American male)
- "Yes, I would hope that my giving would have some impact on my culture, if my culture does something for others." (Caucasian male)
- "I do give to organizations that do not have an impact on my culture, causes I care about—the humane society, children's organizations, and war-torn countries." (Hispanic/Latino female)

Attitudes toward recognition varied widely, even among respondents from the same racial/ethnic group.

When asked to identify with a culture or cultures, all respondents chose at least two cultures that they identified with. Some respondents chose a religious affiliation as an identified culture, others chose to identify by the generation they represent as an American, and others chose lifestyle as a cultural identifier. Only one respondent did not provide any identifying culture(s).

The following pages list the interview questions and selected answers to each question. Respondent answers are separated according to race, but within each race category the responses are listed in no particular order.

INTERVIEW QUESTIONS

FAMILY GIVING PATTERNS

(1) While growing up, what did you learn from your parents and other adults about philanthropy?

(2) From whom did you learn about philanthropy, or giving and sharing, to help others in need?

(3) Was your family's approach to philanthropy considered unusual for your culture? Please describe.

(4) How did/do family members give of their time to help others?

(5) How did/do family members volunteer time at nonprofit organizations?

CULTURAL GIVING PATTERNS

(6) Are nonprofit organizations a part of your culture? Please describe.

(7) Is philanthropy encouraged in your culture? Please describe.

(8) What cultural traditions play a role in your decision to donate time and/or money?

(9) Generally, do you give to organizations that do not have an impact on your culture?

(10) What motivates people in your culture to give? Are you an example of these patterns?

(11) What role does public recognition play in philanthropy in your culture? Is it important for people in your culture to be recognized for their philanthropy?

(12) Have you noticed changes in giving patterns in your culture—say, over the past 10 or 20 years?

(13) Overall, how would you rate your culture's philanthropic habits: very poor, average, generous, or very generous?

(14) Please name the culture(s) you consider yourself a part of.

PERSONAL GIVING PATTERNS

(15) How much do you research an organization before donating to it?

(16) What prompts you to give to a particular organization (i.e., the cause, your personal involvement, involvement of friends, personal solicitation, direct mail or advertising, etc.)?

(A) Are you more likely to give to an organization from which you or someone you know has benefited?

(B) Are you more likely to give directly to individuals in need?

(17) Are there biases, traditions, or norms in your culture that would keep you from donating to certain causes or groups? If yes, how likely are you to support a cause that your culture would disagree with?

PERSONAL INFORMATION

Respondent Data

1. Caucasian; male; 50+; Jewish American
2. Caucasian; female; 50+; Jewish
3. Filipino American; female; 30+; Roman Catholic
4. Caucasian; male; 30+; Roman Catholic
5. Hispanic/Latino American; female; 40+; undisclosed
6. Cuban American; male; 30+; Roman Catholic
7. Caucasian/Native American (Chippewa); female; 50+; Christian/Animist
8. African American; male; 50+; Unitarian
9. Caucasian; male; 50+; Protestant
10. Chinese American; female; 50+; Protestant
11. Chinese American; male; 60+; Christian
12. African American; male; 50+; Christian
13. Hispanic; female; 30+; Roman Catholic

Male:	7	Catholic:	3
Female:	6	Protestant:	6
Gay:	2	Undisclosed:	1
African American:	2	30–39:	4
Asian American:	3	40–49:	1
Hispanic:	3	50–59:	6
Native American:	1	60–69:	1
Jewish:	2		

FAMILY GIVING PATTERNS

> While growing up, what did you learn from your parents and other adults about philanthropy?

African American

- While growing up, my parents were very involved in civic activities. They involved my brother, my sister, and I in those activities, so we grew up understanding and seeing first-hand philanthropy and voluntarism.

- My early education about philanthropy was in terms of volunteer service to what are now termed *community-based organizations* and gifts of cash to the church.

Asian American

- Nothing.

- Growing up, *philanthropy* was not a word in our household. This is not to say that we were not taught to give. Rather, the focus of giving was different. When I was young (high school) my dad would often talk about how once I got a job I would be able to send money to cousins in Mindanao. These cousins lived in a rural area where agriculture was the way of life. He encouraged me to financially assist in their education.

- I learned from my parents and other adults that philanthropy was for older, wealthy white people, not something regular people (like ourselves) did.

- We have done some volunteer work. I was always told that there were people less fortunate. My mother demonstrated to me, through her generosity toward others, that if she did not have the resources, she would help in other ways. We helped, only we didn't call it philanthropy.

- My father and mother encouraged me to give to the Junior Red Cross drives at my elementary school. They wanted me to help children with needs greater than ours.

- From the church/neighborhood center I attended in Chinatown, I learned about stewardship when I was in middle school. We were encouraged to give not only money, but to volunteer to work with the younger children. I started actively volunteering when I was thirteen years old, and I haven't stopped.

Native American

- Taking care of others was important, especially if you had more than you needed.

Hispanic/Latino

- Almost nothing. I knew what it was to get help, since my mother and I were immigrants who arrived with nothing. But I never gave it any thought, and my only recollections are that it was "government" help. I did not even know what a nonprofit organization was until I began to work in a fundraising office of a hospital. They explained to me what nonprofit meant, and I began to learn about organized philanthropy.

Caucasian

- Taught to give generously and regularly to our church (Baptist).
- Faith-based giving was paramount in our household; both the saving of nickels and dimes to give to the "poor orphans in Hungary" or the "starving children in Africa" and to our own small community church. My earliest allowance, which I earned by doing a lot of chores, was clearly expected to be only partly for myself. The rest went to the church and missionary projects in little white envelopes that I filled with coins, licked shut, and placed in the collection plate myself.
- I learned by taking hot meals to a sick woman whose husband had "gone off" that it could be hard to take charity from someone you know. I learned from volunteering as a Junior Grey Lady in our community hospital that you could brighten someone's day with a small act like arranging flowers or adjusting a window blind.
- My parents' circle participated in several fundraising shows to raise money to remodel and expand the temple. They wrote and performed

satirical songs and skits. My dad was on a committee that would decide whether members were paying sufficient temple dues, based on perceived income. They would call on members to get them to increase their gifts. This must have been difficult in a small town where everyone knew everyone.

- When my father died, I was an adult and I learned it was the practice of the temple members to provide food to the family during the funeral period. They had a committee and provided us a list of who would be bringing what meals. This was not an issue of poverty; it was to care for the family during a difficult time, and I assume this practice also went on when I was a kid.

- When I became active in the temple's youth group, it was natural for me to organize fundraisers also. We would "import" kosher delicacies from Chicago and deliver them to members, for a small profit.

- In participating in state and regional youth group activities, I gained the concept of giving money to support social justice causes as part of the biblical injunction to pursue justice. You may be interested to know that, as part of modern bar/bat mitzvahs, some kids are donating a portion of their gifts (often cash) to charity.

- The clearest memory I have regarding philanthropy in our family was my mother's weekly contribution to the Catholic Church we attended. She was completely faithful about this. If we were out of town one Sunday, she made an additional contribution the next week.

- One of my earliest memories of volunteerism was my father's involvement in Lion's Club. I recall how my brothers and I would join him several times a year, well before dawn, by installing large American flags in front of all the businesses on the main street in Sutter Creek, the small town where I grew up. There were dozens of flags that fit into pre-formed holes in the sidewalk, and we did this for every civic holiday.

From whom did you learn about philanthropy, or giving and sharing, to help others in need?

African American

- I learned about philanthropy or giving and sharing to help others from my parents.

- This knowledge came from a variety of sources over a lifetime—early from my parents, grandparents, and other family members. Later, I adopted the creed of my fraternity, "service to mankind." Finally, from the professional positions that I held in the alumni and development departments at my university and other nonprofit organizations for which I worked as a volunteer, staff member, and/or consultant. The need to be philanthropic became paramount.

Asian American

- No one in particular.

- My parents are very generous when it comes to family. I suppose I learned about giving from them. However, they do not actively support social causes or nonprofit organizations.

- I learned from reading about the Carnegies, Rockefellers, etc.

- I learned about philanthropy as a recipient. When I was seven, I was diagnosed with a heart problem that required hospitalization. My parents could not afford the cost of the medical care, and a community agency at a local hospital covered my medical costs.

Hispanic/Latino

- I only learned of this in retrospect. In other words, once I learned there was such a thing as philanthropy, I began to reflect that as a child I must have received much help that my mother and I would not have been able to get without philanthropy. I did remember members of my father's family giving me Christmas gifts and the like, which I thought was nice since I really didn't know them and they really had no obligation other than family ties. I learned and thought of how my mother and I lived with a friend of the family for several years when we first arrived here. But learning and reflecting on these things did not happen until I was in my 20s, after I had already taken a job in a fundraising office.

Native American

- From my parents and the Democratic Party, trade union, and the church.

Caucasian

- From my relatives, and from my church as a child. It was a community church, nominally Congregational, that served as the only church in our tiny community. Ministers from the Pacific Union Theological Seminary in Berkeley and from Africa and Asia often came to stay and teach for a while, giving me a global worldview that I would never have had within my own family. In elementary school as well, we learned about the "starving children in Hungary"—Once my classmates and I proposed we send all our uneaten sandwiches to them; a suggestion not well received by our second-grade teacher.

- I learned about philanthropy from my college (after I graduated, and they started asking me for money). From my experience as a Peace Corps volunteer I learned about volunteering. My wife has also taught me a great deal about philanthropy and fundraising.

- I don't think there was any one person from whom I specifically learned about philanthropy. What did shape me, however, was growing up in a small town where, whether you help a nonprofit agency or not, everyone seems to look out for other people. I did learn charitable-type values that, later in life, I easily translated into making donations and volunteering my time.

Was your family's approach to philanthropy considered unusual for your culture? Please describe.

African American

- I did not consider my family's approach to philanthropy to be unusual for my culture because I did not associate it with culture, nor did my family refer to it as a cultural activity, but as an activity natural to humankind.

- No. There were examples all around of giving, both in my family and among my family's friends.

Asian American

- When growing up, we were a struggling Chinese immigrant family in the poor South during the 1930s and '40s. The Chinese in Augusta, Georgia, during that period were recipients of philanthropy, mainly from the First Baptist Church of Augusta that sought to convert the Chinese immigrants.

- I think my family's approach to philanthropy was in line with their culture. Their sense of giving was very family-oriented.

- No, I don't believe so. We didn't have much money to spare when I was growing up, and I remember that instead of giving my brother and me Christmas gifts, my parents would use the money for gifts for other family members. This was a form of giving and sharing that was natural to our culture.

Hispanic/Latino

- No. Government was seen as the source of help, but the reality is that when you are poor you don't think of philanthropy as something you give—perhaps my mother thought of philanthropy from the perspective of a recipient. I would say that in retrospect, I am aware that our Cuban-American culture was very strong in its commitment to help each other. You hired Cubans, you gave them clothes or old televisions/radios, etc. People gave to people directly. Everyone was in need and everyone helped each other. Everyone tried to help with jobs in particular, such as with referrals to open jobs.

Native American

- Not for whites. Many Native Americans are not in a position to give money, particularly to outside organizations.

Caucasian

- No, not at all. We were typical white, middle-class, church-going suburbanites.

- No. This was the standard Protestant approach to community-based charity. My mother's people descended from Quakers and had a strong sense of giving a hand-up instead of a "handout." There were many post-depression "hobos" who came through looking for meals from the nearby railroad tracks where they hopped off and on trains, and camped in the eucalyptus groves. My mother sent them to my grandfather next door, who would make them hoe a row of vegetables or chop some wood before giving them a hot meal, which they ate sitting on the porch steps. I remember feeling uncomfortable when they were sitting outside, often unwashed and scraggly looking, but this is what all the farm families did.
- No, I think our family's support of our church, schools, and community organizations was quite typical of my culture.

How did/do family members give of their time to help others?

African American

- Explained in previous question.
- My mother was very active in church, civic groups, and her alumni organization. My wife and I have been consistent donors to a range of nonprofit organizations that work on behalf of causes in which we believe. However, more importantly, we have tried to instill a sense of giving of time and resources in our son who has also worked as a volunteer for several groups.

Asian American

- Being poor ourselves, giving was not part of my family's activities, with one exception. The Chinese community in the 1940s, being recent immigrants from China, was loyal to the Nationalist (KMT) struggle against Japan and bought KMT bonds to support that effort. The bonds became worthless and in effect turned out to be gifts.
- They didn't/don't, really. The only volunteer things my parents did were activities that were required of parents when I was a student at a Catholic school. They had to complete about five hours a week of

school service (i.e., drive to games, correct papers, help out with lunch).

- Not while I was growing up. My father worked six or seven days a week, and my mother's job was to take care of my brother and me. They didn't have any time to volunteer.

Hispanic/Latino

- If we are talking about the present, then of course acculturation and success has had a very strong effect. Most of my family members participate greatly in their Catholic Church activities, and volunteer and give throughout the church. They do not give in generous terms when compared against their American counterparts in terms of giving to "American Traditional" organized charity. However, they continue to generously help new friends and family that have arrived from Cuba. This includes time and money. They tend to give to causes that help Cuban immigrants—such as Brothers to the Rescue (flights over the water searching for Cuban rafters).

Native American

- Help animal shelters, zoo, collect newspapers and towels for vet, help animals at horse farm.

Caucasian

- Primarily to our church. Singing in the choir was considered volunteering for my parents.
- As a child, it seemed we all worked very hard most of the time. There was a difference between what was for our family—babysitting sisters and cousins, helping cousins move irrigation pipes in the fields, doing extensive house and yard work at a very early age—and what was for others, such as painting the church social hall, making curtains for the Sunday School classroom, earning Blue Bird beads by visiting the sick and elderly shut-ins. I liked the latter better because it seemed to bring more approval and less criticism, and gave me a chance to be with nonrelative adults. Both my parents and most of my friends' parents seemed to be endlessly going to PTA, church board, and Women's

Club, Grange, Volunteer Fire Department, and other meetings. My parents did less than most because we had a large family, seven people, and there was always so much to do at home.

- As adults, my sisters and I have all had the sad opportunity to assist ill and dying friends with trips to the hospital, visits, and household chores and, for me, with the actual task of dying. We all help nieces, nephews, friends, and each other in countless ways—applying to colleges, making small gifts or large loans in times of need.

- I suspect there were volunteer programs to help sick and elderly members of the temple (all Jews belonged), but I don't have any specific memories.

- It is simply a part of my family that we help others. If others are in need, you help and you do so without making judgments about a person and without seeking acknowledgment for your deeds. I can think of one recent example. My Catholic parish needed two large banner-holding units. They were going to require some engineering because they needed to include holders not just for the banners but also for a row of bells. They also required a unit so that they could be freestanding during Mass. Although my father is not a parishioner at my church and he has never even been to Mass here, he agreed to build the units because he understands the importance of this organization to me.

How did/do family members volunteer time at nonprofit organizations?

African American

- With respect to volunteering time with nonprofit organizations, my family was involved with the church, YWCA, YMCA, NAACP, Girl Scouts, Cub Scouts, Boy Scouts, Red Cross, the arts, and various other community-related civic and social organizations.

- Nonprofit organizations are a part of my culture, which is African American; however, I will have to say that my experience through my parents and community activities was cross-cultural. Therefore, not only were nonprofit organizations a part of the African-American culture, but also a part of the culture generally that we were and that I am involved with.

- We have served on boards, on committees, and in nondescript positions for several organizations.

Asian American

- They didn't/don't. I volunteer for a few organizations and have been doing so for years. When I first started volunteering, this confused my parents. They didn't seem to understand the value or concept of volunteering. For them, time is money—why give time when there are no monetary benefits?

- I am the only member of my family (parents and brother) to actively volunteer, something I've been doing since I was a teenager. My range of volunteer activities has been fairly wide. I believe that volunteering is an essential component of my philanthropy, and when I am asked to help or serve, I look to see if I can really be useful to the organization, and if I believe I can, I'll find a way to help or serve. I, however, do look carefully at the organization's motivations for asking for my involvement and my level of interest in the organization, as I have no interest in serving on a board to fill a "diversity" quota.

Hispanic/Latino

- Only through church activities, such as at church bazaars, and active participation in church building and planning events.

Native American

- Nursing home, museum.

Caucasian

- I don't believe there were any 501 C-3 organizations in my small community. The work was through the organizations like the ones I mentioned earlier. People gave lots of time, labor, and very little money. There were Scout troops and Red Cross volunteers, but the paid leaders and the headquarters and fundraising drives were far away. Today, the two of us sisters who converted to Judaism do a fair amount of volunteering and the rest do little to my knowledge. Many relatives serve on community boards, and one aunt is on the national board of Habitat for Humanity.

- The temple had a b'nai b'rith for men, a sisterhood organization for women, and a youth group. It was assumed that everyone would participate as a committee member, officer, volunteer, etc. My dad was also very proud for being on the park commission for our town.

- My parents are involved with a local organization that cares for seniors and disabled persons. They help with several events hosted by the organization throughout the year, including baking at least twelve dozen cookies every Valentine's Day for a special party. My sisters, one is a registered nurse, the other is a dental hygienist, volunteer at clinics to provide free medical and dental care to disadvantaged youth. My brother is very involved in his Chamber of Commerce and a fraternal organization, the Native Sons of the Golden West. He recently completed a term as president of the latter group. I am very involved at my Catholic parish, where I am presently serving on a search committee to hire a new parish administrator, and will be facilitating a daylong leadership retreat for parish committees. I am also a member of the planning committee for a formal fundraising dinner.

CULTURAL GIVING PATTERNS

> Are nonprofit organizations a part of your culture? Please describe.

African American

- Historically, people of African descent have established their own faith-based organizations and mutual aid societies, as well as fraternal organizations, committed to community service. Also, in the mid-1800s, educational institutions were founded bi-racially by and for Freedmen, who later took over the governance and management of many of these organizations. As needs in other areas became more acute, people of African descent created other types of nonprofit organizations. The tradition of all these organizations has been one of nondiscrimination and working across racial, ethnic, and cultural lines for the betterment of society.

Asian American

- I'm not sure. In the Philippines, the equivalent of nonprofit organizations would probably be NGOs (nongovernmental organizations). Here in the Bay Area, I notice that there are Filipino social organizations that are registered as nonprofits. My parents belong to one. The organization is made up of individuals in the Bay Area who are all from the same small town in the Philippines. The group gets together socially and tries to raise funds or do projects to help out the town.

- I'm a third-generation Chinese American who was raised in a neighborhood where there were few other Asian families. My parents' concerns were economic stability, self-sufficiency, and social acceptability, so nonprofits were not a big part of our lives as supporters.

- Currently, yes. Both my wife and I are part of the community that promote Asian-American cultural, history, and art in the Bay Area, like the Kearny Street Workshop and the Angel Island Immigration Station Foundation and the Angel Island Association. I also volunteer my time to inner-city nonprofit groups like Destiny Arts Center of Oakland.

Hispanic/Latino

- Donating in the Hispanic culture has always meant "a handout" to the poor or sick. Literally handing people change on the streets—not a very effective method for addressing social problems. Usually people give through the church; it greatly influences how and where people give.

- Not as visibly and organized as in American culture. They are mostly grassroots efforts to help others. Nonprofits are not ingrained as organized charity, they are simply a group of people creating an organized way of helping others or supporting a cause. They did exist in Cuba so it isn't entirely new—for example "La Liga Contra el Cancer" (League Against Cancer) was big in Cuba and is big in Miami. Of course, with time the question asked here becomes muddled. Are they a part of our current Cuban-American culture? Yes, definitely. By this time every-one here is familiar with the nonprofit, but mainly through groups that were affiliated with the church or with immigrant causes. And the Cuban-American culture is now acculturated enough to partici-pate even in United Way, Red Cross, and the other mom and apple-pie charities, although not with any great enthusiasm.

Native American

- For Caucasian side, yes. For Native American, no. Help comes from your family.

Caucasian

- If a church is a nonprofit, then yes. The church was the cornerstone of my family's activities while I was growing up.

- I have worked, volunteered, and contributed to nonprofit organiza-tions my entire adult life. I have served as volunteer, board member, staff, executive director, and for the past 18 years as a full-time con-sultant and trainer with nonprofits. I have volunteered since I was very young. I have been a contributor to a number of causes, as well as a volunteer, all my adult life.

- Reform congregations, which are the majority of Jewish congregations worldwide, operate as religious nonprofits. Most have a number of organizations such as the Brotherhood and Sisterhood that exist to fund-raise for the local temple and Jewish community, and Hadassah and others that raise money for Israel. At one time in the '90s, I read a re-port that said the largest source of income in the State of Israel was con-tributions from American Jews. I don't know if this figure still holds.

- Jews have always supported civil rights and first amendment rights, since our own have been historically threatened. Organizations such as the NAACP, Southern Poverty Law Center, and ACLU have large numbers of Jewish supporters. After African Americans, the second most numerous ethnic group active in the civil rights movement from Mississippi Freedom Riders to behind-the-scenes supporters of the Black Panthers (attorneys and bail fund donors) were Jewish. Politi-cal action and political causes often dominate our giving.

- Yes, definitely, but these organizations may be more obvious to me because I work in the nonprofit industry. Nonprofits account for a substantial segment of the American economy. I personally feel that without nonprofit organizations people in dire need in our society would go unaided.

Is philanthropy encouraged in your culture? Please describe.

African American

- I believe that philanthropy is encouraged in my culture primarily through the church; however, it is also encouraged generally. I feel, however, that in the African-American culture we believe that it should be greater, and wish that could be greater.

- All of the organizations I talked about earlier have had volunteer and financial support from the people that they were founded to support, as well as from many of the organizations and individuals that have supported other nonprofit organizations. Moreover, all of these organizations have received support from people of African descent. Also, people of African descent have been donors and volunteers to and with the mainstream nonprofit organizations.

Asian American

- I don't know. Within my own upbringing in a Filipino immigrant household, it was not encouraged.

- Yes. Within the American-born community of Chinese Americans that I'm familiar with, there is definitely encouragement to be philanthropic, generally for specific causes. Philanthropy as a general practice is a personal economic matter, which, in my opinion, is not something many in my culture are comfortable discussing in public.

- I am defining my culture to be separate from my root country heritage and to be that of a first-generation Asian American from pre-1965 immigrants. (Post-1965 Chinese immigrant Asian Americans fit into a different category.) Many of us who have seen the struggles of our parents are motivated to give back to the community. Both of my grown children also have this attitude.

Hispanic/Latino

- Yes, but personal philanthropy, not necessarily organized philanthropy. You help those you know, those who are connected to your family, because it is your duty and your pride. Giving through organized methodologies has developed through acculturation, but it isn't yet totally in the heart. However, put the story of a child from Cuba who needs an operation on television or especially radio, and you will get hundreds and hundreds of checks (e.g., I am currently helping a few children in this situation—and one child received over 500 checks in one day, ranging from $10 to $2,000, totally from a couple of radio spots). Philanthropy as an obligation of a "good citizen" is not a part of our culture.

Native American

- White, Caucasian part, yes. Native Americans, not to 501-C-3, but to individuals, churches, etc.

Caucasian

- To me, my culture is my religious background, which is Baptist, which is not necessarily the mainstream culture I grew up in. I was encouraged to make all my financial contributions through my church and its missionary work.

- It is not only encouraged, it is required. *Tzdakah* is the Hebrew word for "charity." The concept is as old as our religion. It is written in the Talmud that even the poorest of the poor, those receiving charity, are commanded to give charity. Throughout history Jews have been in the forefront of fundraising, first in our own communities and for our own causes and now internationally. I heard this interesting comment from a well-known professional colleague in 1998. "Since Jews are no longer limited to serving Jewish-only groups, they have flocked to gentile philanthropy in such great numbers that if you took out all of the Jews in philanthropy in New York, 90 percent of the organizations' doors would close."

- Absolutely. In small orthodox temples, members are asked on the holiest day of the year to stand up and make pledges to the organization. Of course, people are competitive and try to outperform each other. I have never seen this practice myself, but I have been told about it.

- Yes, I feel philanthropy is encouraged in my culture, but even more so, I feel it is expected. Nonprofits are a major part of our society, from arts and culture, to social service and religion, we are impacted by nonprofits every day. I was thinking the other day about the "Free Shakespeare in the Park" that happens every summer at Golden Gate Park, and the "free" concerts that happened every Tuesday and Thursday at Old St. Mary's Cathedral, where I used to work. Although these are free events, most people expect that they will be asked to support the events financially. Although no one is turned away if they cannot donate, there is clearly a sense that without financial contributions, the events would not take place.

> What cultural traditions play a role in your decision to donate time and/or money?

African American

- The cultural traditions that play a role in my decision to donate time and/or money are those that are central to the African-American culture—giving and helping others.

- African Americans are the only group of people in this country who were brought to this continent without their consent, enslaved, had all elements of their history, traditions, and religions taken from them, and threatened with death or dismemberment if they tried to be free, vote, learn, or practice their original religions. It was under these conditions that they were forced, at first clandestinely, and later, under varying degrees of suppression, to support the organizations founded by and for them. This tradition has been recognized in many families over the years. That recognition has influenced my decisions about giving.

Asian American

- None.

- I suspect that some of the Chinese-American traditions of helping the elderly and the young, as well as the concept of reciprocity, affect my giving patterns. It is deeply ingrained in me to show respect for my elders and to support the needs of the young. Beyond that, however, I think the "cultural" component of having worked in fundraising for over 25 years has in itself affected my decision making on giving.

Hispanic/Latino

- Philanthropy is not encouraged in my culture.

- I give and participate in things that friends and family participate in, and that the need is apparent and close. I give to things that touch my family and my past history, knowing what my mother went through and what it is like to know so little and have so little. Culturally, like most Cuban Americans, I give to United Way and the like only when forced. Culturally, this feels way too distant and organized and unfeeling and unemotional.

Native American

- Care for the earth and all that dwell on it, they are equal to me in their right to live here in dignity.

Caucasian

- I never thought of it as "cultural." Others in my life donated time and money, and I did the same. I see it as the "give back" principle. It was done for me, so I do it for others, and I also want to set the example for my own children. Regarding giving money, my wife and I are donors. I give to organizations whose issues I agree with (Amnesty, Habitat), and I give to my church. There are numerous other organizations we support throughout the year, and the decision to give to them is based on what they're using our money for, how well we know the organization, and their ability to send us a thank-you letter on a timely basis.

- Certainly belonging to the synagogue is an important element of charity. Because we do not collect funds through a weekly offering, we have dues structures that require everyone to pay their fair share. This often becomes the largest contribution a Jewish person is making and may cut into the decision and ability to give to other causes.

- Certainly I would not volunteer or give to a cause that I believed to be anti-Semitic or that showed insensitivity to my identification as a Jew. I don't give to appeals with Christmas or Easter themes. If a Jewish person is leading an organization or on a committee, I am more apt to take note. I want groups to be sensitive to my holidays and not expect me to attend events on Friday nights or during Yom Kippur.

- I donate quite a bit of time and funds to my temple, but I have a political as well as a cultural rationale for this philanthropy. I wish to support the existence of progressive Jewish organizations.

- I feel in my culture there is an attitude of giving back to your community, especially if you have been helped in the past. There is also a sense of dependence and reliance on one another, which naturally leads to a desire to help. Although in many ways our fast-paced, high-technology society desensitizes our feelings of helping, I still feel it is part of human nature to help someone in need.

> Generally, do you give to organizations that do not have an impact on your culture?

African American

- My involvement in philanthropy and voluntarism is cross-cultural; therefore, it does have an impact cross-culturally.

- It is difficult to say which organizations do not have an impact on my culture, but if the question is intended to mean organizations that do not focus exclusively on people of African descent, the answer is yes. When I was in my early thirties, I was elected to the Board of Directors of the USO of Metropolitan Washington D.C. I was only the third African American to serve on that board. I served on that board for 17 years, two as its second African-American president. This was an organization that served a relatively small number of African Americans at the time, not because they were excluded, but rather because many of them did not avail themselves the services of the USO. The number of African Americans did increase over those years.

Asian American

- Mostly culturally related, but also to the inner-city organizations in Oakland (California).

- Generally I give to organizations that are concerned with causes I care about. These organizations do not necessarily have an impact on my culture.

- The majority of my giving is to organizations outside of my culture. My interests and the organization's ability to meet its stated needs determine my giving. I support many human service organizations. Among them are services to the elderly, international adoption. I also provide occasional support to an AIDS program, and a few homeless shelters. I am considering establishing a donor-advised fund for the management of my charitable giving.

Hispanic/Latino

- I do give to organizations that do not have an impact on my culture, causes I care about—the humane society, children's organizations, and war-torn countries.

- Yes, if it related to my experiences in ways that I could draw parallels. But it is likely that I would give only to things that I thought would have a direct impact on things that I thought were important— like anyone else. Since my culture is a part of me and my geographic area (Florida), it is likely this would have a major impact.

Native American

- Yes, but to those that save my animals, brothers and sisters, and mother earth.

Caucasian

- Yes, I would hope that my giving would have some impact on my culture, if my culture does something for others.

- Yes, I do. Judaism is my faith, but I also identify with a broader culture that I think of as "people who care," cross-cultural and beyond borders. I identify with liberal, feminist, pro-working class and cultural organizations of many different types. I buy coffee that supports a Nicaraguan health collective, for example, because I believe in workers' rights and want to contribute to ameliorating some of the misery caused by U.S. policy in Central America.

- Between a third and a half of my giving is to arts organizations or social justice/political causes that do not arise out of my culture.

- Yes, I give to "non-Caucasian" organizations. For many years, I have given a small annual donation to the Omega Boys Club, a San Francisco-based organization that assists young African-American men in attending college. While the work of the Omega Boys Club has no direct impact on my life, their mission creates a stronger society for everyone.

> What motivates people in your culture to give? Are you an example of these patterns?

African American

- I believe that people as well as specific causes motivate people within my culture to give. Yes, I believe that I am an example of those patterns.

- I have not observed the reasons for people of African descent to be philanthropic to be much different from the giving of Americans of other cultures—primarily in response to a perceived need to advance society. From the studies I have seen, people of African descent have patterns of giving that follow national trends.

Asian American

- I think giving in my culture is based on social and family ties. It may also be motivated by appearances/looking good. Not necessarily to set an example, but to "look good." This response is based on my own personal experience being brought up in a Filipino immigrant household. I don't know how representative this experience is of the Filipino culture as a whole.

- There's a historical pattern of giving to assist neighbors in need within my culture. I believe that tradition continues today. Services for elders, concern for the welfare of children, and mutual assistance efforts are vital components of Chinese-American philanthropy. People are motivated to give because they care.

Hispanic/Latino

- Latino people are motivated to give for the same reasons others are: recognition and betterment of the lives of "their" people. I am not necessarily an example of these patterns.
- Direct need, having a need to pull yourself up because you lost everything. Very little motivation to help those that won't help themselves. Children and family are very big. Injustice by government gets a huge reaction and giving response (e.g., the Elian Gonzales saga).

Native American

- Which of my cultures? White or Native American? I think I'm not an example of either.

Caucasian

- They/we give because it's the right thing to do. You never know when you are going to need help. I feel fortunate/privileged, and I want to help those not as fortunate. People in my particular defined culture give because faith, personal beliefs, scripture, and the teachings of Jesus lead us.
- The ethical imperative to give and give as much as possible is deeply ingrained in Jewish culture. For the past 54 years, giving to Israel has been a key element of Jewish philanthropy, one that I do not share in. However, my giving to liberal, civil rights, and social justice groups and support of diverse, particularly African-American–led organizations, is fairly typical of my generation.
- We give because we have always given. The tradition arose both from strong biblical injunctions to care for the widows, clothe the naked,

etc. and also because the survival of the Jewish community has often required the more fortunate to care for the less fortunate. These factors are important to my giving, but they are not the only factors.

- I feel the strongest motivators are a desire to help others and to give back to your community. Yes, I am clearly an example of these patterns. I recently graduated from the University of San Francisco. I credit this institution with helping me grow professionally and personally, and I feel much of this growth would not have happened without my positive experiences at USF. Consequently, I give to USF whenever I am asked.

What role does public recognition play in philanthropy in your culture? It is important for people in your culture to be recognized for their philanthropy?

African American

- I believe that public recognition does play a role in philanthropy with respect to my culture, but much less than other cultures. I believe this is a case primarily because the amount of wealth in the African-American culture is significantly less; and therefore, the level of individual giving is not given the same kind of recognition as major gifts in other cultures. It is very important for people in my culture or any culture to be recognized for their philanthropy.

- Public recognition of philanthropy is used as the carrot on the stick for many people of all cultures to give and to give at certain levels. However, some cultures do encourage their members to be anonymous donors.

Asian American

- Not personal recognition per se, but publicity is important because it helps solicit more support.

- Recognition is very important to the older member of the Chinese-American community. There is a strong social infrastructure in Chinese-American society, and that structure includes recognizing key individuals for their generosity. It would not be uncommon to have a major donor not only expect appropriate recognition, but for this donor to "script" the form of acceptable recognition. On the other hand, I believe that there are also those Chinese Americans with a different perspective on cultural traditions, who would shy away from elaborate forms of public recognition. Personally, I don't expect recognition for most of my giving. If I am making a significant gift, then I do expect some form of personal recognition.

- I believe it's important. Growing up, my mom placed much importance on how one was perceived by others.

Hispanic/Latino

- On a grassroots level, not too much, just average. However, in the acculturated Cuban-American community of today, much higher than in mainstream American culture. Organized fundraising by Cuban Americans/Latin Americans in South Florida very much feeds on recognition, big parties, lots of visibility. It's sort of parallel to Maslow's hierarchy—these people have now reached a point that they've made it enough to give, but not enough to give without recognition. Imagine, you arrive or grow up poor, you make it big and now are in a position to help others. You are proud of it, and want people to know that you've made it and that you are now a big important chief. Everyone is competing for recognition—and most people also want it if it helps their businesses because they aren't so successful that they can simply sit back and rest. Recognition has to be blasted.

- Public recognition is important. Latinos have a lot of pride and want to be recognized.

Native American

- Whites usually want it. Native Americans usually not. Pretty important for Native Americans not to be singled out for any reason.

Caucasian

- I was surprised to learn this about myself: in the case of a few organizations where I have been an active participant, the recognition for giving was very important to me. Is recognition important to people in my culture? Classic Jewish joke: Why can't the Israelis get a space shuttle off the ground? Answer: Too many donor plaques.

- As a consultant who has worked on synagogue capital campaigns, I can only say "It depends." The older generation for the most part likes recognition in the form of naming opportunities. Arguments over plaqueing and memorial wall placement tend to dominate certain phases of these campaigns. There certainly are people who respond well to competitive giving, wanting to be in the same level as Dr. So-and-So. Many Jews of all generations adhere to Maimonides' admonition that the greatest charity is a secret that only God knows. Hence, there are many large, anonymous donations from Jews. Anonymous or very quiet charity is common in Jewish communities. At some level, I think we all want to be known, recognized for our contributions, whether it is by a small group, the larger community, or by Adonai alone.

- Public recognition is certainly a major aspect of philanthropy in my culture. While a number of donors want to remain anonymous, there are certainly those donors who desire recognition. I do feel much of this is due to the nonprofit industry wishing to recognize their donors rather than the donors themselves actually seeking it. Personally, if I were never publicly acknowledged for my giving, that would be fine with me. My giving is motivated by a desire to help rather than a need to be recognized.

Have you noticed changes in giving patterns in your culture—say, over the past 10 or 20 years?

African American

- The changes that have occurred took place as new organizations were formed. For example, as new organizations were created to address inequities in civil and social rights and to stress equal justice for all, they received support from African Americans as well.

- Yes, I have noticed changes in giving patterns in my culture of the last 10 or 20 years. During that time, African Americans have gained increasing income and wealth and participation in all social, cultural, and civic activities, therefore enabling and creating greater participation in giving.

Asian American

- Yes. As Asian-American generations mature and become more economically secure I see more giving back to the community.
- There's more generosity now, but there's also more wealth.

Hispanic/Latino

- I do believe that Latinos in this country are adopting American-style giving patterns. Things are changing. They are gaining a new perspective on social issues. While they are closely tied to family and religion—they do not feel a sense of civic duty. The wealthy put up walls to shelter themselves from the poor, the problems in their community. They seem to think that the family lives in a mansion surrounded by walls—just beyond the walls is trash everywhere, homeless children, and incredible poverty. They shut themselves off from it and take care of "their own."

- Tremendous and monumental changes based on acculturation and success. Cuban Americans have now made it by the thousands. Twenty years ago they were beginning to lay the foundations of their success, and didn't have leftover funds for others (although recognitions/status was important, which is why South Florida is a big-time status area—with BMWs, Rolexes, etc., even if they could barely make their payments). Now these same people have made it, some have sold their businesses, some have more than enough equity and income. Having made it also has meant that these people have had to join the mainstream, so they have to play ball by the rules. In other words, you are a rich businessman, you give to United Way because you are supposed to and you need to be able to mingle with the American crowd, which you do business with.

Native American

- Depends on if these are people who are more acculturated. I think greater access to wealth for some has made for greater philanthropy.

Caucasian

- As Jews are more and more accepted and assimilated into other cultures, our giving has expanded. The farther we are from the Holocaust and the more frustrated we become with the political situation in Israel, the more difficult it is to raise funds for those causes. Younger Jews are often resentful of the traditional temple board expectations regarding contributions, and one result is that memberships have declined nationwide. The sense of pressure and obligation sometimes obliterates the invitation to contribute and the joy of giving. There is a Jewish renewal effort among the American Hebrew Congregations to make worship more meaningful, and certainly increasing membership is one hoped-for result.

- I don't pay that much attention to that. I think it's turned more inwards—more domestic causes. Used to be more motivated to give outside their community.

- Not qualified to say.

- Certainly as the economy grows stronger, giving increases. But while giving has increased—thanks in part to the booming high-technology industry—I have not really seen any changes in giving patterns, i.e., religious causes still draw a majority of the money, less "glamorous" causes seem to struggle to survive.

> Overall, how would you rate your culture's philanthropic habits: very poor, average, generous, or very generous?

African American

- The giving of African Americans seems to follow national trends, and the range is from average to very generous.

- I would rate my culture's philanthropic habits as generous to very generous, and the reason why I say that is that when you look at the giving for religious purposes, and when you look at the per capita income, and you compare that to the per capita income of those making significant amounts of money, I conclude that my culture is very generous.

Asian American

- Average.

- With family (and extended family), giving is very generous. Outside, I can't comment.

- Average.

Hispanic/Latino

- Poor to average.

- Very generous in terms of direct giving and helping others. Average in terms of organized philanthropy for the general community. This defies some classification yet is obvious—people give to what they care about deeply, and as a culture Cuban Americans give generously to what they care about deeply, and give lightly to everything else because they have no ingrained obligation to give for giving's sake.

Native American

- Generous to each other.

Caucasian

- Generous to very generous.

- Overall, I believe that Jews are very generous. There are exceptions of course, but a great number of Jews, including secular, nonreligious Jews, have dedicated their lives to philanthropy, establishing schools and foundations. Most do extensive volunteer work. Many well-known entertainment and business figures of Jewish heritage are known as big donors. Giving is considered part of being successful, at whatever level is possible for oneself.

- Very generous.
- Generous.

Please name the culture(s) you consider yourself a part of.

African American

- African American.
- I consider myself to be part of the African-American culture; however, as I have indicated I believe that I am cross-cultural largely because of my upbringing, beliefs, and involvement.

Asian American

- First-generation Asian American from pre-1965 immigrants.
- Filipino-American family culture.
- Chinese American third generation.

Hispanic/Latino

- Not specified.
- Cuban American.

Native American

- Chippewa—not all Indians are alike, and Caucasian.

Caucasian

- American.
- Reform Jewish and Pioneer American.
- Progressive Jewish. I didn't address philanthropy in the other culture I belong to—gay and lesbian culture.
- Caucasian.

PERSONAL GIVING PATTERNS

How much do you research an organization before donating to it?

African American

- Most of my giving has followed my other involvement with the organizations—volunteer, staff member, and/or consultant—or with recommendations from family members or friends.
- Before giving to an organization my research is thorough. I like to know that my giving is going to be "invested" wisely.

Asian American

- Until I'm comfortable with the cause and the people involved.
- Not very much.
- My research comes from becoming involved with the organization before giving to it. For those organizations I am not directly involved with, I rely on family and friends, and instinct.

Hispanic/Latino

- Not too much.
- Not much. If I give it's because I know it and trust it because of who is involved or what it has accomplished.

Native American

- Thoroughly. I work too hard to waste money.

Caucasian

- Not thoroughly, but I try to know something about it.
- I give almost exclusively to local organizations that I have worked with or know people with, so I know a great deal including salaries, fundraising costs. I am likely to have seen their audits.

- I have only made major gifts to an organization where I have been an active participant in governance.

- I really do not research an organization very much. I give small amounts so I am not as concerned that a large amount of money will be unwisely utilized. I typically trust an organization to be a good steward of my gift; however, bad publicity certainly does affect my giving. For example, despite being Catholic, I will not give to Catholic Charities, even though I firmly believe in their efforts to help numerous organizations. They have, at times, received bad press questioning their handling of funds, so I feel better about giving directly to the organizations helping people in need, rather than to an "umbrella" organization.

> What prompts you to give to a particular organization, i.e., the cause, your personal involvement, involvement of friends, personal solicitation, direct mail or advertising, etc.?
> (A) Are you more likely to give to an organization from which you or someone you know has benefited?
> (B) Are you more likely to give directly to individuals in need?

African American

- A. Yes; B. Neither more or less likely. My giving usually is in response to my understanding of the need and my ability to help.

- Prompting me to give to an organization can be any number of things, such as the cause, personal involvement, involvement of friends, personal solicitation, direct mail or advertising—in essence, all of the above. However, I must say that I am not given over to advertising generally. I do my research and make sure again that I am giving/investing wisely. A. Yes , I am more likely to give to an organization from which I or someone I know has benefited. B. I am less likely to give directly to individuals in need. I prefer to give to organizations that are helping individuals in need.

Asian American

- Mainly the cause. A. Yes. B. Only if I know the situation of the individual.

- The cause, my personal involvement, and involvement of friends. A. Yes. B. Yes.

- The cause and the need. A. Very likely. B. Not likely. I prefer to give to organizations, although I am concerned about unnecessary overhead within some organizations.

Hispanic/Latino

- The cause must be something I personally value. A. No, not necessarily. B. Yes, I probably would not give to any religious organization.

- The cause and my involvement is number one, the involvement of friends is likely to move me to give but not too much. Personal solicitation (which has to be handled with care as compared to standard fundraising methodology) will only get a small response if other factors are not there. I never give to direct mail or advertising or phone calls. A. Absolutely. Seeing is believing. B. I give to people in need who have arrived from Cuba, but do believe that giving to organizations that help many people is more important.

Native American

- The cause, reputation of the organization. A. No. More inclined to give where "liberal" causes are the focus and "minority" groups are included. B. No.

Caucasian

- A. Yes, definitely. I give mainly to the Catholic Church and the University of San Francisco because both organizations have played pivotal roles in my personal development. I am glad to have the opportunity to support both organizations. B. I will occasionally give directly to an individual; however, my preference is to give to an organization because I recognize that my small contribution can effectively be combined with other gifts to help a broader range of people.

- The cause. A. I imagine yes, but not a primary motivation. B. No.

- My personal involvement, direct benefit to a friend, such as using Hospice services, and commitment to the social ideals I hold are primary motivations. I often give to small grassroots groups because a small gift can have greater impact. Many of my gifts are self-initiated, not in response to an appeal. I have never begun a donor relationship with direct mail as the first contact; there has to be a more personal experience. I make political contributions, which are not deductible but are an important part of my giving, of both time and money. I buy advertising in programs and often a "brick for the wall" on capital campaigns in the name of my business. I consider these marketing expenses more than charity. I am pretty likely to make a small pledge to almost any friend or relative who is running, biking, or kayaking for charity. I am simply in awe of friends who have done the 700-mile AIDS ride. A. Yes, if it's an organization that seems well run and shares my values. On the other hand, when a close friend's husband died in a tragic accident last year, I could not bring myself to make a contribution to his favorite charity as requested, because it is an organization I consider extremist in its approach to animal welfare. Nor would I give to an evangelical Christian church if asked by surviving family members.

- The cause, although I give token amounts to organizations that my friends solicit for. A. A little. B. No.

Are there biases, traditions, or norms in your culture that would keep you from donating to certain causes or groups? If yes, how likely are you to support a cause that your culture would disagree with?

African American

- Based on the experiences of people of African descent, I would not support any organization that did not espouse equality and fair treatment of all people.

- I am not unlike anyone else in that I can be influenced by not giving to organizations or causes that have had or currently have biases, or a negative impact with respect to my culture.

Asian American

- Yes. I will not support a cause that is racist or promotes superiority of a particular race or group.

- I don't think so.
- Not biases or norms from within my culture; but certainly my own biases play an important part of my philanthropic decision making. I make my own decisions, and therefore do not feel any obligation to my culture's perceptions on giving. I do not support organizations that promote racial intolerance or superiority. I do not support the NRA, or organizations that tolerate violence.

Hispanic/Latino

- I am definitely likely to give to an organization that my culture would disagree with. I take the good from being a part of the culture, but leave the rest behind, especially when it comes to giving.
- Is definitely a macho culture, so gays do not fare well. Neither do liberal causes, or anything that could be remotely linked to communism. *Remotely* is a big word in this case. Homelessness does not fare well because they are perceived as losers who don't get their butts up, so do welfare causes and African-American causes related to welfare, welfare mothers, etc. It is still a rather old-fashioned culture, so mental health is still a hidden problem. The arts are not big in terms of priority of giving. Government handout-type programs do not resonate at all with Cuban Americans. I personally would be highly unlikely to give to many things that my culture would disagree with, but like many Cuban Americans am acculturated enough to not include gays and homeless causes in this. I would be likely to give to anything that I personally believed in, and would not be affected by cultural restraints (although perhaps I would keep quiet about it).

Native American

- I'm a person of mixed ethnic heritage. I was raised as a white, middle-class woman, and so most of my values were learned as part of the "majority" culture. White people think I'm white. Few people understand being from two traditions. Because much of what we think is racially motivated behavior is cultural and, therefore, learned. It's not inherited. A white person living on a reservation has more in common with the Native Americans there than Native American or white living in the white culture.

Caucasian

- Despite a desire to help, I certainly feel there are some causes that do not get funding because of people's biases. AIDS is a perfect example. When the disease became prominent in the early 1980s there was a feeling that this was a "gay" disease. Why should mainstream America contribute to help cure a disease that seemingly only affected a small minority people who seemingly contracted the disease through practices that were not accepted by the majority of our society? Even though public opinion has been greatly reversed since the disease's inception, there still is some lingering stigma about contributing to organizations involved in AIDS care and research.

- I wouldn't give to a cause that promotes harm or violence. An example: an organization collecting money for Irish homeland, but the dollars could be used to buy arms for the IRA.

- I donate to many causes that Orthodox Jewry disagrees with and decline to donate to some projects, like the Holocaust museum, which many Jews support. I think the role of culture for me is to create a framework for evaluating a situation. But, hopefully, I make my own decision. For example, I am less likely to support popular charities and more likely to look for those that lack a broad base of support. Is that itself a cultural trait? I don't think so.

- I don't give to organizations that believe their religion is the only one, that they have the answer for all of the people. Many people mistakenly think that Jews believe this but it is not part of our tradition nor is attempting to convert others. Any group, such as the Boy Scouts, that discriminates on the basis of gender, sexual orientation, religion, ethnicity, or other identity does not get my support. In general, I would not support any organization that is offensive to the average Jewish person.

CHAPTER 8

Case Studies

Each of the six case studies in this section reflects a distinct diverse fundraising experience. Discussion questions that follow each case are designed to facilitate debate and further examination. These cases reflect both actual and fictional circumstances, and some names and locations are not specifically identified.

The first case study, "The Elephant in *Our Turn*'s Living Room," takes a multiethnic look at fundraising for health issues in a predominantly low-income African-American community.

"A Capital Campaign for a Roman Catholic Chinese School" presents an interview with a junior fundraiser, a Caucasian in a Catholic-run Chinese School in the Chinatown of a large city who is working on the school's first capital campaign where the volunteer leadership is Chinese, but the staff is predominantly Caucasian.

"Sisters of African Descent" introduces an organization founded 50 years ago by a small group of African-American women teachers. The case looks at the evolution of the organization, as well as its growth and fundraising efforts leading them to engaging counsel for a feasibility study, only to be told that the findings did not support readiness for such a campaign.

The First Nations People case study, "Insider Outsider: Major Gift Fund-Raising Among Some First Nation's People," reflects on the cultural implications of Native American philanthropy through the experiences of a Native American–Caucasian fundraiser working for a small college in the Midwest. The college campaign encourages gifts of cash and real estate, and the Native American beliefs about the significance of the land emerge as personal challenges to the fundraiser.

Jackson Memorial Hospital is located in Miami, Florida, and the author of "Involving Cuban-Americans in South Florida Charities" is the president of the hospital foundation. With a large Cuban-American population, Jackson Hospital engages in culturally appropriate fundraising activities designed to increase Cuban-American participation. The case identifies the challenges the hospital faces in raising money from multiple constituencies while acknowledging that attracting Cuban-American donors is important.

"Successful Fund-Raising for India's 5H Program" uses the example of a special musical event organized by South Asians to provide financial support to a youth leadership organization based in India. Volunteer leadership for this event comes from successful technology executives in Silicon Valley.

THE ELEPHANT IN *OUR TURN*'S LIVING ROOM

Michael L. Edell*

This case raises issues facing executive directors, development directors, boards of directors, and communities. It focuses on the moral and ethical dilemmas of fundraising for controversial causes, and their impact on African-American residents of a small town called Greenview, particularly on a respected nonprofit organization, *Our Turn.*

Our Turn, a nonprofit organization located in the small California community of Greenview, provides programs to empower Greenview's youth and families to overcome the plagues of violence, drugs, and crime. Seventy percent of Greenview's ethnically and culturally diverse population is African American.

Between 1991 and 1997, Greenview's community spirit had suffered as a result of growing racial insularity, gang violence, drugs, and crime. *Our Turn* was founded in 1996 by a group of Greenview's families and several local churches, of which some children had lost their lives. Sophia Williams, a longtime Greenview resident who was the youngest of six children raised by a father who earned money for his family by doing sharecropping work and a mother who did domestic work, was one of the founders. She became

---

*The material contained in this case does not necessarily represent actual people, institutions, or conditions.

Our Turn's executive director after earning a master's degree in nonprofit administration.

For many, *Our Turn* symbolizes the power of the family in taking back the community from the elements that threaten to destroy it. The residents took great pride in restoring safety and in reconstructing a positive image among neighboring cities that had begun to equate Greenview with violence, drugs, and crime.

Our Turn was only three years old when Sophia's daughter, Claire, lost her battle to HIV/AIDS, after years of injection drug abuse. At Claire's funeral, tears rolled down Sophia's face as she spoke about losing her daughter and how she planned to dedicate her life to stopping AIDS from taking any more lives in Greenview. At an *Our Turn* board meeting two months later, Sophia proposed an annual campaign to raise $150,000 for an HIV/AIDS educational awareness and prevention program targeting at-risk youth.

As Sophia spoke about the campaign, several board members remained silent and looked at each other with concern. The board voted to discuss the campaign at its next meeting and asked Sophia to prepare a report on the pros and cons of taking on a controversial issue such as HIV/AIDS. They also requested a detailed plan on how she would raise the funds.

As she left the building Sophia turned to her new director of development, Doris Clayton, and said, "First thing in the morning, start doing some research on the HIV/AIDS epidemic and its impact on the black community. This is one cause worth fighting for." Doris had noticed the concerned stares from several board members during the meeting and was less confident that Sophia's campaign would be an easy sell.

Meanwhile, several board members held a "meeting after the meeting" and shared their concerns that HIV/AIDS, albeit an important public health concern, was not part of *Our Turn's* mission. Some felt that Sophia was trying to alter *Our Turn*'s mission to memorialize her daughter.

"This organization is about crime, drugs, and violence," said Fred Jones, a Greenville resident for more than 30 years. "AIDS is the public health department's problem, not ours."

"*Our Turn* should focus on restoring the family and its values, not on how to engage in immoral activities safely," added the Rev. Sampson, pastor of Shiloh Christian Center. The discussion ended with an informal understanding that Sophia's fundraising campaign most likely would be voted down at the next board meeting.

Our Turn was no stranger to controversial issues. Its mission initially focused only on violence and crime among youth and families. One year later, Sophia struggled to include the word "drugs" in the mission statement, arguing that drugs were so often the cause of violence and crime.

"It is time for the black community to start talking about the 'elephant in the living room,'" she said, referring to how some families ignore issues such as substance abuse that have a dominant presence in the home.

The community responded positively after *Our Turn* included anti-drug programs for youth. Testimonials from former drug addicts whose lives were turned around were heard frequently at community meetings and churches throughout Greenview. But some listeners felt that too much attention was being given to drugs and that recovering addicts and alcoholics with compelling stories only glorified substance abuse.

Doris Clayton came to *Our Turn* as an intern while earning her development director certificate through an online program offered by a local university. She found that working at *Our Turn* was the perfect opportunity to apply the many fundraising principles taught by seasoned development professionals at the university.

She found herself deeply moved while conducting research on HIV/ AIDS among African Americans. She was shocked to learn that in the year 2000, AIDS was the leading cause of death among African Americans age 25 to 44. She also found that more African Americans were reported with AIDS than any other racial/ethnic group; blacks accounted for 35 percent of all HIV cases, although they make up only 13 percent of the population; 63 percent of new AIDS cases in children under 13 years of age were African American; and black babies made up almost two-thirds of the new pediatric AIDS cases. (*Source*: Congressional Black Caucus Foundation, 2001.)

Doris drafted a direct mail solicitation highlighting the HIV/AIDS problem among African Americans and the importance of community action to integrate HIV awareness and prevention with substance abuse treatment and education. Doris's letter further related that Greenview's HIV/AIDS statistics closely resembled national findings.

Sophia liked Doris's letter immediately and felt it would be even more compelling if it included the faces and words of Greenview residents courageous enough to lend their names to the campaign's plea to help end to drugs, violence, and HIV/AIDS in the community. Sophia and Doris were encouraged to find that several HIV-positive clients in *Our Turn* who had a history of crime and drug and alcohol use were eager to give testimonials to further HIV/AIDS awareness in the community. Sophia mailed a draft of the letter to the board of directors for advance review and discussion at its next monthly meeting.

The reaction to the letter started only days after it was mailed.

"Isn't it bad enough that our black brothers and sisters in Greenview are so often stereotyped as drug addicts and gang members?" said board member Betty Clark. "This campaign will demean our community by depicting us as diseased."

The Rev. Jacobs, board member and pastor of the prosperous Trinity Baptist Church, remarked that "AIDS is a reflection of the immorality that has overtaken our community. We must fight this with prayer, not our hard-earned money," he said.

Not all board members were as critical of the direct mail piece.

"Why can't *Our Turn* take a positive spin on this campaign and portray Greenview African Americans as self-sufficient and responsible?" asked successful businessman Steve Adams. "Our community needs to be empowered first so we can address the AIDS problem. We can't just ask them to write a check to solve this problem."

Board president Katherine Dickson agreed. "This is part of what *Our Turn* stands for," she said. "We identify the problem and then take immediate action. Greenview solutions for Greenview problems."

The Rev. Templeton was quick to respond to the outcries of the local clergy. "If AIDS is God's punishment for immoral people, does that mean that breast cancer is His punishment against women?" she said. "It is a time to put our judgments aside and reach out with compassion to those in their time of greatest need." It was well known that Rev. Templeton served on a national faith-based coalition to raise awareness about HIV/AIDS among minority communities.

Sophia was distraught. It seemed as though each day her board of directors became more divided. She knew in her heart that *Our Turn* had the track record and expertise to address HIV/AIDS in Greenview. As she looked out the window of her office, she saw a small playground filled with young girls playing jump rope. She thought of her daughter and searched her heart for the right thing to do about the elephant in Greenview's living room.

Acknowledgments

Special thanks to the leadership, clients, and staff of the following organizations and individuals whose insights and contributions were part of the development of this case study:

AIDS Community Research Consortium, Redwood City, California

Benjamin J. Bowser, Ph.D., California State University—Hayward

Sandra Burnett, Mission Hospice, San Mateo, California

The Rev. Mary Frazier, Bread of Life Worship Center, East Palo Alto, California

Marsha L. Howard, Cultural Diversity Training Specialist, Redwood City, California

Carla Hudson, Economic and Social Opportunities, Inc., San Jose, California

Roger Shaff, MPH, International Health Programs, Santa Cruz, California

Sally Smith, Management Consultant, Palm Springs, California

William Washington, DPA, MPH, CHES, San Jose State University, California

Discussion Questions

1. Was it right for Sophia to suggest modifying her agency's mission based on the loss of her daughter? Why or why not?

2. What steps should *Our Turn* have taken to make the community more aware of the HIV/AIDS problem in Greenview?

3. What are some of the different cultural approaches Sophia could have used to make the "elephant" more accepted in this diverse community?

4. What role(s) could other ethnic groups in Greenview have in supporting a new mission for *Our Turn*?

5. Given that HIV/AIDS was a controversial subject in this community, what would be the advantages and disadvantages of beginning with small programs and then scaling up as the organization and its leadership gained more experience in the area?

A CAPITAL CAMPAIGN FOR A ROMAN CATHOLIC CHINESE SCHOOL

Anonymous

In 1998, Michael C. accepted a junior fundraising position for a capital campaign being conducted by an urban Catholic elementary school located in a Chinese-American neighborhood. A Caucasian, Michael was unfamiliar with most of the traditions and structures of the Chinese culture. He was recently interviewed about his experiences of working in fundraising in an organization primarily serving an ethnic culture different from his own.

Q: *To begin with, tell me about the school, St. Ambrose.*

A: St. Ambrose is small, just a few hundred students in kindergarten through eighth grades. Parents who send their children to the school are foreign-born immigrants and long time residents, including first-, second-, and third-generation Chinese Americans. I should note that many of the children do not live near the school, and some even travel from other cities. But there is a strong tie to St. Ambrose, especially if their parents and grandparents attended there, so the families are willing to travel great distances each school day. And, despite the school's Roman Catholic affiliation, most of the school children—approximately 80 percent—are not baptized Catholics.

Q: How long has St. Ambrose existed?

A: St. Ambrose has served this particular Chinese community since the early 1900s. It began as a social service center, with a group of Roman Catholic priests reaching out to the Chinese community who were limited in employment and housing opportunities by the segregation laws of the time. The priests taught new immigrants English and practical techniques of how to live and succeed in America. In the 1920s, an elementary school was added, and later a Chinese cultural school was formed so that American-born Chinese children could learn of the cultures and traditions of their parents, grandparents, and ancestors. This was especially important since many of the households were—and still are—multigenerational.

Q: *Why was St. Ambrose conducting a capital campaign, and what was the goal?*

A: The school was housed in an outdated building that required extensive renovations to bring it up to code for safety and Americans with Disabilities requirements. The renovations would have resulted in a loss of 25 percent of usable space in the already overcrowded facility, and would have cost over half as much as a brand-new building. The community was polled, and it was determined that a new, modern building was a better alternative to repairing a 70-year old structure. The campaign goal was $7 million.

Q: *Was there support for the campaign from everyone in the community?*

A: I was not involved with the campaign during the planning phases, but I do not believe there was much opposition to the project. The prospect of a modern facility with state-of-the-art computer and technological enhancements, along with twice as much space for classrooms and recreational facilities, was certainly a compelling argument. It is also important to point out that the school had not—at least in recent history—conducted a capital campaign, so I feel the community was well suited financially to raise the funds.

Q: *Were you apprehensive about working in an organization with a culture with which you were not familiar?*

A: No, not at all, because I accepted the position thinking that the biggest challenge would be to help raise the $7 million goal. I never thought of myself as a minority, a Caucasian working at a Chinese organization or that there would be challenges involved with that. There were only a handful of Caucasians working at St. Ambrose. Most of the administration and faculty were Chinese, and practically every student was Chinese. Interestingly, though, the two highest-ranking staff members were Caucasian: the director (a Roman Catholic priest of Irish-American descent) and the principal. Of course, being in positions of authority and being older they were treated with great respect. My manager, the senior fundraiser (also a Caucasian), commented to me shortly after I began, "You will never be fully accepted here." At first, that comment hurt a bit. But soon I understood what she meant. I had no affiliation with St. Ambrose prior to coming to work there, so I'm sure I appeared to many people like a stranger.

Q: *What were you most unprepared for?*

A: Clearly I was unprepared for the strict hierarchical structure with which the campaign was run. The chair, a doctor very well known and respected in the local medical community, spent time in the military, so the campaign was run with what I considered a militaristic precision. Meetings always began and ended on time, and there was a rigid formality in everything we did. Every meeting, no matter how big or small, had an agenda. This hierarchical structure, I came to understand, is quite common in the Chinese culture.

Q: *How so?*

A: Let me first give you my definition of hierarchy: an organization where the structure is clearly defined with a series of horizontal levels with varying degrees of authority and responsibility. The higher positions have more power, the lower ones less, and those on the bottom are expected to show respect to those above them. I came from a more laterally oriented structure where I could always voice my opinion. When I first came to St. Ambrose, however, I was frequently interrupted by the chair and was expected to stop talking and defer to the chair. It was maddening to me, to be interrupted. I allowed it to stifle my creativity and felt discouraged about sharing my ideas. I recognize that this may have had less to do with my ethnicity and more to do with my age: I was over 20 years younger than the chair. In fact, now that I think about it, I feel my age was probably the main reason, since Asian campaign volunteers who were the same age as me but higher on the campaign structure treated me as a peer and as someone who was equally committed to the campaign.

Q: *Did the challenges you had in dealing with the hierarchical structure affect others or the smooth operation of the campaign?*

A: I don't believe so. While this was unusual to me, I found it nonetheless to be highly effective, especially since most of the donors to the campaign were Chinese, especially the older donors solicited for major gifts. They were familiar with the structure and expected it.

It was a format with which they would be familiar and comfortable, and illustrated that the campaign leadership clearly respected its constituencies. And remember that this is a Catholic organization, which is also based on hierarchy. Since all the volunteers were either Chinese or Catholic—most were both, actually—they were familiar with a structured environment.

Q: *How did you deal with the feelings of being the "outsider"?*

A: Let me first say that many of the feelings I had, I now realize, were of my own creation. But in a way, the feelings challenged me to do my best work. I didn't want to be perceived as an outsider *and* someone who is not very effective at fundraising. The feelings helped me to focus my energies and to look at ways I could positively help the campaign instead of dwelling on the negative, stagnating thoughts of not being accepted because I was not of Chinese descent. It also helped that I am Catholic, that I at least fit into one of the major segments of the community. And I lived near the school, on the border of the Chinese area of the city. Because of this, I was often seen by people affiliated with the school as I walked through the area and as I patronized local Chinese merchants.

Q: *Was your role in the campaign clearly defined?*

A: I was clearly expected to have a "behind the scenes" role and to ensure that the volunteers, particularly the chair and director, were well prepared for their meetings and visits. In many ways my position was more secretarial and administrative rather than managerial and professional. At first, I really didn't like this. For example, I am a good writer and can easily draft a variety of fundraising letters. But when I began at St. Ambrose, our chair would leave lengthy voice-mail messages for me and I was expected to transcribe the letters verbatim. I thought that my skills were not being used adequately. After writing and editing a few issues of the campaign newsletter, my writing responsibilities increased. Again, I felt it was a case of actions speaking louder than words, and that I had to clearly demonstrate my loyalty before I was permitted to take on more responsibilities.

Q: *It sounds as though the chair of the campaign was quite involved?*

A: He was a volunteer, but from the level of his involvement and the amount of time he devoted to the campaign, you would think he was a paid staff member! My past experiences had led me to believe that the "chair" is more of a ceremonial position, someone who lends his or her name to letters and solicits wealthy friends and colleagues. Yes, the St. Ambrose chair did those things, but he was definitely "hands on" when it came to running the campaign. Although I technically reported to the director, practically all of my work direction came from the chair. He got people—donors and volunteers—to say yes. In fact, I recall one volunteer saying to me, "How can we say no, when he is doing so much?" I truly feel he is the main reason the campaign is so successful. The community made a very wise decision in selecting him.

Q: *Why did the chair do so much?*

A: He was an alumnus of the school, so that was certainly a motivating force. I learned in the Chinese culture that you always remember your roots, the places where you came from. I heard at St. Ambrose that is the reason why schools and hospitals with Chinese constituencies are successful with fundraising activities, because so many lives began and were nurtured at those organizations. I even found donors who didn't attend St. Ambrose but had parents or grandparents who did, and that was as strong a motivation to give as if the donors had attended St. Ambrose themselves. I also feel the chair was following a theme in the Chinese culture of "saving face," of not allowing your words or actions to disgrace your family name. Because of this, I feel he worked very hard to ensure that the word *failure* was never associated with the campaign. But ultimately, I believe the chair was so involved because that is his nature, that if he is in charge of a project he will be completely involved.

Q: *What else did you learn at St. Ambrose about how to run a capital campaign?*

A: I learned the importance of internal commitment, of ensuring that everyone involved with the organization believed in the work of the campaign. This was clearly evident at St. Ambrose. When campaign activities disrupted class schedules—which didn't happen often—the teachers were happy to accommodate our needs, as they believed in what the campaign staff was trying to accomplish. More specifically, at the completion of a phone-a-thon, one alumnus said I was to call him whenever I needed help. "Anything for St. Ambrose," he said. That was a feeling echoed throughout my time there. I also learned that you need to be sensitive to and aware of unique cultural traditions, such as the impoliteness of asking people about their financial resources, how it is insulting to ask a Chinese person to sign their name to a pledge, and not talking about death, since it can be a taboo subject to many Chinese people.

Q: *Regarding your last point, death as a taboo subject, how do you approach planned giving in the Chinese community?*

A: I feel that your approach is no different from discussing the subject with any other community. You wouldn't meet a potential donor one minute and talk about their estate plan the next. The relationship needs to be cultivated and nurtured, and each and every case needs to be handled differently, but I do feel that Chinese donors—particularly the older generations—need to be approached very sensitively. St. Ambrose had only a few planned giving participants, at least that we were aware of. But in many ways I feel the lack of participants had less to do with a reluctance to discuss planned giving and more a desire to look after the donor's children.

Q: *Is the St. Ambrose campaign a success?*

A: Absolutely! The only major delays the campaign encountered were with finalizing building plans and permits, delays that were caused by an inordinate amount of civic bureaucracy, not by the campaign. The fundraising aspect of the campaign has been most successful. Yes, the money may not have come in as quickly as was hoped and we encountered some plateaus, but in analyzing the history of the campaign, of what was accomplished from a relatively small group of donors and without a major, region-wide publicity and marketing program, I feel the campaign is a success.

Q: *So it sounds as though the campaign was basically a positive experience for you, yet you left after less than two years and before the goal was reached. Why?*

A: Another opportunity came my way to get a substantial raise in salary and that would provide opportunities to focus primarily on my development writing skills. It would also give me more visibility in the local fundraising community, and being relatively new to the field, I felt that was very important. Still, I am very happy with what I accomplished at St. Ambrose and still help the campaign financially.

Q: *You spoke earlier about how you felt loyalty was a highly regarded trait in the Chinese culture. When you announced your departure, did you encounter any feelings of disloyalty?*

A: Absolutely not. Everyone understood my reasons for leaving and appeared very happy for me. I do feel it has helped that although I am no longer an employee of the campaign, I do continue to support the effort financially. I have also attended a couple of school events where my presence reinforces my interest in the school and my support of its endeavors.

Q: *Would you work in a similar environment again?*

A: Yes. The commitment and dedication of the volunteers and the community made my fundraising job much easier. The community was eager to help because they knew the result of their efforts would culminate in a new school providing great opportunities for their children and for future generations. And the challenges I encountered made me stronger personally and made me a much better and more effective fundraiser. I learned many skills and techniques there. For example, I used to call older people by their first name when I was meeting them for the first time or addressing them in a letter. While at St. Ambrose, I learned it was a sign of respect to address people you just met as "Mr." and "Mrs." I still follow this rule today and find it to be a simple but very effective tool in fundraising.

Q: *What advice would you give to others who begin working in organizations that predominantly serve ethnicities other than their own?*

A: I feel that the basics of fundraising are the same. You need the same skills regardless of the type of constituency. I feel it is important for the person to know that there may be some resistance if you are the one actually asking for the gifts and in charge of recruiting and motivating volunteers. I would definitely find one or two mentors who can help you understand the ethnic culture in which you are working, and with whom you can ask questions and share experiences. I also feel it is a good idea to get very involved in the community and its activities, rather than just work "9-to-5." But do you know any fundraiser who does work regular hours?

Discussion Questions

1. Michael thinks that fundraising concepts are the same regardless of the community being served. Do you agree or disagree?

2. Michael said he thought the hierarchical structure of the campaign was similar to structures in the Chinese culture. Is this an accurate comparison?

3. What are some demonstrations of respect in different cultures, and how are they similar to or different from those in the Chinese culture?

4. Do levels of hierarchy exist in all major fundraising endeavors, particularly capital campaigns, or is St. Ambrose unusual?

5. Michael provided some advice to people working with ethnic groups that are different from their own ethnicity. What additional advice would you give?

SISTERS OF AFRICAN DESCENT

Samuel N. Gough, Jr.

In 1941, three African-American women who met in college and later became teachers in Washington, D.C., founded the Sisters of African Descent in Washington, D.C. They initially met to exchange information about teaching and as a social outlet. As World War II began to escalate, they became increasingly more concerned about the plight of other African-American women, whom they felt were not being given equal employment opportunities in the growing war economy. They expanded their small circle of friends to 18 other women, and by 1943, they were alternating their monthly meetings at the homes of their members. By 1964, there were more than 1,000 members of the Sisters of African Descent.

As the group grew, so, too, did the members' interest in other areas affecting the lives of African-American women throughout the country. In addition to career advancement, health and education emerged as the fore-most issues for the focus of their interest.

At the beginning of 1944, there were 41 members, with nine of them now living in other cities on the East Coast after being relocated because of marriages and/or careers. Even though these nine women were not meeting monthly with the other 32 members, they continued to stay in contact with one another by mail, telephone, and job-related and/or per-sonal travel either to Washington, D.C., or to the cities where members lived. The members in other cities began to recruit like-minded African-American women to become members.

By the end of 1944, there were 48 members in Washington, D.C., and 96 members in six other cities—Boston, New York, Baltimore, Richmond, Charlotte, and Atlanta. These groups were called chapters. There had to be at least 10 members in a city to form a chapter. The organization was struc-tured locally and regionally.

The Washington, D.C., chapter met monthly. The other chapters met as prescribed by their individual bylaws. Annual meetings were held each June in Washington, D.C. Each chapter was allowed two voting members. These two members per chapter, elected by their respective chapters for three-year terms, formed the governing board of the organization.

In 1944, the Sisters of African Descent incorporated as a nonprofit or-ganization. The organization stated its mission as:

> The Sisters of African Descent is a national, non-profit organization headquartered in Washington, D.C., that seeks to ameliorate disadvan-tages that Negro women have endured in obtaining educational and ca-reer opportunities and in gaining access to adequate health care.

The Sisters of African Descent still was an entirely volunteer-run orga-nization. In its bylaws, provisions were made for six officers—president, first vice-president, second vice-president, recording secretary, corresponding secretary, and treasurer. The chapters also had the same officers.

When World War II ended in 1945, thousands of servicemen and women returned to civilian life. These veterans were given first preference in obtaining jobs and with continuing their education. The Sisters of African Descent saw an even greater need to focus its efforts on seeking equity for African-American women, both veterans and nonmilitary. It was at this time that fundraising proved necessary.

Traditionally, the members used their own resources, money they had raised from friends and small special events to implement programs that advanced the goals set forth by their organization's mission. As the organization grew, members realized more money was needed to make significant progress.

In 1957, the Sisters of African Descent applied for and was granted tax-exempt status by the federal government. Soon after, appeals for support were broadened to offer donors tax-deduction benefits. In furtherance of the mission, three primary programs were launched:

- The Sisters of African Descent Scholarship Program that allowed young women with high-school grade point averages of 3.5, or better, to apply for scholarships that included full tuition, room and board, books, and a modest stipend for one year. If they maintained their academic standing at, or above, that level for the next three years, the scholarships were renewed throughout their undergraduate studies. There could be as many as 18 scholars in any one year.

- The Careers for Women Program linked women of any age who were entering the workforce or who sought advancement in their current jobs to be mentored by other women who were successful in those same fields. Participants were matched by career fields and geographic locations. The parameters for the mentoring were set by an advisory committee made up of Sisters of African Descent members. All mentors and protégées met at the annual meeting of the Sisters of African Descent to share information and to broaden the network.

- Healthy Sisters provided information and referrals to women on health and wellness matters. Workshops and seminars were sponsored and conducted in all the cities where chapters were located.

By 1964, the organization had grown to more than 1,000 members with chapters in 17 cities. The Washington, D.C., chapter remained the largest. The first staff person was hired as executive secretary, and space was rented for an office.

The executive secretary was charged with keeping the records of the organization, maintaining the membership lists for all the chapters, collecting annual dues, making arrangements for the annual meetings, maintaining the three primary programs, and coordinating all volunteer efforts.

The monies to pay the salary of executive secretary, to rent space, and to operate the office came from the annual dues that each chapter paid. As time passed, the need to raise money to continue and expand programs as well to hire more staff and increase the operating budget became evident. Therefore, the executive secretary was given the added responsibility of raising funds.

Initially, members were sent two annual fundraising appeals, one in April and the other in late November. Annual donors received a semi-annual newsletter and public recognition for their gifts with the publication of their names and the issuance of certificates based on the size of their gifts.

However, after three years, the chapters began to complain that by asking for more money each year from the members, the amount of money that could be raised for chapter activities was decreasing. Many of these activities had expanded into the area of civil rights and social justice.

In 1968, the entire country was in upheaval following the death of Dr. Martin Luther King, Jr. The chapters began to initiate programs to strengthen family unity and community cohesiveness. Education and job training took center stage. Child care and job training centers, before- and after-school programs, and the Sisters of African Descent Scholarship Program became paramount. Less time and attention was paid to the Healthy Sisters Program.

During the 1970s and 1980s, new programs evolved, headquarters hired three additional staff members, the membership grew to more than 3,000 women, and eight new chapters were formed. Chapter dues and the annual solicitation of members accounted for 55 percent of the organization's annual budget. The remaining 45 percent came from foundations that supported specific programs; a few corporations that provided small to medium-sized grants, restricted and unrestricted; and a few wealthy individuals.

In 1991, at the annual meeting, the chapters voted to explore launching a capital campaign to purchase a headquarters building and to start an endowment. The executive secretary selected a development consulting firm to determine if it was feasible to raise funds for these two purposes and if it was feasible, how much money could be raised and from whom.

A year later, the executive secretary reported to the members on the results of the consulting firm's findings.

In summary, that report drew the following conclusions:

- The Sisters of African Descent were not ready to launch a capital campaign because they did not have the lead gifts identified that would be needed for success, adequately trained staff to conduct a campaign, sufficient support from the governing board, or the necessary support systems to sustain the level of accounting required.

- The governing board needed to better understand its responsibility as a board and as individuals in a capital campaign.

- The Sisters of African Descent needed to do more to let its members know what was taking place at the national office and chapters across the country. The semiannual communication from the national headquarters now was only sent to donors.

- The organization needed to broaden its outreach to a wider range of individuals and organizations by letting them know what has been done and what needed to be done.

- There needed to be a series of cultivation events over a 15-month period that would focus on enlarging the pool of potential donors.

- At the end of the 15 months, a modified study needed to be conducted to determine the size of a goal and to identify potential donors to a capital campaign.

The governing board of the Sisters of African Descent accepted the report without comment.

Discussion Questions

1. Given the era during which this African-American group was organizing and growing, what types of pressure—social, economic, and historical—must the original leaders have encountered?

2. The organization was in operation for about 20 years before they began to actively solicit funds from outside their membership ranks. Should they have waited this long?

3. What types of corporations do you suppose supported the group with "small- to medium-sized grants"?

4. Nearly 50 years after beginning operation, a consulting firm determined the organization would not be able to successfully implement

a capital campaign. What could the organization have done differently in its first 50 years to be ready for a major fundraising effort?

5. The only way this organization will survive is if they change their mission to focus on the struggles of all women, not just those of African-American descent. Do you agree or disagree with this statement? If the group changed its mission, what are some responses or reaction that they may expect from longtime donors?

INSIDER-OUTSIDER: MAJOR GIFT FUNDRAISING AMONG SOME FIRST NATIONS PEOPLE

Prudence S. Precourt, Ph.D., CFRE

The campus of Sweet Home College was lovely that spring morning when Dave first visited during his job interview. Situated in a rural agricultural community in the South, the immediately adjacent town was almost exclusively inhabited by First Nations people who were primarily of a single tribal[1] affiliation.

While many people from this community had received degrees from the college, most had not. Originating out of a student body that was almost totally local First Nations people, the campus voluntarily embraced integration in the early 1950s. The number of students from outside the community gradually grew, so by the time of Dave's interview, most students were Caucasian. The remainder of the student body was comprised of First Nations people, African-American, and international students. The administration contained a substantial number of First Nations people, while the faculty was comprised primarily of nonlocal Caucasians. The staff was almost completely local First Nations people. The board of trustees was almost totally made up of First Nations people.

The town of Sweet Home was tightly knit. Most of the staff, faculty, and administration could trace their roots back into the community. Many educated local people had left the area. Some stayed and took what employment they could find, often below their level of education and ability. Of those who left, some later returned. Returnees often found it challenging being accepted in their hometown. Such people were thought of as having turned their backs on their roots by leaving, although promising job prospects were most often away from the community. Some returnees had married outside their community and outside their racial and cultural heritage. These individuals generally found it difficult to become part of the community again.

New employees of the college relocated to Sweet Home or to surrounding counties. Most of these new arrivals choose to live outside Sweet Home in towns and cities that offered more resources, which were more racially mixed, and which had smaller numbers of First Nations people. Like all new arrivals, Dave was often asked where he had decided to live. When he answered with the name of a nice fairly large city just north of the campus community, he was surprised by the reaction of those talking to him. As time went on and the question kept being asked, Dave realized that not only had he come from the outside, but he had also chosen to live on the "outside," as perceived by the residents of Sweet Home. Even among themselves, local people recognized other local First Nations people as somewhat different when they lived in other communities.

For the local community, the college was a complex symbol. Local alumni functions, including homecoming, were attended by as many local residents as graduates. For the First Nations people in the community and on campus, the boundaries between town and campus did not exist.

In the South, there is a great respect for the family home that is often part of a farmstead. It is a symbol of pride, heritage, and connectedness to the land. The eldest living direct descendants of the original family owner usually live in the family home on the property. Their children often occupy trailers or smaller dwellings located on the same property, clustered around the farm's other buildings.

For First Nations people, the connection to the land goes deeper. Before European contact, these peoples depended on the land, rivers, forests, and wildlife for survival. This mode of survival was reinforced by the spiritual beliefs of the First Nations people.

Dave himself was of Caucasian and Chippewa ancestry. Although he did not know of this heritage until he was an adult, he had always felt a connectedness to the land. When he discovered his great-grandfather had married a full-blooded Chippewa, Dave felt things about him that now made sense. He was proud of his heritage and wanted to identify with both parts of it. Although he had never seen a reservation or been called Indian, he was happy to be moving into a community with which he felt a kinship.

When Dave arrived, there was considerable discussion about where he was going to live and if he was going to buy a home. Dave's understanding of his new colleagues and community members' inquiries was that people wanted to learn if he was serious about becoming a part of the community. As time went on, the question about where he was thinking of living became the more serious of the two.

From the frequency of the question, Dave felt there was more to the question than simple interest. Shortly after his arrival, Dave had the chance to ask the chair of the faculty governance committee about these questions. Dr. Roberta Brown was not from the area, but had lived and worked there for 20 years. She explained to Dave that people were trying to find out about his interest and loyalty to the local community. The surrounding, larger towns and cities had a greater range of appropriate housing and more resources than the small town where the campus was located. In the end, Dave decided to live outside the campus town in the next closest town that had a hospital, movie theaters, a number of restaurants, and the regional shopping center. Besides, the commute to campus took him through beautiful countryside. It also took him into a community that had a majority population that was Caucasian.

Dave soon began attending social and business events to network and get to know local leaders, donors, and prospects. The most frequently asked question at this time became "You're not from around here, are you?" Dave sounded exactly like what he was, a northerner from a big city who talked too fast. Despite his Chippewa roots, he was clearly not a local. Understanding the meaning of this question, Dave tried to be more visible in the community.

Dave now got questions about where he went to church and where his wife was. Dave was Episcopalian and single. Local people knew that the only Episcopalian church in the whole area was in a nearby town that was predominately Caucasian.

Keeping in mind that he was hired to manage a campaign, Dave's efforts at networking indicated some of the major factors that needed to be in place for the campaign to be a success. The plan was a good one, executed by a large, well-reputed consulting firm that was headquartered in the state's capital. He was concerned that no feasibility study had been done, but there was an excellent program audit that seemed to indicate that resources were in place to be successful. The closest towns of any size were at least 30 minutes away, yet they contained potential new donors and significant wealth with no other competing educational institutions. From the apparent enthusiasm of the campus, the town, and the surrounding areas and given the modest track record of prior fundraising, Dave thought the projected goals were a reasonable stretch.

Dave began to produce the college's first annual report that contained an honor roll of donors. For various reasons, the college had not produced a report in many years. Working with the publications staff, he began outlining the standard parts of his report. He gave special attention to the selection of compelling stories of how donors' gifts were used to make significant positive differences. The development staff was then asked to identify specific gifts and donors whose stories would illustrate these points. As staff members began to contact the selected donors, Dave noted a distinct trend. Of the six donors selected for profiling, none had wanted their names associated with such an article, although two had agreed that referring to them as anonymous donors was all right. To meet his deadline, Dave decided to go ahead with the stories about the anonymous gifts, reallocating his unused space to more photos and larger type. He was puzzled by the response this project had gotten.

Dave also began reorganizing his staff and hiring new members. Because of the low salary levels he was working with and the relative remoteness of the campus, his searches produced very small pools of appropriately credentialed candidates. At last, he completed his search and hired two new fundraisers. One of these people had good qualifications, came from Chicago, and was an African American. The other was a native of the state capital. When both individuals had relocated to the area, each one chose to live outside the campus town. With the addition of these two new employees, Dave felt he had done a great job assuring that his staff reflected the diversity of the First Nations people. He had roughly equal numbers of men and women who represented Caucasian, African-American, First Nations, and Hispanic populations. This was a diverse staff working in one of the most diverse areas of the United States.

While he addressed the most important issues in establishing a well-managed, high-performing development program, Dave also reviewed the current membership of the board of trustees, particularly the development committee with whom he would be working. He discovered that all of the trustees were born in and still lived in or near the town of Sweet Home. They were all First Nations peoples.

After visiting with all of the members of the development committee and most of the remaining trustees, Dave was satisfied that he knew what his primary challenges would be. The first challenge would be to interest the members of the development committee in enhancing their fundraising skills and commitment through a continuing program of trustee development. However, the development committee felt that it was Dave's responsibility to do all the fundraising. But the chair of the committee was supportive of Dave's plan to provide learning opportunities for committee members about fundraising and other trustee responsibilities.

Dave also thought that having more than half of the trustee positions on his committee vacant was a benefit and a challenge. It was a benefit in that it gave him the opportunity to fill those positions with people who brought wider geographic and social networks to the committee.

Dave concluded that his best strategy now would be to use the vacant development committee positions to fill both the trustee and advisory committee roles. The chair of the nominations committee, Sara, was very supportive of the need to bring new people onto the development committee. She knew the best fundraising connections would be through people from outside Sweet Home. Sara began to help Dave locate nominees from areas across the state where Sweet Home College had significant enclaves of stakeholders with access to substantial wealth.

Dave and Sara agreed that all current development committee members would serve out their current terms if they wished. They worked hard at recruiting the right people. The development committee was somewhat hesitant at first, but was gracious to each new trustee candidate as they went through the approval process. As time went on, more support came from previously untouched parts of the state. Money and donors were coming from everywhere, leaving local support in the minority. The development committee was pleased.

Dave had planned for a local giving strategy as he had anticipated that the new major donors would ultimately bring in more support as, in general, they had greater financial resources. Since Sweet Home was occupied primarily by families ranging from below poverty level to modest middle-class incomes, Dave knew the financial success of the campaign rested on their ability to attract outside investors. He planned to rely on trustees with local community connections and to use his diverse fundraising staff to support them.

Preparation began for the first prospect-screening session. Lists were compiled and reviewed by the staff and appointments were made with four respected local community leaders, people who were very well thought of locally, who had some resources, and who had financial resources in their community. Dave planned to staff these sessions along with one of his new staff members, Ralph, the director of development, who was an African American from Chicago.

While planning their strategy, Dave and Ralph thought there would be great potential in starting a real estate program for gifting property as part of their major gift strategy in light of the fact that there were many valuable family farms. The children of many of these families, having moved away for better opportunities, would not be returning to take up farming. As most local wealth was tied up in these lands, Dave and Ralph planned to make this program an integral part of the campaign.

Dave scheduled the first lunch meeting for himself, Ralph, and the locally born president of the Sweet Home Bank, Mel. They wanted to explain their plans and enlist his help in recruiting three other local screeners. They were surprised by Mel's extreme reluctance to identify potential screeners. He suggested meeting each person individually at a location away from Sweet Home. When Ralph and Dave explained that working in small groups was often more productive because of the stimulation offered by working with others from the screening committee, Mel still advised against it. He strongly felt that if local people found out some of "their own" were giving out information about other people's wealth, the community would be very unhappy. Mel declined to be identified with such a committee. He did offer three new prospect names and suggested three others whom Dave and Ralph could talk about assisting in screening. Dave and Ralph did pursue screening sessions, but they worked individually, as Mel suggested. The list of names collected was small, and no one agreed to help solicit funds or real estate. Although Dave had both Caucasian and First Nations heritage, he seemed to be making no greater progress than Ralph. On some days, he was sure that he was not doing as well as Ralph.

Dave and Ralph continued soliciting volunteers and gifts. They did well in the major metropolitan areas. When working in Sweet Home, they both felt uncomfortable. Ralph felt the most ill at ease. Although people were polite to him, he found he was not included in social activities. When Ralph and his Caucasian wife attended the first Sweet Home College holiday dinner dance, the only further invitations they got were for official college functions.

With no local people willing to participate visibly in soliciting major gifts, Dave and Ralph shouldered those responsibilities, along with the other development staff members. The college president was born in Sweet Home, but had been educated and lived away from there for most of his life; he also delegated all fundraising to the development staff. Dave and Ralph received a cordial local reception, but they never produced any significant local gifts. All major gifts came from outside Sweet Home. When they approached suggested prospects for gifts of real estate, their reception was cordial and, perhaps, cool. After soliciting their first gift of property, rumors quickly spread about their intentions and it became more difficult to find people who would talk to them. It also became harder to find local people to attend social events at the president's home. Local people were increasingly reluctant to accept an invitation. Many residents of the largest, closest, and wealthiest community in the area, which was a short distance away, feared coming into what many of the Caucasian wealth-holders feared was a crime-ridden, dangerous community.

The campaign did conclude just over goal, but the local community was not happy, despite increased scholarship opportunities for local students and more jobs created by the construction financed by the campaign.

A Cultural and Historical Setting of the First Nations People

Who are the people of the First Nations?

First Nations people are often mistakenly referred to as Native Americans or Indians. The term *First Nations* emphasizes the fact that these are individuals whose direct ancestors were residents of North America before contact by Christopher Columbus.[2]

This is far from a complete definition as the indigenous people of what are today called Canada, the United States, and Mexico were highly diverse groups. People residing in these areas before European contact spoke a variety of languages, all of which were not related to the languages of the Old

World. In fact, a great many were not related to each other. The political and social complexity of these groups ranged greatly in complexity and size. Although First Nations people are commonly referred to as "tribes," the traits that identify a group as such are sometimes difficult to categorize.[3]

Before contact with the Old World, First Nations people lived in widely ranging environments from dry deserts to the lush coastal forests. They made their living fishing, hunting, collecting, trading, and farming. Some lived nomadic or seminomadic existences while others lived in large, permanent settlements with distinctive architecture. Even during pre-Columbian times, the original inhabitants of North America were mobile and, in some places, maintained significant trading networks. The indirect, and often direct, trade of goods also brought other kinds of contact, so that before Europeans, many native peoples were of mixed blood, being from different indigenous stocks.

With the arrival of Columbus, the mixture of the local gene pool increased so that today the definition of who is or is not a Native American/Indian/First Nations people is even more complex. Are you an indigenous person if your family is mixed Tewa and Navajo blood? Are you one if you are Tewa and Caucasian Irish?[4] Where the line is drawn is a subjective matter relative to the person doing the defining and subject to the definition.

While the history and social organization of each indigenous group was highly varied before European contact, the situation after contact was even more complex.

There is no single way to accurately generalize about all First Nations people. The experience of living on a reservation is very different from living in a cosmopolitan urban setting away from ongoing contact with First Nations cultures. Many of these indigenous cultures were and are male centered, but not all.[5] So, while the daily tasks that women and men performed in traditional cultures (i.e., women gave birth, reared the children, and managed the living area; men hunted or farmed and defended their homes and families), the relative important spiritual, and political roles of the genders could be very different.

However, we can still outline some broad characteristics of many First Nations cultures, keeping in mind that there is still great variability with respect to individuals and groups. Despite media stereotyping, First Nations cultures tend to:

- Incorporate spirituality as part of daily life
- View themselves, animals, rain, stars, moon, sun, etc., as part of the earth
- Not maintain a concept of individual ownership
- Prize cooperation and sharing
- Value respect for older members of the group
- Place a high priority on maintenance of the orderliness and balance of the group in its natural and social setting
- Respect humility
- Believe that expressing thoughts indirectly is proper behavior

Although this is a highly generalized inventory, there are some interesting general trends for examining philanthropy among First Nations people. As the cultural expectation was that individuals used resources but did not own them, the idea of practicing philanthropy by giving these things away is not an indigenous concept. The desired behavior was sharing, cooperating, and providing for others, particularly blood relatives.

First Nations people traditionally existed in interdependent living situations where sharing and cooperation were prized and encouraged. In this context, seeking individual recognition was directly contrary to the values of humility and group cohesiveness. In a traditional First Nations culture, the contemporary American striving for individuality, personal recognition, and isolation didn't make sense.

Today, the vast majority of First Nations people live in cities. They and the people around them grapple with the issues of what it means to be an Indian/Native American/First Nations people. There is no single answer that applies equally well to everyone; nor is there an answer that is true for all times. "There's more than one way to be an Indian . . ."[6]

Discussion Questions

1. Why was the constituency so interested in where Dave lived? Why were those who lived outside Sweet Home looked upon differently from those who lived in the town?

2. Even if he did not live in Sweet Home, what are some other ways in which Dave could demonstrate his loyalty to the college and the community?

3. The author noted that an honor roll of donors had not been prepared in many years. A few sentences later the author notes that most donors did not want to be publicly acknowledged. What could Dave do to counteract the possible perception that a lack of public acknowledgment equates to a lack of support for the college? Can you think of a few different cultures that have different thoughts about being publicly recognized for their support of an organization? How does this change a major fundraising program?

4. The author details the difficulties that Dave and Ralph experienced when soliciting major gifts of money and property. As the solicitations continued, community members grew even more reluctant to give to or even meet with the fundraisers. What could Dave and Ralph have done differently to educate the community about their intentions? How does this desire for anonymity affect the traditional "quiet phase" of a capital campaign?

5. At the end of the case, the notes mention that the community was not happy with the campaign. What could the fundraisers have done early in the campaign to avoid such unhappiness? What issues need to be resolved before future fundraising endeavors are undertaken?

INVOLVING CUBAN AMERICANS IN SOUTH FLORIDA CHARITIES

Rolando D. Rodriguez, CFRE
Jackson Memorial Foundation
Jackson Memorial Hospital, Miami, Florida

The Setting—South Florida

Hispanic Americans have had an enormous impact on South Florida in a relatively short period of time. Starting with the Cuban influx in the 1960s, and continuing on as the new gateway to Latin America, the community has grown into one of the most predominantly Hispanic areas in the United States. Over 50 percent of the community is now of Hispanic origin, with the largest segment of Cuban background.

These Cuban Americans, who came to South Florida fleeing communist oppression, included a large subset of well-educated and successful businessmen and professionals. They formed the nucleus of a successful and influential ethnic group who have educational and income levels comparable to mainstream American society. Philanthropically, however, Cuban Americans have not been as involved as in other areas, and have not been perceived as strong participants.

Building a Diverse Hospital Foundation

Jackson Memorial Hospital (JMH) has over 1,600 beds, making it one of the largest teaching hospitals in the country. It is the only Miami hospital receiving public tax dollars and responsible for all indigent health care. At the same time, it also doubles as the principal teaching hospital for the University of Miami Medical School. Until 1990, the hospital had no fundraising foundation or other development resource, leaving this opportunity solely in the hands of the University of Miami (UM) Medical School.

In the late 1980s, the community faced a crisis in trauma care. As the public hospital, JMH committed to raising private dollars for the creation of a new trauma center. The Jackson Memorial Foundation was created whose first mission would be to raise $28 million to create a world-class trauma center. It was clear that in order to succeed, Hispanic-American support had to be enlisted.

The foundation began with a very small but powerful group of leaders representing various constituencies of the community. While many Hispanic groups made up the cultural landscape, it was clear that targeting Cuban Americans—the largest and wealthiest group of Hispanic Americans—was the most important priority. This was not an exercise in cultural sensitivity, it was a clear marketing decision aimed at present and future goals for success.

Jackson Memorial Hospital's positioning as the local public hospital, serving the indigent, was its major strength. Its image and history was strongly tied to the African-American community, but it could not be denied that many Cuban Americans had been served in their time of great need. This appeal had never been used to attract Cuban-American support.

While it would be important to appeal to Cuban Americans, it could not come at the price of losing other strong potential constituencies. This specific objective—reach Cuban Americans but don't alienate others—became the bedrock of the organization's long-term strategy.

Enlisting Cuban Americans

At the time of this effort, 1991, very little major Hispanic support existed for mainstream philanthropic institutions in South Florida, especially at the major gifts level. Hispanics were perceived as not as willing to reach out philanthropically. This unenlightened viewpoint did not take into account that Cuban Americans had arrived in this country with little or no economic assets and that it had taken time for them to reach higher economic levels. It also didn't take into account the millions of dollars that were being given by Cuban Americans to the causes they most cared about but that were not obvious to the mainstream community.

Was giving to United Way an accurate barometer of Cuban-American philanthropic support? Or was it better measured through giving to an inner-city child care center run by the Catholic Church? Was giving in response to a Red Cross mailing (in English) reflective of real Cuban-American support, or was it perhaps more accurate to assess the thousands of dollars raised on Spanish-language radio to help recently arrived families? Did a major private nonprofit hospital desiring Cuban-American support find an ungenerous Hispanic response, or had they looked first to their board of directors to see if they had any Cuban Americans serving in leadership positions? Little true effort had been given to studying or resolving these issues.

The foundation approached the problem with a different perspective. It was first noted that Cuban Americans had now been in South Florida for almost 30 years and were highly acculturated and increasingly successful financially. Fifteen years before, they had been working hard to build their businesses and assets. Now these same people had grown-up children, many who had been born in the United States, and strong ties to the local community. They were ready and waiting to participate.

Having involved Cuban Americans on its board and staff, it had an intrinsic perspective of the community. Having served the Cuban-American community, the hospital had a case. The leadership and staff also understood that Cuban Americans did indeed often give money to causes—but amazingly, they gave to causes they were involved in and deeply cared about (and to causes that often the mainstream community did not even know existed).

Strategic Exposure

The first public exposure to the campaign was boosted by the world-famous entertainer Julio Iglesias, who was persuaded to perform at a benefit black-tie event. Mr. Iglesias, who had a home in Miami Beach, had survived and recuperated from a major traumatic auto accident while in his youth and was therefore interested in the cause. Julio Iglesias, of course, was well known by Hispanic Americans for his music, while his celebrity stature was also a lure to the entire community. ("Attract Hispanics, but don't turn off Anglos.")

This first event—which raised over $1 million—clearly helped set the stage for an organization that would be strongly geared to attracting Hispanic Americans.

As the campaign evolved beyond a volunteer activity, it became clear that a strong staff was necessary for the long haul. It was at this time that the board chose to hire a Cuban-American executive director who had spent most of his life in South Florida, yet had roots and cultural ties beneficial to the effort.

As a public facility, JMH had never attempted to attract philanthropic support, nor taken any steps to position itself attractively for this purpose. Property taxes, as well as a half-penny sales tax, supported its budget for the care of the indigent. Recognition did not exist—indeed, it was highly discouraged. Only the UM Medical School had a major presence in philanthropy.

What the hospital was known for, however, was its policy of caring for all residents who came through its doors. People with no resources, people with life-threatening illnesses, mothers with critically ill children, victims of violent crime—all those in need—would be cared for at little or no cost. And there was now a need, a need to create a trauma center that would care for all people, rich and poor alike, for an entire community.

How could Cuban Americans not resonate with this mission? Almost all had experienced arriving in this country penniless and at the mercy of fate. Many, had experienced a need for medical care for themselves and for their children, and whether they had received it at JMH or elsewhere, they remembered what it was to be in this exposed position.

Eight years later, the words of one Cuban-American supporter who made a landmark $5 million gift to the children's hospital at JMH serve as a reminder: "I came to this country with nothing, and I remember my child being sick and needing care, and my not being able to do what was needed. I don't want any other mother to go through this."

At the time of the foundation's creation, many other local organizations had begun to make their first efforts to attract Cuban Americans and other Hispanics. Most of these organizations, however, had strongly entrenched leadership and little or no true (nontoken) Cuban-American involvement. The foundation had no such encumbrances.

The foundation set out to be among the first to be truly successful. Several strategies helped make this possible, including developing high-energy, high-visibility social events, enlisting up-and-coming Cuban-American leadership, and creating a business atmosphere conducive to the social business style of Cuban Americans.

Events

Miami's social and philanthropic community places heavy emphasis on high-profile events and recognition. *Understated* is rarely descriptive of Miami. Events that would appeal to the desired constituency would therefore have to be highly energetic and to have elements designed specifically to appeal to Cuban Americans.

For example, should a gala have musicians play the foxtrot or the merengue? Could you employ one band that played both types of music, or more subtly, could you find a band that could play a waltz and yet not play an elevator-music version of salsa? (The answer: No, not at the beginning because such bands didn't yet exist.) How loud is too loud? Figuring out the right formula for such questions would be key in order to attract and mingle both crowds.

Events were planned to be high-glamour and celebrity conscious. Consequently, the first event after the Julio Iglesias gala was an overnight cruise on a Norwegian caribbean cruise ship, with Diana Ross as the hostess. The chairman of the event was the Cuban-American wife of a prominent Cuban-American board member, with a co-chair who was a respected African-American business leader. (Eight years later, this Cuban-American wife was the very successful chair of the entire foundation.)

A second concert black-tie gala by Mr. Julio Iglesias soon followed, also chaired by two prominent Cuban-American couples. These high-profile events laid the groundwork for much current leadership, having attracted Cuban Americans who made the first major Cuban-American individual gift to a subsequent campaign ($500,000), as well as involving two future board chairs, both highly successful Cuban Americans. These events also kept the interest of the mainstream community, which was by that time pioneering what the rest of America has been discovering in the last year or so—that Hispanics were *in*.

Are You Early or Are You Late?

A second component critical to the involvement of Cuban-American leadership was to mold the foundation's business style to be attractive to the group, while not alienating others. It was apparent to the staff from the onset that the no-nonsense let's-get-down-to-business style that is a hallmark of American business practice would do wonders to turn off Cuban-American involvement.

Time issues, for example, were deliberately more relaxed than the customary American model. A meeting called for 2:00 P.M. was not expected to start precisely on time. Committee chairs who were not Hispanic had to learn to allow for some variation, or risk making it unpleasant to the Hispanic volunteers they desired to attract. Much effort was made to comfort those accustomed to the "start on time or else" credo and to educate them that being a little late was not disrespectful, but simply a cultural trait that did not value rigidity and have an obsession with punctuality.

Fundraising events were once again a key element in the time warp phenomena. An event called for 7 P.M. would often bring a group that arrived on time, followed by the Hispanic group much closer to 8 P.M. Planning would take into account that a 6:30 P.M. gala would have a small, uninitiated crowd that arrived precisely on time (usually recent immigrants from North America), with a much larger group that arrived closer to 8 P.M. If the gala chair called for dinner to start precisely at 8 P.M., she would find herself dining almost alone. If your gala leadership was Cuban American and you planned for a 6:30 P.M. receiving line, you would be standing there alone.

Diversity meant adjustment.

Attractive Cause

To specifically attract Hispanic Americans, the foundation chose as its next major project the development of JMH's children's hospital. While children are a cause that resonates with any group, it is especially attractive to the family-oriented Hispanic American. This was particularly true for children who were low-income and/or indigent, reminding the Cuban Americans of the times they themselves had been in a position of such need. It was obvious that an emerging group of wealthy Cuban-American young women, primarily in their 30s and with children of their own, had only now begun to be recognized. Many of these women had an interest in community participation and recognition for the successes of their family, but had not yet found high-level groups who welcomed their leadership and participation.

The foundation's answer was to create a group dedicated to the children's hospital. Cuban-American women with small children were specifically targeted as key leaders. This, of course, not only served to attract the women, but also their husbands, who also became a part of the foundation's activities in a number of ways. Again, the group was carefully designed not to deliver the message that it was for Cuban Americans only. Its founding co-chairs were, for example, a Cuban American and a Jewish American. Balance would be maintained, although it was harder to achieve since this group was born with Cuban-American leadership.

Media

Another oft-ignored component important to attracting Hispanic Americans was the proper use of Hispanic media. Radio and print media were particularly of value, since many outlets existed that targeted older Hispanics as well as the bilingual acculturated Hispanics. It is telling that one of the primary social publications covering philanthropy in South Florida—for both Anglos and Hispanics—is a high-quality Spanish-language fashion magazine that only recently began including English translations in the back.

The foundation made special efforts to seek coverage in a number of Spanish-language print media. These media were more interested in social affairs than the larger mainstream print media and were much easier to approach successfully. As a result, it was not unusual for the Hispanic-American group—who were exposed to both mainstream and Hispanic media—to be more aware of media coverage and recognition of events and programs than the non-Hispanic group.

Special efforts were also made to find projects that would specifically expose the foundation to the older Hispanic community that used radio as their primary source of information. For example, the foundation participated in the raising of funds in radio marathons to benefit critically ill children from Cuba or Latin America. The goodwill and name recognition gained from these efforts continue to be significant.

Conclusion

For years, the Cuban-American community had been thriving in South Florida. To many, this community did not appear to participate in helping others. But what wasn't easily seen was the huge number of grassroots causes that did receive their support. They had not seen the millions raised on Spanish radio from the thousands of people who would send in their checks, from $5 to $5,000. Their incorrect conclusion was that Cuban Americans were not philanthropic because it was not a part of their cultural makeup and because this philanthropy did not go to the Red Cross, United Way, Salvation Army, and other traditional organizations.

With time and effort, using the obvious but often ignored rules of fundraising, this perception was overcome. Involve potential donors in leadership positions. Recruit their friends and neighbors. Find credible spokespersons, especially those who make leadership gifts. Design efforts that appeal to their background, history, and interests. Communicate to them where they listen and read, and in a manner that they will understand. Start early and remember that those who may not have it all now may have plenty later. Be open to new leaders and leadership styles. Ask for the gift.

In the new millennium, more and more South Florida charities have begun to find the formula for success. Cuban-American participation in local charities is greater than ever and still growing. The process of philanthropic assimilation is well on its way, and South Florida is on the cusp of a successful philanthropic marketplace that bodes well for the rest of the country.

Discussion Questions

1. Hispanics are, as of 2001, the largest minority group in the United States according to the U.S. Census. How will this fact affect fundraising by Hispanic organizations such as Jackson Memorial Hospital?

2. The author states, "It was clear that in order to succeed, Hispanic-American support had to be enlisted." Why? Is it always critical that a particular ethnic group must be the predominant supporters of an organization that supports its culture?

3. The author refers to the importance of not alienating other cultural constituencies by focusing too much on soliciting Cuban Americans. What are some ways the fundraisers could attract non–Cuban-American donors? What are some ways these types of donors could be alienated?

4. Is it likely that a non–Cuban American living outside of Miami would have absolutely no interest in donating to the hospital? What could the fundraisers do to successfully solicit this donor?

5. The author mentions many times that care was taken not to alienate non–Cuban-American donors. Yet social events and meetings were run strictly in a format familiar to Cuban Americans. Is this a contradiction? Should the campaign leadership have forced events to begin on time? If you agree, how would this clash with the predominant cultural traditions of the constituency?

SUCCESSFUL FUNDRAISING FOR INDIA'S 5-H PROGRAM

Janice Gow Pettey, Editor

In June 2000, a benefit concert was held at a large cathedral in a California city, featuring some of India's top musicians. The proceeds of the event were directed to a pilot program recently launched in rural India to train young adults in health, hygiene, and life-skills education. This leadership development program provides three months of training for young people, who must share their knowledge in at least 10 additional villages.

Four hundred young adults, ages 20 to 30, have already completed the training and are utilizing the skills acquired through the 5-H program—health, hygiene, homes, harmony in diversity, and human values. Each participant will educate 800 to 1,200 residents per village. The goal of 5-H is to train enough young leaders during the next three years to touch the lives of 10 million to 14 million people. 5-H was founded by a spiritual master from India who founded the International Association for Human Values, the umbrella organization for 5-H.

Several Silicon Valley professionals actively support 5-H through fundraising events like the benefit concert in San Francisco. One of those professionals, a 30-year-old executive for a high-tech company, volunteers as the West Coast coordinator of the International Association for Human Values. He states, "It gives me enormous satisfaction to make a difference in so many people's lives. Life is not just to climb up the corporate ladder and make your million bucks." In addition to his volunteer work, he donates regularly toward the living expenses of one of the youth leaders in India. Because it is a grassroots effort, overhead costs are minimal, so contributions like his directly fund the youth leader's training and community work in India.

(*San Francisco Chronicle*, June 16, 2000).

Discussion Questions

1. Can you name some other organizations that raise money in the United States but that exclusively fund programs in other countries?

2. What percentage of U.S. donors to this organization do you suppose are of Indian descent?

3. What are some techniques this organization could use to reach non-Indian donors? How could the organization advertize the concert to attract a broader base of possible donors?

4. Are there cultures in the world to which U.S. donors might not be receptive to giving to, no matter how important the cause?

Population by Race and Hispanic Origin, for the United States, Regions, Divisions, and States, and for Puerto Rico, 2000

United States Region Division State Puerto Rico	Total population	Race							Hispanic or Latino (of any race)	White alone, not Hispanic or Latino
		One race						Two or more races		
		White	Black or African American	American Indian and Alaska Native	Asian	Native Hawaiian and Other Pacific Islander	Some other race			
United States	281,421,906	211,460,626	34,658,190	2,475,956	10,242,998	398,835	15,359,073	6,826,228	35,305,818	194,552,774
NORTHEAST	53,594,378	41,533,502	6,099,881	162,558	2,119,426	20,880	2,429,670	1,228,461	5,254,087	39,327,262
New England	13,922,517	12,050,905	719,063	42,257	374,361	5,316	448,315	282,300	875,225	11,686,617
Maine	1,274,923	1,236,014	6,760	7,098	9,111	382	2,911	12,647	9,360	1,230,297
New Hampshire	1,235,786	1,186,851	9,035	2,964	15,931	371	7,420	13,214	20,489	1,175,252
Vermont	608,827	589,208	3,063	2,420	5,217	141	1,443	7,335	5,504	585,431
Massachusetts	6,349,097	5,367,286	343,454	15,015	238,124	2,489	236,724	146,005	428,729	5,198,359
Rhode Island	1,048,319	891,191	46,908	5,121	23,665	567	52,616	28,251	90,820	858,433
Connecticut	3,405,565	2,780,355	309,843	9,639	82,313	1,366	147,201	74,848	320,323	2,638,845
Middle Atlantic	39,671,861	29,482,597	5,380,818	120,301	1,745,065	15,554	1,981,355	946,161	4,378,862	27,640,645
New York	18,976,457	12,893,689	3,014,385	82,461	1,044,976	8,818	1,341,946	590,182	2,867,583	11,760,981
New Jersey	8,414,350	6,104,705	1,141,821	19,492	480,276	3,329	450,972	213,755	1,117,191	5,557,209
Pennsylvania	12,281,054	10,484,203	1,224,612	18,348	219,813	3,417	188,437	142,224	394,088	10,322,455
MIDWEST	64,392,776	53,833,651	6,499,733	399,490	1,197,554	22,492	1,417,388	1,022,468	3,124,532	52,386,131
East North Central	45,155,037	36,826,856	5,405,448	177,014	880,635	13,686	1,123,544	727,884	2,478,719	35,669,945
Ohio	11,353,140	9,645,453	1,301,307	24,486	132,633	2,749	88,627	157,885	217,123	9,538,111
Indiana	6,080,485	5,320,022	510,034	15,815	59,126	2,005	97,811	75,672	214,536	5,219,373
Illinois	12,419,293	9,125,471	1,876,875	31,006	423,603	4,610	722,712	235,016	1,530,262	8,424,140
Michigan	9,938,444	7,966,053	1,412,742	58,479	176,510	2,692	129,552	192,416	323,877	7,806,691
Wisconsin	5,363,675	4,769,857	304,460	47,228	88,763	1,630	84,842	66,895	192,921	4,681,630
West North Central	19,237,739	17,006,795	1,094,315	222,476	316,919	8,806	293,844	294,584	645,813	16,716,186
Minnesota	4,919,479	4,400,282	171,731	54,967	141,968	1,979	65,810	82,742	143,382	4,337,143
Iowa	2,926,324	2,748,640	61,853	8,989	36,635	1,009	37,420	31,778	82,473	2,710,344
Missouri	5,595,211	4,748,083	629,391	25,076	61,595	3,178	45,827	82,061	118,592	4,686,474
North Dakota	642,200	593,181	3,916	31,329	3,606	230	2,540	7,398	7,786	589,149
South Dakota	754,844	669,404	4,685	62,283	4,378	261	3,677	10,156	10,903	664,585
Nebraska	1,711,263	1,533,261	68,541	14,896	21,931	836	47,845	23,953	94,425	1,494,494
Kansas	2,688,418									

SOUTH	100,236,620	72,819,399	16,905,092	725,919	1,922,407	51,217	3,889,171	1,847,015	11,586,696	65,927,794
South Atlantic	51,769,160	37,283,595	11,026,722	233,192	1,101,965	25,762	1,175,288	922,636	4,243,946	34,575,917
Delaware	783,600	584,773	150,666	2,731	16,259	283	15,855	13,033	37,277	567,973
Maryland	5,296,486	3,391,308	1,477,411	15,423	210,929	2,303	95,525	103,587	227,916	3,286,547
District of Columbia	572,059	176,101	343,312	1,713	15,189	348	21,950	13,446	44,953	159,178
Virginia	7,078,515	5,120,110	1,390,293	21,172	261,025	3,946	138,900	143,069	329,540	4,995,637
West Virginia	1,808,344	1,718,777	57,232	3,606	9,434	400	3,107	15,788	12,279	1,709,966
North Carolina	8,049,313	5,804,656	1,737,545	99,551	113,689	3,983	186,629	103,260	378,963	5,647,155
South Carolina	4,012,012	2,695,560	1,185,216	13,718	36,014	1,628	39,926	39,950	95,076	2,652,291
Georgia	8,186,453	5,327,281	2,349,542	21,737	173,170	4,246	196,289	114,188	435,227	5,128,661
Florida	15,982,378	12,465,029	2,335,505	53,541	266,256	8,625	477,107	376,315	2,682,715	10,458,509
East South Central	17,022,810	13,113,106	3,418,542	57,850	136,378	5,741	121,441	169,752	299,176	12,967,670
Kentucky	4,041,769	3,640,889	295,994	8,616	29,744	1,460	22,623	42,443	59,939	3,608,013
Tennessee	5,689,283	4,563,310	932,809	15,152	56,662	2,205	56,036	63,109	123,838	4,505,930
Alabama	4,447,100	3,162,808	1,155,930	22,430	31,346	1,409	28,998	44,179	75,830	3,125,819
Mississippi	2,844,658	1,746,099	1,033,809	11,652	18,626	667	13,784	20,021	39,569	1,727,908
West South Central	31,444,850	22,422,698	4,536,428	434,877	684,064	19,714	2,592,442	754,627	7,043,574	18,384,207
Arkansas	2,673,400	2,138,598	418,950	17,808	20,220	1,668	40,412	35,744	86,866	2,100,135
Louisiana	4,468,976	2,856,161	1,451,944	25,477	54,758	1,240	31,131	48,265	107,738	2,794,391
Oklahoma	3,450,654	2,628,434	260,968	273,230	46,767	2,372	82,898	155,985	179,304	2,556,368
Texas	20,851,820	14,799,505	2,404,566	118,362	562,319	14,434	2,438,001	514,633	6,669,666	10,933,313
WEST	63,197,932	43,274,074	3,076,884	1,187,989	5,003,611	304,246	7,622,844	2,728,284	15,340,503	36,911,587
Mountain	18,172,295	14,591,933	533,283	614,553	353,429	38,508	1,541,704	508,885	3,543,573	12,883,812
Montana	902,195	817,229	2,692	56,068	4,691	470	5,335	15,730	18,081	807,823
Idaho	1,293,953	1,177,304	5,456	17,645	11,889	1,308	54,742	25,609	101,690	1,139,291
Wyoming	493,782	454,670	3,722	11,133	2,771	302	12,301	8,883	31,669	438,799
Colorado	4,301,261	3,560,005	165,063	44,241	95,213	4,621	309,931	122,187	735,601	3,202,880
New Mexico	1,819,046	1,214,253	34,343	173,483	19,255	1,503	309,882	66,327	765,386	813,495
Arizona	5,130,632	3,873,611	158,873	255,879	92,236	6,733	596,774	146,526	1,295,617	3,274,258
Utah	2,233,169	1,992,975	17,657	29,684	37,108	15,145	93,405	47,195	201,559	1,904,265
Nevada	1,998,257	1,501,886	135,477	26,420	90,266	8,426	159,354	76,428	393,970	1,303,001
Pacific	45,025,637	28,682,141	2,553,601	573,436	4,650,182	265,738	6,081,140	2,219,399	11,796,930	24,027,775
Washington	5,894,121	4,821,823	190,267	93,301	322,335	23,953	228,923	213,519	441,509	4,652,490
Oregon	3,421,399	2,961,623	55,662	45,211	101,350	7,976	144,832	104,745	275,314	2,857,616
California	33,871,648	20,170,059	2,263,882	333,346	3,697,513	116,961	5,682,241	1,607,646	10,966,556	15,816,790
Alaska	626,932	434,534	21,787	98,043	25,116	3,309	9,997	34,146	25,852	423,788
Hawaii	1,211,537	294,102	22,003	3,535	503,868	113,539	15,147	259,343	87,699	277,091
Puerto Rico	3,808,610	3,064,862	302,933	13,336	7,960	1,093	260,011	158,415	3,762,746	33,966

Source: U.S. Census Bureau, Census 2000 Redistricting Data (P.L. 94-171) Summary File for states and Census 2000 Redistricting Summary File for Puerto Rico, Tables PL1 and PL2.

Population by Race and Hispanic Origin, for All Ages and for 18 Years and Over, 2000

	All ages		18 years and over	
Subject	Number	Percent of total population	Number	Percent of population 18 years and over
RACE				
Total population	**281,421,906**	**100.0**	**209,128,094**	**100.0**
One race	274,595,678	97.6	205,158,752	98.1
White	211,460,626	75.1	161,862,337	77.4
Black or African American	34,658,190	12.3	23,772,494	11.4
American Indian and Alaska Native	2,475,956	0.9	1,635,644	0.8
Asian	10,242,998	3.6	7,777,999	3.7
Native Hawaiian and Other Pacific Islander	398,835	0.1	271,656	0.1
Some other race	15,359,073	5.5	9,838,622	4.7
Two or more races	6,826,228	2.4	3,969,342	1.9
HISPANIC OR LATINO AND RACE				
Total population	**281,421,906**	**100.0**	**209,128,094**	**100.0**
Hispanic or Latino (of any race)	35,305,818	12.5	22,963,559	11.0
Not Hispanic or Latino	246,116,088	87.5	186,164,535	89.0
One race	241,513,942	85.8	183,468,581	87.7
White	194,552,774	69.1	150,525,687	72.0
Black or African American	33,947,837	12.1	23,337,573	11.2
American Indian and Alaska Native	2,068,883	0.7	1,382,972	0.7
Asian	10,123,169	3.6	7,702,895	3.7
Native Hawaiian and Other Pacific Islander	353,509	0.1	244,010	0.1
Some other race	467,770	0.2	275,444	0.1
Two or more races	4,602,146	1.6	2,695,954	1.3

Source: U.S. Census Bureau, Census 2000 Redistricting Data (P.L. 94–171) Summary File for states, Tables PL1, PL2, PL3, and PL4.

Population by Race, Including Combinations of Two Races, 2000

Race	Number	Percent of total population
Total population	**281,421,906**	**100.0**
One race	274,595,678	97.6
Two or more races	6,826,228	2.4
Two races	6,368,075	2.3
White; Black or African American	784,764	0.3
White; American Indian and Alaska Native	1,082,683	0.4
White; Asian	868,395	0.3
White; Native Hawaiian and Other Pacific Islander	112,964	—
White; Some other race	2,206,251	0.8
Black or African American; American Indian and Alaska Native	182,494	0.1
Black or African American; Asian	106,782	—
Black or African American; Native Hawaiian and Other Pacific Islander	29,876	—
Black or African American; Some other race	417,249	0.1
American Indian and Alaska Native; Asian	52,429	—
American Indian and Alaska Native; Native Hawaiian and Other Pacific Islander	7,328	—
American Indian and Alaska Native; Some other race	93,842	—
Asian; Native Hawaiian and Other Pacific Islander	138,802	—
Asian; Some other race	249,108	0.1
Native Hawaiian and Other Pacific Islander; Some other race	35,108	—
Three or more races	458,153	0.2

Source: U.S. Census Bureau, Census 2000 Redistricting Data (P.L. 94–171) Summary File for states, Table PL1.

Population by Race with Comparisons, 2000

Subject	Race alone[1] (minimum population)		Race in combination only[2]		Race alone or in combination[3] (maximum population)	
	Number	Percent of total population	Number	Percent of total population	Number	Percent of total population
	(1)	(2)	(3)	(4)	(5)	(6)
RACE						
Total population[4]	**281,421,906**	**100.0**	**281,421,906**	**100.0**	**281,421,906**	**100.0**
Number of race responses[4]	*274,595,678*	*97.6*	*14,168,760*	*5.0*	*288,764,438*	*102.6*
White	211,460,626	75.1	5,470,349	1.9	216,930,975	77.1
Black or African American	34,658,190	12.3	1,761,244	0.6	36,419,434	12.9
American Indian and Alaska Native	2,475,956	0.9	1,643,345	0.6	4,119,301	1.5
Asian	10,242,998	3.6	1,655,830	0.6	11,898,828	4.2
Native Hawaiian and Other Pacific Islander	398,835	0.1	475,579	0.2	874,414	0.3
Some other race	15,359,073	5.5	3,162,413	1.1	18,521,486	6.6
HISPANIC OR LATINO AND RACE						
Total population[4]	**281,421,906**	**100.0**	**281,421,906**	**100.0**	**281,421,906**	**100.0**
Hispanic or Latino (of any race)[4]	35,305,818	12.5	35,305,818	12.5	35,305,818	12.5
Not Hispanic or Latino[4]	246,116,088	87.5	246,116,088	87.5	246,116,088	87.5
Number of race responses[4]	*241,513,942*	*85.8*	*9,590,697*	*3.4*	*251,104,639*	*89.2*
White	194,552,774	69.1	3,625,126	1.3	198,177,900	70.4
Black or African American	33,947,837	12.1	1,435,914	0.5	35,383,751	12.6
American Indian and Alaska Native	2,068,883	0.7	1,375,817	0.5	3,444,700	1.2
Asian	10,123,169	3.6	1,456,325	0.5	11,579,494	4.1
Native Hawaiian and Other Pacific Islander	353,509	0.1	394,640	0.1	748,149	0.3
Some other race	467,770	0.2	1,302,875	0.5	1,770,645	0.6

[1] One of the following six races: (1) White, (2) Black or African American, (3) American Indian and Alaska Native, (4) Asian, (5) Native Hawaiian and Other Pacific Islander, (6) Some other race.

[2] In combination with one or more of the other five races listed. For example, a person who is "White *and* Black or African American" is included both with White and with Black or African American.

[3] Alone or in combination with one or more of the other five races listed. Numbers for the six race groups may add to more than the total population, and the six percentages may add to more than 100 percent because individuals may be of more than one race. For example, a person indicating "American Indian and Alaska Native *and* Asian *and* Native Hawaiian and Other Pacific Islander" is included with American Indian and Alaska Native, with Asian, and with Native Hawaiian and Other Pacific Islander.

[4] The total population, the Hispanic or Latino population, and the Not Hispanic or Latino population are not affected by whether data on race are for race alone, for race in combination only, or for race alone or in combination. The numbers by race do not add to the total population in column 1, column 3, and column 5, and the percentages do not add to 100 percent in column 2, column 4, and column 6. This is because the numbers by race are counts of particular types of responses by race. The numbers are not counts in which each person is included once and only once. The number of race responses is shown in italics.

Source: U.S. Census Bureau, Census 2000 Redistricting Data (P.L. 94–171) Summary File for states, Tables PL1 and PL2.

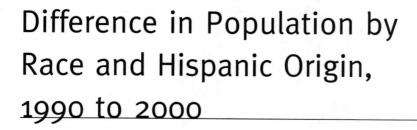

Difference in Population by Race and Hispanic Origin, 1990 to 2000

Subject	1990 Census		Census 2000		Differences between 1990 and 2000			
					Using race alone for Census 2000		Using race alone or in combination for Census 2000	
	Number	Percent of total population	Race alone[1]	Race alone or in combination[2]	Numerical difference (2000 minus 1990)	Percent difference (based on 1990)	Numerical difference (2000 minus 1990)	Percent difference (based on 1990)
	(1)	(2)	(3)	(4)	(5)	(6)	(7)	(8)
RACE								
Total population[3]	**248,709,873**	**100.0**	**281,421,906**	**281,421,906**	**32,712,033**	**13.2**	**32,712,033**	**13.2**
White	199,686,070	80.3	211,460,626	216,930,975	11,774,556	5.9	17,244,905	8.6
Black or African American	29,986,060	12.1	34,658,190	36,419,434	4,672,130	15.6	6,433,374	21.5
American Indian and Alaska Native	1,959,234	0.8	2,475,956	4,119,301	516,722	26.4	2,160,067	110.3
Asian	6,908,638	2.8	10,242,998	11,898,828	3,334,360	48.3	4,990,190	72.2
Native Hawaiian and Other Pacific Islander	365,024	0.1	398,835	874,414	33,811	9.3	509,390	139.5
Some other race	9,804,847	3.9	15,359,073	18,521,486	5,554,226	56.6	8,716,639	88.9
HISPANIC OR LATINO AND RACE								
Total population[3]	**248,709,873**	**100.0**	**281,421,906**	**281,421,906**	**32,712,033**	**13.2**	**32,712,033**	**13.2**
Hispanic or Latino (of any race)[3]	22,354,059	9.0	35,305,818	35,305,818	12,951,759	57.9	12,951,759	57.9
Not Hispanic or Latino[3]	226,355,814	91.0	246,116,088	246,116,088	19,760,274	8.7	19,760,274	8.7
White	188,128,296	75.6	194,552,774	198,177,900	6,424,478	3.4	10,049,604	5.3
Black or African American	29,216,293	11.7	33,947,837	35,383,751	4,731,544	16.2	6,167,458	21.1
American Indian and Alaska Native	1,793,773	0.7	2,068,883	3,444,700	275,110	15.3	1,650,927	92.0
Asian	6,642,481	2.7	10,123,169	11,579,494	3,480,688	52.4	4,937,013	74.3
Native Hawaiian and Other Pacific Islander	325,878	0.1	353,509	748,149	27,631	8.5	422,271	129.6
Some other race	249,093	0.1	467,770	1,770,645	218,677	87.8	1,521,552	610.8

[1] One of the following six races: (1) White, (2) Black or African American, (3) American Indian and Alaska Native, (4) Asian, (5) Native Hawaiian and Other Pacific Islander, (6) Some other race.

[2] Alone or in combination with one or more of the other five races listed. Numbers for the six race groups may add to more than the total population and the six percentages may add to more than 100 percent because individuals may indicate more than one race. For example, a person indicating "American Indian and Alaska Native *and* Asian *and* Native Hawaiian and Other Pacific Islander" is included with American Indian and Alaska Native, with Asian, and with Native Hawaiian and Other Pacific Islander.

[3] The differences between 1990 and 2000 for the total population, the Hispanic or Latino population, and the Not Hispanic or Latino population are not affected by whether data on race are for race alone or for race alone or in combination. The Hispanic or Latino population may be of any race.

Source: U.S. Census Bureau, 1990 census.

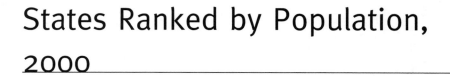

States Ranked by Population, 2000

Rank	Area	Census Population		Change, 1990 to 2000	
		April 1, 2000	April 1, 1990	Numeric	Percent
1	California	33,871,648	29,760,021	4,111,627	13.8
2	Texas	20,851,820	16,986,510	3,865,310	22.8
3	New York	18,976,457	17,990,455	986,002	5.5
4	Florida	15,982,378	12,937,926	3,044,452	23.5
5	Illinois	12,419,293	11,430,602	988,691	8.6
6	Pennsylvania	12,281,054	11,881,643	399,411	3.4
7	Ohio	11,353,140	10,847,115	506,025	4.7
8	Michigan	9,938,444	9,295,297	643,147	6.9
9	New Jersey	8,414,350	7,730,188	684,162	8.9
10	Georgia	8,186,453	6,478,216	1,708,237	26.4
11	North Carolina	8,049,313	6,628,637	1,420,676	21.4
12	Virginia	7,078,515	6,187,358	891,157	14.4
13	Massachusetts	6,349,097	6,016,425	332,672	5.5
14	Indiana	6,080,485	5,544,159	536,326	9.7
15	Washington	5,894,121	4,866,692	1,027,429	21.1
16	Tennessee	5,689,283	4,877,185	812,098	16.7
17	Missouri	5,595,211	5,117,073	478,138	9.3
18	Wisconsin	5,363,675	4,891,769	471,906	9.6
19	Maryland	5,296,486	4,781,468	515,018	10.8
20	Arizona	5,130,632	3,665,228	1,465,404	40.0
21	Minnesota	4,919,479	4,375,099	544,380	12.4
22	Louisiana	4,468,976	4,219,973	249,03	5.9
23	Alabama	4,447,100	4,040,587	406,513	10.1
24	Colorado	4,301,261	3,294,394	1,006,867	30.6
25	Kentucky	4,041,769	3,685,296	356,473	9.7
26	South Carolina	4,012,012	3,486,703	525,309	15.1
27	Oklahoma	3,450,654	3,145,585	305,069	9.7
28	Oregon	3,421,399	2,842,321	579,078	20.4
29	Connecticut	3,405,565	3,287,116	118,449	3.6
30	Iowa	2,926,324	2,776,755	149,569	5.4
31	Mississippi	2,844,658	2,573,216	271,442	10.5
32	Kansas	2,688,418	2,477,574	210,844	8.5
33	Arkansas	2,673,400	2,350,725	322,675	13.7
34	Utah	2,233,169	1,722,850	510,319	29.6
35	Nevada	1,998,257	1,201,833	796,424	66.3
36	New Mexico	1,819,046	1,515,069	303,977	20.1
37	West Virginia	1,808,344	1,793,477	14,867	0.8
38	Nebraska	1,711,263	1,578,385	132,878	8.4
39	Idaho	1,293,953	1,006,749	287,204	28.5
40	Maine	1,274,923	1,227,928	46,995	3.8
41	New Hampshire	1,235,786	1,109,252	126,534	11.4
42	Hawaii	1,211,537	1,108,229	103,308	9.3
43	Rhode Island	1,048,319	1,003,464	44,855	4.5
44	Montana	902,195	799,065	103,130	12.9
45	Delaware	783,600	666,168	117,432	17.6
46	South Dakota	754,844	696,004	58,840	8.5
47	North Dakota	642,200	638,800	3,400	0.5
48	Alaska	626,932	550,043	76,889	14.0
49	Vermont	608,827	562,758	46,069	8.2
(NA)	District of Columbia	572,059	606,900	−34,841	−5.7
50	Wyoming	493,782	453,588	40,194	8.9
(NA)	United States	281,421,906	248,709,873	32,712,033	13.2

Source: U.S. Census Bureau, Census 2000 Redistricting Data (P.L. 94–171) Summary File and 1990 Census.

States Ranked by Percent Population Change, 1990 to 2000

Rank	Area	Census Population		Change, 1990 to 2000	
		April 1, 2000	April 1, 1990	Number	Percent
1	Nevada	1,998,257	1,201,833	796,424	66.3
2	Arizona	5,130,632	3,665,228	1,465,404	40.0
3	Colorado	4,301,261	3,294,394	1,006,867	30.6
4	Utah	2,233,169	1,722,850	510,319	29.6
5	Idaho	1,293,953	1,006,749	287,204	28.5
6	Georgia	8,186,453	6,478,216	1,708,237	26.4
7	Florida	15,982,378	12,937,926	3,044,452	23.5
8	Texas	20,851,820	16,986,510	3,865,310	22.8
9	North Carolina	8,049,313	6,628,637	1,420,676	21.4
10	Washington	5,894,121	4,866,692	1,027,429	21.1
11	Oregon	3,421,399	2,842,321	579,078	20.4
12	New Mexico	1,819,046	1,515,069	303,977	20.1
13	Delaware	783,600	666,168	117,432	17.6
14	Tennessee	5,689,283	4,877,185	812,098	16.7
15	South Carolina	4,012,012	3,486,703	525,309	15.1
16	Virginia	7,078,515	6,187,358	891,157	14.4
17	Alaska	626,932	550,043	76,889	14.0
18	California	33,871,648	29,760,021	4,111,627	13.8
19	Arkansas	2,673,400	2,350,725	322,675	13.7
20	Montana	902,195	799,065	103,130	12.9
21	Minnesota	4,919,479	4,375,099	544,380	12.4
22	New Hampshire	1,235,786	1,109,252	126,534	11.4
23	Maryland	5,296,486	4,781,468	515,018	10.8
24	Mississippi	2,844,658	2,573,216	271,442	10.5
25	Alabama	4,447,100	4,040,587	406,513	10.1
26	Oklahoma	3,450,654	3,145,585	305,069	9.7
27	Indiana	6,080,485	5,544,159	536,326	9.7
28	Kentucky	4,041,769	3,685,296	356,473	9.7
29	Wisconsin	5,363,675	4,891,769	471,906	9.6
30	Missouri	5,595,211	5,117,073	478,138	9.3
31	Hawaii	1,211,537	1,108,229	103,308	9.3
32	Wyoming	493,782	453,588	40,194	8.9
33	New Jersey	8,414,350	7,730,188	684,162	8.9
34	Illinois	12,419,293	11,430,602	988,691	8.6
35	Kansas	2,688,418	2,477,574	210,844	8.5
36	South Dakota	754,844	696,004	58,840	8.5
37	Nebraska	1,711,263	1,578,385	132,878	8.4
38	Vermont	608,827	562,758	46,069	8.2
39	Michigan	9,938,444	9,295,297	643,147	6.9
40	Louisiana	4,468,976	4,219,973	249,003	5.9
41	Massachusetts	6,349,097	6,016,425	332,672	5.5
42	New York	18,976,457	17,990,455	986,002	5.5
43	Iowa	2,926,324	2,776,755	149,569	5.4
44	Ohio	11,353,140	10,847,115	506,025	4.7
45	Rhode Island	1,048,319	1,003,464	44,855	4.5
46	Maine	1,274,923	1,227,928	46,995	3.8
47	Connecticut	3,405,565	3,287,116	118,449	3.6
48	Pennsylvania	12,281,054	11,881,643	399,411	3.4
49	West Virginia	1,808,344	1,793,477	14,867	0.8
50	North Dakota	642,200	638,800	3,400	0.5
(NA)	District of Columbia	572,059	606,900	−34,841	−5.7
(NA)	United States	281,421,906	248,709,873	342,712,033	13.2

Source: U.S. Census Bureau, Census 2000 Redistricting Data (P.L. 94–171) Summary File and 1990 Census.

Anthropology and the Concept of Race

NORMAN C. SULLIVAN
MARQUETTE UNIVERSITY

It has long been known that humans in various regions of the world have different physical attributes. Early observers of the natural world, such as Herodotus and Pliny the Elder, recognized some of these differences and thought that they could assign behavioral attributes to the races they identified. The practice of classifying humans, on the basis of physical features, continued on an informal basis until the empirical scientists of the eighteenth century began to generate formal classificatory systems with trait lists (Brues 1977). Numerous schemes were developed that purported to classify humans into "natural" groups. However, the scheme that has endured was developed by Johann Blumenbach. He classified people on the basis of skin color and cranial capacity and determined that there are five races among humankind (African, American Indian, Asian, European, and Southeast Asian). Obviously, Blumenbach's scheme has been modified over the years, but many people still believe that there are five or six races of humans that correspond to the major geographical regions of the world.

A basic and fundamental issue is that anthropologists simply do not believe that there is any biological reality to the concept of race (Molnar 1998). It is, of course, recognized that humans look different from one another in a variety of traits like skin color, body form, nose shape, shape of the lips, hair form, and so on. It is also true that humans are variable in more subtle ways, as in the variation that occurs in all proteins of the body as well as DNA sequences. A problem arises when attempting to use this variation to classify people into race categories. There is no consistent cluster of traits, among the thousands of anatomical and biochemical features that can be assembled, which can be used to say that one group of people are distinct from another group (Garn and Coon 1968). This is a basic fact, and its recognition makes it clear that there is not one single group of people who can be identified as being unique from all other groups and, therefore, members of a race. Rather, all so-called races are simply types in classificatory schemes that exist in our minds. These schemes have no biological basis and are imposed on the natural world.

With an appreciation of this basic fact, it can be understood that any number of different races can be, and have been, created in any classificatory scheme that is developed. If one scheme is based on skin color, one set of races will be identified. If hair form is added to skin color for a second classificatory scheme, a wholly different set of races will be identified. Add to this a third trait and a new set of races emerges, and so on, for any number of features that are used in the classification. For example, in southern India there are many people with skin color that is essentially the same as many people in sub-Saharan Africa. If a race classification is created on the basis of skin color alone, then there would be a single race of people with dark skin in Africa and southern India. However, the people of southern India have facial features and hair that more closely resemble European populations than they do Africans. As a result, if a second trait is added to the classification, there are now two races. The number of races that are identified will be determined by the number of traits used in the classification. Does a classification scheme with 10 traits have a biological reality not possessed by a scheme that uses only 9 traits? It simply doesn't matter if one trait is used or 1,000 traits are used to create the type. They are all equally arbitrary. Moreover, the traits themselves are arbitrarily selected. Does skin color provide a better basis for classifying humans than hair form? Why not use a biochemical marker instead? The traits that have traditionally been used to identify human races were selected because they were convenient, not because they were useful markers of distinctively different groups of people.

Geneticists have provided a rigorous set of attributes for documenting human variation. Data on more than one dozen genes have been studied in many populations around the world. These data make it possible to begin to document the amount of genetic variation that exists within and between populations. These studies have unequivocally demonstrated that there is more variation within populations than there is between populations. There is simply more genetic variation among Europeans than between Europeans and Africans, and vice versa (or any other combination of races that might be constructed). This underscores two important points in the biological history of the human species. The first is that every person in the world derives from a small ancestral African population. Most geneticists and archaeologists would propose that the ancestral population existed sometime around 100,000 years ago and that much of the diversity seen in contemporary humans has a recent origin (Lewin 1997). The second important point is that geneticists have shown that, even after the divergence of humans from the ancestral African population, there has been a regular genetic exchange across population boundaries (Cavalli-Sforza et al. 1994).

There is still an insidious legacy of the race concept. The scientists who made the first attempts at establishing an empirical basis for races did so in a sociocultural context in which it was acceptable to ascribe behavioral attributes and capabilities along with physical features in their classificatory schema (King 1981). The result was that different human groups were stated to have different propensities of behavior or different capacities of intellect. The linking of intellectual capacity and behavior served as a justification, in the United States, for enacting legislation that permitted sterilization, created immigration quotas for specific groups, and allowed indeterminate sentencing in the U.S. criminal justice system (Gould 1983, 1985; Kevles 1985).

By the 1930s laws were enacted in 41 of the 48 states that permitted the sterilization of people who were thought to be defective, particularly those who were said to be "imbeciles" or "idiots." The idea was to stop people with mental impairment from reproducing in order to eliminate their inferior genes from the population. As recently as the 1970s, 27 states still had sterilization laws. It should be noted that the law was not used exclusively against people of any specific biological heritage and that a court-ordered sterilization for diminished intellectual capacity has not taken place for decades. Nonetheless, it is a part of our past and must not be forgotten.

The immigration laws of the 1920s also developed out of the notion that different populations had different capacities. The idea was that certain "races" were inferior and should be kept out of the country to block the introduction of their inferior traits to the people already living in America.

The "inferior races" scheduled for exclusion included people from Asia, eastern and southern Europe as well as Jews, among others.

Indeterminate sentencing was made part of the criminal justice system because it allowed judges some discretion in the application of law. However, the practice was also supported by people who believed that criminals are born and that they are inferior by their nature. The idea was to put away bad people for as long as possible, even for a relatively minor crime. By contrast, occasional criminals may be good people who have fallen into crime by accident. If convicted of similar crimes, the occasional criminal could be given a shorter sentence than the "natural-born" criminal. Advocates of the idea that some people have a criminal nature were convinced that they could easily decide who is inherently good or bad as seen in traits of the face, shape of the skull, length of the arms, distribution of head hair, and shape of the feet (the same attributes often used to define "race").

The "scientific" tradition of denigrating people from various biological backgrounds continues, and every few years there is another treatise that claims to demonstrate one or another human group consistently behaves better or worse than another group or that there are different intellectual abilities among human populations. The ethnographic literature conclusively shows that any such claims are without foundation. No doubt, there will continue to be publications that claim to demonstrate the higher refinement of one human population over another. These works will be cloaked in the respectability of graduate degrees and academic affiliation. Nonetheless, they will all be characterized by a fundamental misunderstanding of the biology of human differences and a fundamental confusion of biology and ethnicity.

INTELLIGENCE, BEHAVIOR, AND HIERARCHY OF RACIAL GROUPS

There have been those who claim that there are different levels of intelligence among different "racial groups." Samuel Morton, an anatomist active in the mid-nineteenth century, thought that he was able to prove that Europeans had the largest cranial capacity of any "race" (and, therefore, the greatest ability) and that they were followed, in order, by Asians and Africans. Steven Jay Gould, in *The Mismeasure of Man*, showed that Morton falsified his data. In recent years, several researchers from well-respected universities have raised the issue once more by arguing that, when given IQ tests, Americans of African descent do not score as well, on average, as Americans of European descent. They draw the conclusion that African-derived peoples are not as intelligent as European-derived peoples.

These assertions are based on several fundamental misunderstandings. First, intelligence is elusive and there are difficulties in defining it, let alone measuring it. Many IQ tests in the past were based on questions with a cultural bias. Current tests do not have the same degree of bias, but there are other problems. The scores that an individual gets on the test can vary significantly from one day to the next. In addition, IQ test scores will be substantially higher for people who take the test one at a time, with an examiner, as opposed to people taking the test in a group. Children who take an IQ test after they have had breakfast do better than children who have not been fed before the test. In short, there is overwhelming evidence to show that IQ scores are strongly associated with the social environment. Children growing up in nurturing and protective families score higher on the tests than children who lack those advantages. The fact of the matter is that IQ tests were developed in the first place only to identify children who needed remedial help in school subjects—the tests were not designed to measure intelligence.

If some researchers make the claim that there are differences of intelligence between different ethnic groups, then they must explain a fundamental fact of evolution. How did it happen? Why did natural selection favor increased intelligence for populations in some environments and not in others? This is especially problematic in light of the regular genetic exchange that has taken place between sub-saharan Africa, North Africa, the Near East, and Europe.

These misconstructions were ultimately based on the ideas of a few scientists who thought that they had an absolute truth to communicate. As Jacob Bronowski said: "It was done by arrogance. It was done by dogma. It was done by ignorance."

REFERENCES CITED

Brues, Alice M. *People and Races*. New York: Macmillan, 1977 (reissued 1990, Waveland Press, Prospect Heights, IL).

Cavalli-Sforza, Luigi, Paolo Menozzi, and Alberto Piazza. *The History and Geography of Human Genes*. Princeton, NJ: Princeton University Press, 1994.

Garn, Stanley M., and Carleton S. Coon. On the number of races of mankind. In *Readings on Race*, pp. 9–16, ed. by Stanley M. Garn. 2nd ed. Springfield, IL: Charles C. Thomas, 1968.

Gould, Stephen Jay. *The Mismeasure of Man*. New York: W. W. Norton and Co., 1981.

___. Science and Jewish Immigration. In *Hen's Teeth and Horse's Toes*, pp. 291–302, assembled by Stephen Jay Gould. New York: W. W. Norton and Co., 1983.

___. Carrie Buck's Daughter. In *The Flamingo's Smile*, pp. 306–318, assembled by Stephen Jay Gould. New York: W. W. Norton and Co., 1985.

Kevles, Daniel J. *In the Name of Eugenics*. Berkeley: University of California Press, 1985.

King, James C. *The Biology of Race*. Berkeley: University of California Press, 1981.

Lewin, Roger. *Patterns in Evolution. The New Molecular View*. Scientific American Library. New York: W. H. Freeman and Co., 1997.

Molnar, Stephen. *Human Variation. Races, Types and Ethnic Groups*. Upper Saddle River, NJ: Prentice Hall, 1998.

Notes

Introduction

1. Michael Barone, "American Dreamers," *U.S. News and World Report,* Vol. 128, No. 3 (April 3, 2000), p. 27.
2. Ibid.
3. Marilyn Fischer, "Respecting the Individual, Valuing Diversity," *Critical Issues in Fund Raising* (New York: John Wiley & Sons, 1995), p. 68.
4. Ibid., p. 67. See also Michael O'Neill and William L. Roberts, *Giving and Volunteering in California* (San Francisco: University of San Francisco, 1995), p. 51.
5. Refer to *NSFRE Fund Raising Dictionary* (New York: John Wiley & Sons, 1997).
6. James Joseph, *Remaking America: How the Benevolent Traditions of Many Cultures Are Transforming Our National Life* (San Francisco: Jossey-Bass, 1995), p. 7.
7. Ibid., p. 9.
8. K. Chappell, "The Washerwoman Philanthropist," *Ebony* Vol. 51, No. 2 (December, 1995), p. 84.
9. *U.S. Census, 2000.*

Chapter 1

1. As quoted by Jean E. Fairfax in "Black Philanthropy: Its Heritage and Its Future," *Cultures of Giving: Heritage, Gender, Wealth, Values* (San Francisco: Jossey-Bass, 1995), p. 9.
2. Emmett D. Carson, "African Philanthropy on the Rise," *Philanthropy News Digest,* Vol. 6, No. 27 (June 27, 2000).
3. See John Hope Franklin and Alfred A. Moss, Jr., *From Slavery to Freedom: A History of African Americans,* Seventh Edition (New York: McGraw-Hill, 1994), pp. 1-67.
4. Ibid.
5. Claud Anderson, *Dirty Little Secrets About Black History, Its Heroes, and Other Troublemakers* (New York: PowerNomics Corporation of America, 1997), pp. 65-66.
6. Emmett D. Carson, Ph.D., *A Hand Up: Black Philanthropy and Self-Help in America* (Washington, DC: Joint Center for Political and Economic Studies, Inc., 1993), pp. 7-15.
7. Ibid.
8. Cited in Charles H. Wesley, Ph.D., *The History of Alpha Phi Alpha: A Development in College Life* (Washington, DC: Howard University Press, 1957), pp. xxiii–xxiv.
9. Ibid.
10. Jean E. Fairfax, "Black Philanthropy: Its Heritage and Its Future," *Cultures of Giving: Heritage, Gender, Wealth, Value* (San Francisco: Jossey-Bass, 1995), pp. 9, 13, 15.
11. Ibid., p. 12.
12. Ibid., p. 15.
13. Anderson, p. 191.
14. Ibid.

15. Cheryl Hall-Russell and Robert H. Kasberg, *African-American Traditions of Giving and Serving: A Midwest Perspective* (Indianapolis: Indiana Center on Philanthropy, 1997), pp. 3–4.

16. Ibid.

17. "America 2000: A Map of the Mix," *Newsweek* (September 18, 2000), p. 48.

18. Data from U.S. Census Bureau, United States Department of Commerce.

Chapter 2

1. Stella Shao,"Asian American Giving," *Cultures of Giving II,* No. 8 (San Francisco: Jossey-Bass, Summer 1995), p. 54.

2. Juanita Tamayo Lott, Speech delivered at Conference on "Asian Pacific Americans and the Nonprofit Sector," Institute for Nonprofit Organization Management, University of San Francisco, at Hyatt at Fisherman's Wharf (June 19, 1997).

3. Harry H. L. Kitano and Roger Daniels, *Asian Americans: Emerging Minorities*, Revised (Upper Saddle River, NJ: Prentice-Hall, 2000), p. 91.

4. Ibid., p. 112.

5. Ibid., p. 118.

6. Ibid., p. 166.

7. Ibid., p. 105.

8. James W. Loewen, *The Mississippi Chinese* (Cambridge, MA: Harvard University Press, 1971), p. 27.

9. Ronald Takaki, *A Different Mirror: A History of Multicultural America* (Boston, MA: Little Brown and Company, 1993), p. 194.

10. "The Chinese of the Mendocino Coast" (Mendocino, CA: The History Company, 1990), p. 5.

11. Hubert Howe Bancroft, *History of California, Vol. 6*, Chapter VII (San Francisco: The History Company, 1884–1890), p. 124.

12. Charles J. McClain, Jr., "The Chinese Struggle for Civil Rights in Nineteenth Century America: The First Phase, 1850-1870," *California Law Review*, Vol. 72 (1984), pp. 544, 555.

13. Takaki, p. 201.

14. Stuart Creighton Miller, *The Unwelcome Immigrant: The American Image of the Chinese, 1752–1882* (Berkeley, CA: University of California Press, 1969), p. 190.

15. Ibid., p. 17.

16. Him Mark Lai, Genny Lim, and Judy Yung, *Island: Poetry and History of Chinese Immigrants on Angel Island, 1910–1940* (Seattle: University of Washington Press, 1980), Island Poem #23, p. 60.

17. Coined in 1966 by sociologist William Petersen, initially applied only to Japanese Americans.

18. Kitano and Daniels, p. 51.

19. Ronald Takaki, *In the Heart of Filipino America: Immigrants from the Pacific Islands* (New York: Chelsea House, 1994), p. 65.

20. H. Brett Melendy, *Asians in America: Filipinos, Koreans and East Indians* (Boston: Twayne Publishers, 1977), p. 53.

21. Ibid., p. 93.

22. Takaki, *A Different Mirror*, p. 252.

23. Ibid., p. 256.

24. Harry H. L. Kitano, *Japanese Americans: Evolution of a Subculture* (Englewood Cliffs, NJ: Prentice-Hall, 1976), p. 3.

25. Takaki, *A Different Mirror*, p. 268.

26. Ibid., p. 472.

27. Ibid., p. 275.

28. Sucheng Chan, *Asian Americans: An Interpretive History* (New York: Twayne Publishers, 1991), p. 122.

29. Ibid., p. 124.

31. Ibid., p. 139.
32. Kitano and Daniels, p. 113.
33. Karen Isaksen Leonard, *The South Asian Americans* (Westport, CT: The Greenwood Press, 1997), p. 69.
34. Ibid., p. 31.
35. Ibid., p. 41.
36. Ibid., p. 45.
37. Ibid., p. 78.
38. Ibid., p. 69.
39. *India-West,* cited in Leonard, (January 25, 1991, October 1, 1993, April 22, 1994). No article or author information given.
40. *India-West*, January 25, 1991.
41. Leonard, p. 77.
42. Ibid., p. 80.
43. Bradford Smith et al., *Philanthropy in Communities of Color* (Bloomington, IN: Indiana University Press, 1999), p. 4.
44. Ibid., p. 33.
45. See Jessica Chao, "Asian American Philanthropy: Expanding Circles of Participation," *Cultures of Caring: Philanthropy in Diverse American Communities* (Washington, DC: Council on Foundations, 1999), p. 199.
46. Smith et al., p. 94.
47. Kitano and Daniels, 77.
48. Smith et al., p. 123.
49. Ibid.
50. Ibid., p. 128.
51. Ibid.
52. Smith et al., p. 145.
53. Ibid., p. 140.
54. Ibid., p. 144.
55. Jacob Neusner, ed., *World Religions in America* (Louisville, KY: Westminster John Knox Press, 2000), p. 126.
56. See generally Joel Beversliuis, ed., *Sourcebook of the World's Religions,* Chapter 13, "A Portrait" by Dr. Rajwant Singh and Georgia Rangel (Novato, CA: New World Library, 2000), pp. 92-93.

Chapter 3

1. Himilce Novas, *Everything You Need to Know About Latino History,* Revised (New York: Penguin Group, 1998), pp. 171–72.
2. Ibid., p. 172.
3. Ibid., p. 178.
4. Ibid., pp. 179–181.
5. Ibid., 201.
6. James S. Olson, *The Ethnic Dimension in American History* (St. James, NY: Brandywine Press, 1999), p. 205.
7. Novas, p. 204.
8. See generally Novas, pp. 215–228.
9. Ibid., p. 225.
10. Ibid., p. 235.
11. Ibid., p. 240.
12. Manuel G. Gonzales, *Mexicanos: A History of Mexicans in the United States* (Bloomington, IN: Indiana Univeristy Press, 2000), p. 16.

13. Ibid., p. 19.
14. Ibid., p. 26.
15. Ibid., p. 37.
16. Ibid., p. 75.
17. Ibid., p. 134.
18. Ibid., pp. 190–195.
19. Novas, p. 133.
20. Ibid., p. 134.
21. Ibid., p. 136.
22. Ibid., pp. 148–150.
23. Ibid., p. 158.
24. Olson, pp. 257–260.
25. Ibid., p. 257.
26. Herman E. Gallegos and Michael O'Neill, eds., *Hispanics and the Nonprofit Sector* (New York: The Foundation Center, 1991), p. 41.
27. Ibid., p. 43, quoting Bonilla, 1965, p. 1.
28. Ibid., p. 44.
29. Bradford Smith et al., *Philanthropy in Communities of Color* (Bloomington: Indiana University Press, 1999), p. 29.
30. Ibid., pp. 30–31.
31. See later section in this book on remittances.
32. Smith et al., pp. 34–48.
33. Ibid., p. 40.
34. Ibid., p. 48.
35. Ibid., p. 59.

Chapter 4

1. Gordon R. Willey, *An Introduction to American Archaeology, Volume One: North and Middle America* (Englewood Cliffs, NJ: Prentice-Hall, 1966).
2. Ibid., p. 10.
3. Ibid., p. 23.
4. Ibid., p. 23.
5. Ibid., p. 24.
6. Ibid., p. 30.
7. Ibid., p. 24.
8. Ibid., p. 34.
9. Clara Sue Kidwell, "True Indian Giving," *Foundation News and Commentary,* Vol. 31, No. 3 (May/June 1990), pp. 27–29.
10. See generally *U.S. Census Bureau Facts for Features*, 1999.
11. See Rebecca Adamson, "Creating a New Vision for Native American Philanthropy," *Responsive Philanthropy* (Summer 1996), pp. 9–10.
12. See Dagmar Thorpe, "Looking at Philanthropy Through Native American Eyes," *The Journal* (Alexandria, VA: National Society of Fund Raising Executives, Autumn 1989), pp. 17–20.
13. Ibid.

Chapter 5

1. Walter V. Collier, Ph.D., and Associates, *Financing African American Churches: National Survey on Church Giving* (Atlanta, GA: Institute of Church Administration and Management, Interdenominational Theological Center, 1998).

2. Ibid.

3. Ibid.

4. Emmett D. Carson, *Working Papers: Black Volunteers as Givers and Fundraisers* (1990), pp. 6–9.

5. Dr. Joanne Scanlan, *Cultures of Caring: Philanthropy in Diverse American Communities* (Washington, DC: Council on Foundations, 1999), p. 5.

6. Ibid., pp. 7–8.

7. Mary-Frances Winters, "Reflections on Endowment Building in the African-American Community," *Cultures of Caring: Philanthropy in Diverse American Communities* (Washington, DC: Council on Foundations, 1999), p. 109.

8. Ibid., p. 110.

9. Alice Green Burnette, *The Privilege to Ask: A Handbook for African-American Fund Raising Professionals* (Atlanta, GA: Interdenominational Theological Center, 2000), p. 5.

10. Ibid., p. 4.

11. Ibid., p. 9.

12. Taken from mission statement, Association of Fund Raising Officers, Inc., (Washington, DC: 2000), p. 2.

13. See mission statement for National Center for Black Philanthropy. Adopted by board of directors, January 2000.

14. Bradford Smith et al., *Philanthropy in Communities of Color* (Bloomington, IN: Indiana University Press, 1999), p. 9.

15. *Cultures of Caring: Philanthropy in Diverse American Communities* (Washington, DC: Council on Foundations, 1999).

16. Jessica Chao, "Asian American Philanthropy: Expanding Circles of Participation" *Cultures of Caring: Philanthropy in Diverse American Communities* (Washington, DC: Council on Foundations, 1999), pp. 192–195.

17. Smith et al., p. 88.

18. Ibid., p. 105.

19. Ibid., p. 121.

20. Ibid., p. 135.

21. See generally *Hispanic Scholarship Fund Annual Report*, 1999.

22. See generally *Giving USA 2000.*

23. Daniel Villaneuva interviewed in *Ventura Star Bulletin* (March 18, 2000).

24. See Michael Cortés, "Three Strategic Questions About Latino Philanthropy," *Cultures of Giving II: How Heritage, Gender, Wealth, and Values Influence Philanthropy*, ed. Warren Ilchman and Charles Hamilton (San Francisco: Jossey-Bass, 1995).

25. See Ana Gloria Rivas-Vazquez, "New Pools of Latino Wealth: A Case Study of Donors and Potential Donors in U.S. Hispanic/Latino Communities," *Nuevos Senderos: Reflections on Hispanics and Philanthropy*, ed. Diana Campoamor, William A. Diaz, and Henry J. Ramos, (Houston: Arte Publico Press, April 1999).

26. Henry A. J. Ramos, "Latino Philanthropy: Expanding U.S. Models of Giving and Civic Participation," *Cultures of Caring* (Washington, DC: Council on Foundations, 1999), pp. 149–150.

27. Smith et al., p. 28.

28. Ibid., p. 49.

29. Ibid., p. 69.

30. Michael Yellow Bird, "What We Want to Be Called," *American Indian Quarterly,* Vol. 23 (Spring 1999), p. 1.

31. Ibid., p. 4.

32. Ibid.

33. Bureau of Labor Statistics, U.S. Department of Labor, "Preference for Racial and Ethnic Terminology: By Group," Press Release USDL95-2 (October 26, 1995). See also Yellow Bird.

34. See Robert B. Moore, "Racism in the English Language," *Race, Class, and Gender in the United States.*

35. Ibid.
36. Yellow Bird.
37. Mindy Berry, "Native-American Philanthropy: Expanding Social Participation and Self-Determination," *Cultures of Caring* (Washington, DC: Council on Foundations, 1999), p. 36.
38. Ibid., p. 66.
39. Ibid., p. 36.

Chapter 6

1. Bennett J. Sims, *The Meaning of Servant Leadership* (Boston: Cowley Publications, 1997), p. 6. See also Peter M. Senge, *The Fifth Discipline Field Book* (New York: Doubleday, 1994), pp. 3–4.
2. Dagmar Thorpe, "Native Americans in Philanthropy." Paper presented at Pluralism in Philanthropy Roundtable (Washington, DC: Council on Foundations, June 1989).
3. James Joseph, *Remaking America: How the Benevolent Traditions of Many Cultures Are Transforming Our National Life* (San Francisco: Jossey-Bass, 1995), p. 29.
4. Ronald Austin Wells, *The Honor of Giving: Philanthropy in Native America* (Indianapolis: Indiana Center on Philanthropy, 1998), p. 78. See also Black Elk, *The Sacred Pipe,* ed. Joseph Epes Brown, (New York: Penguin Books, 1971), p. 92.
5. Peter Booth Wiley, *A Free Library in This City* (San Francisco: Weldon Owen, 1996), p. 205.
6. Ibid.
7. Ibid., p. 207.
8. See generally Michael L. Radice, "Pursuing the Culturally Specific Donor," *Fund Raising Management* (May 2000), pp. 10–13.
9. National Committee for Responsive Philanthropy, *Grants: Corporate Grantmaking for Racial and Ethnic Communities* (Wakefield, RI: Moyer Bell Publishers, 2000), p. 20.
10. Ibid., p. 85.
11. Ibid., p. 93.
12. Ibid., p. 102.
13. Ibid., p. 112.
14. Ibid.
15. Demetrios G. Papdemetriou, "Myths and Realities," *UNESCO Courier* (November 1998), p 18(5).
16. Jeffrey H. Cohen, "Consequences of Migration and Remittances for Mexican Transnational Communities," *Economic Geography*, Vol. 74, No. 1 (January 1998), p. 26(19).

Chapter 8

1. The term *tribe* can mean several things. In social science literature, it refers to a group of people who are organized into a specific kind of sociopolitical unit. In common usage, it is often used to describe groups of First Nations people/Native Americans/Indians in general.
2. The term *First Nation* is currently not in common use.
3. Wendell H. Oswalt, *This Land Was Theirs* (New York: Wiley, 1978), pp. 16–17.
4. Paula Gunn Allen, *Off the Reservation* (Boston, MA: Beacon Press, 1998), p. 1.
5. Ibid., p. 8.
6. Ibid., p. 13.

Glossary of Racial/Ethnic Terms

[β]**American Indian and Alaska Native**
refers to people having origins in any of the original peoples of North and South America (including Central America), and who maintain tribal affiliation or community attachment. It includes people who indicated their race or races by marking this category or writing in their principal or enrolled tribe, such as Rosebud, Sioux, Chippewa, or Navajo.

[β]**Asian** refers to people having origins in any of the original peoples of the Far East, Southeast Asia, or the Indian subcontinent. It includes people who indicated their race or races as "Asian Indian," "Chinese," "Filipino," "Korean," "Japanese," "Vietnamese," or "Other Asian," or wrote in entries such as Burmese, Hmong, Pakistani, or Thai.

[β]**Black or African American** refers to people having origins in any of the black racial groups of Africa. It includes people who indicated their race or races as "Black, African Am[erican] or Negro," or wrote in entries such as African American, Afro-American, Nigerian, or Haitian.

[α]**Class** refers to a stratum of people within a society who share basic economic, politicial, or cultural characteristics—for example: wealth or its absence, "life chances" in a market situation, kind of labor performed, tastes, family background, linguistic characteristics, or sets of special attitudes and behaviors. Class membership may provide access to power and privilege or other benefits within a social, economic, or political structure.

[α]**Communication** is the transmission of messages from a sender to a receiver in any one of a variety of codes—language, gestures, signs, written symbols, etc.—to which the sender and receiver attach meaning. The aim is to transfer the message with as little loss of meaning as possible. Communication is also a transaction that generates new meanings. Communication through means other than spoken or written language is generally referred to as *nonverbal communication*.

[α]**Cultural relativism** suggests that cultures cannot be judged or evaluated from a single or absolute ethical or moral perspective. Evaluations are relative to the background from which they arise. No culture's values, ethics, or morals as a whole may be judged as

[α]*Source*: Margaret Pusch, ed. *Multicultural Education*. Intercultural Network, Inc., 1981, pp. 3–7.
[β]*Source*: Census 2000.

inherently superior or inferior to another's.

α**Culture** is the sum total of ways of living, including values, beliefs, esthetic standards, linguistic expression, patterns of thinking, behavioral norms, and styles of communication that a group of people has developed to assure its survival in a particular physical and human environment. Culture, and the people who are part of it, interact, so that culture is not static. Culture is the response of a group of human beings to the valid and particular needs of its members. It, therefore, has an inherent logic and an essential balance between positive and negative dimensions.

α**Dialect** is a variety of a spoken language that differs from the standard form of the language and is used by a group of speakers who are set off from others geographically or socially.

α**An ethnic group** is a group of people identified by racial, national, or cultural characteristics. Ethnic group membership is normally determined by birth. Most commonly, ethnic groups are seen as interdependent subunits of larger cultural or political entities. The term *ethnic group* is often applied to groups that have a minority status in the larger society.

α**Identity group** (or role group) is any group of people who share enough characteristics, interests, attitudes, or behaviors to provide an ease of communication and a satisfying sense of relatedness. Identity groups may be based on profession or vocation, family status, avocation, special skills, and so on. Cultures are identity groups but identity groups are not cultures. (A *role*

group is an identity based on a professional, vocational, familial, or some other role.)

α**Intercultural communication** refers to the communication process (in its fullest sense) between people of different cultural backgrounds. It may take place among individuals or between social, political, or economic entities in different cultures, such as government agencies, businesses, educational institutions, or the media. This includes nonverbal as well as verbal communication and the use of differing codes— linguistic or nonlinguistic. Culture is viewed as having a major influence on the communication process.

β**Native Hawaiian and Other Pacific Islander** refers to people having origins in any of the original peoples of Hawaii, Guam, Samoa, or other Pacific Islands. It includes people who indicated their race or races as "Native Hawaiian," "Guamanian or Chamorro," "Samoan," or "Other Pacific Islander," or wrote in entries such as Tahitian, Mariana Islander, or Chuukese.

α**Prejudice** describes hostile and unreasonable feelings, opinions, or attitudes based on fear, mistrust, ignorance, misinformation—or a combination thereof—and directed against a racial, religious, national, or other cultural group.

α**Race** is a somewhat suspect concept used to identify large groups of the human species who share a more or less distinctive combination of hereditary physical characteristics. Within a society racial identification may be used to separate out a culture group for special privileges or disabilities.

α*Source*: Margaret Pusch, ed. *Multicultural Education*. Intercultural Network, Inc., 1981, pp. 3–7.
β*Source*: Census 2000.

[α]A **role group** is an identity based on a professional, vocational, familial, or some other role.

[β]**"Some other race"** was included in Census 2000 for respondents who were unable to identify with the five race categories. Respondents who provided write-in entries such as Moroccan, South African Belizean, or a Hispanic origin (for example, Mexican, Puerto Rican, or Cuban) are included in the "Some other race" category.

[α]A **subculture** is a group of people within a larger sociopolitical structure who share cultural (and often linguistic or dialectical) characteristics that are distinctive enough to distinguish it from others within the same society.

[β]**White** refers to people having origins in any of the original peoples of Europe, the Middle East, or North Africa. It includes people who indicated their race or races as "White" or who wrote in entries such as Irish, German, Italian, Lebanese, Near Easterner, Arab, or Polish.

[α]*Source*: Margaret Pusch, ed. *Multicultural Education*. Intercultural Network, Inc., 1981, pp. 3–7.
[β]*Source*: Census 2000.

Bibliography

Adamson, Rebecca. "Creating a New Vision for Native American Philanthropy." *Responsive Philanthropy* (Summer 1996).

"America 2000: A Map of the Mix." *Newsweek* (September 18, 2000).

American Demographics. Desk Reference Series, No. 1. "American Diversity." Ithaca, NY: American Demographics, Inc., 1991.

Anderson, Claud, Ed.D. *Dirty Little Secrets About Black History: Its Heroes, Troublemakers.* Bethesda, MD: PowerNomics Corp. of America, 1997.

Anderson, Eric, and Alfred A. Moss, Jr. *Dangerous Donations: Northern Philanthropy and Southern Black Education, 1902–1930.* Columbia: University of Missouri Press, 1999.

Anderson, Margaret L., and Patricia Hill Collins, eds. *Race, Class, and Gender: An Anthology.* Belmont, CA: Wadsworth Publishing Company, 1995.

Barringer, Herbert R., Robert W. Gardner, and Michael J. Levin. *Asians and Pacific Islanders in the United States.* New York: The Russell Sage Foundation, 1993.

Bancroft, Hubert Howe. *History of California, Volume 6.* San Francisco, CA: The History Co., 1888.

Barone, Michael. "American Dreamers." *U.S. News and World Report* v. 128 (April 3, 2000).

Bear, Dorothy, and David Houghton. *The Chinese of the Mendocino Coast.* Mendocino, CA: Mendocino Historical Research, Inc., 1990.

Berry, Mindy L. "Native-American Philanthropy: Expanding Social Participation and Self-Determination." In *Cultures of Caring: Philanthropy in Diverse American Communities.* Washington, D.C.: Council on Foundations, 1999.

Beversluis, Joel ed., *Sourcebook of the World's Religions: An Interfaith Guide to Religion and Spirituality.* Novato, CA: New World Library, 2000.

Bonacich, Edna, and John Modell. *The Economic Basis of Ethnic Solidarity: Small Business in the Japanese American Community.* Berkeley: University of California Press, 1980.

Bremner, Robert. *American Philanthropy.* Chicago: University of Chicago Press, 1988.

____. *Giving.* New Brunswick, NJ: Transaction Publishers, 1994.

Burnette, Alice Green. *The Privilege to Ask: A Handbook for African American Fund Raising Professionals.* Atlanta, GA: Interdenominational Theological Center, 2000.

Campoamor, Diana, William A. Diaz, and Henry A. J. Ramos, eds., *Nuevos Senderos: Reflections on Hispanics and Philanthropy.* Houston, TX: Arte Publico Press, 1999.

Campoamor, Diana et al. *The Funders Collaborative for Strong Latino Communities Second Draft Prospectus,* Berkeley, CA: Hispanics in Philanthropy.

Carnegie, Andrew. "The Gospel of Wealth." Bloomington: Indiana University Center on Philanthropy, 1993.

Carson, Emmett D., Ph.D. *A Hand Up: Black Philanthropy and Self-Help in America.* Washington, D.C.: Joint Center for Political and Economic Studies, 1993.

___. "Black Volunteers As Givers and Fundraising." Working Papers. New York: Graduate School and University Center, City University of New York, 1990.

Chan, Sucheng. *Asian Americans: An Interpretive History.* New York: Twayne Publishers, 1991.

Chao, Jessica. "Asian American Philanthropy: Expanding Circles of Participation." In *Cultures of Caring: Philanthropy in Diverse American Communities.* Washington, D.C.: Council on Foundations, 1999.

Chappell, K. "The Washerwoman Philanthropist," *Ebony* (1995).

Choy, Bong-youn. *Koreans in America.* Chicago: Nelson-Hall, 1979.

Cohen, Jeffrey H. "Consequences of Migration and Remittances for Mexican Transnational Communities." *Economic Geography* v. 74, n. 1 (Jan. 1998).

Cohen, Lucy M. *Chinese in the Post-Civil War South: A People Without a History.* Baton Rouge: Louisiana State University, 1994.

Collier, Walter V., Ph.D., and Associates. *Financing African American Churches: National Survey on Church Giving.* Atlanta, GA: Institute of Church Administration and Management, Interdenominational Theological Center, 1998.

Cortés, Michael. "Three Strategic Questions About Latino Philanthropy." In *Cultures of Giving II: How Heritage, Gender, Wealth and Values Influence Philanthropy.* Ed. Warren Ilchman and Charles Hamilton. New Directions for Philanthropic Fundraising. San Francisco: Jossey-Bass Publishers, 1995.

Cultures of Caring: Philanthropy in Diverse American Communities. Washington, D.C.: Council on Foundations, 1999.

Cultures of Giving: How Region and Religion Influence Philanthropy. Ed. Charles H. Hamilton and Warren F. Ilchman. San Francisco: Jossey-Bass, 1995.

Cultures of Giving II: How Heritage, Gender, Wealth, and Values Influence Philanthropy. Ed. Charles H. Hamilton and Warren F. Ilchman. San Francisco: Jossey-Bass, 1995.

Deloria, Vine Jr. *God Is Red: A Native View of Religion.* Golden, CO: Fulcrum Publishing, 1994.

Fairfax, Jean E. "Black Philanthropy: Its Heritage and Its Future." In *Cultures of Giving: How Heritage, Gender, Wealth, and Values Influence Philanthropy.* Ed. Charles H. Hamilton and Warren F. Ilchman. San Francisco: Jossey-Bass, 1995.

Finberg, Barbara. "Asian Pacific Americans and the Independent Sector." Speech delivered at Conference on Asian Pacific Americans and the Nonprofit Sector. San Francisco, CA, 1997.

Fischer, Marilyn. *Ethical Decision Making in Fund Raising.* New York: Wiley, 2000.

___. "Respecting the Individual, Valuing Diversity." In *Critical Issues in Fund Raising.* New York: Wiley, 1995.

Franklin, John Hope. *Race and History: Selected Essays 1938–1988.* Baton Rouge: Louisiana University Press, 1989.

Franklin, John Hope, and Alfred A. Moss, Jr. *From Slavery to Freedom: A History of African Americans.* New York: McGraw-Hill, 1994.

Gallegos, Herman E., and Michael O'Neill, eds. *Hispanics and the Nonprofit Sector.* New York: The Foundation Center, 1991.

Giving USA 1999: The Annual Report on Philanthropy. New York: AAFRC Trust for Philanthropy, 1999.

Gonzales, Manuel. *Mexicanos: A History of Mexicans in the United States.* Bloomington: Indiana University Press, 2000.

Gonzalez-Pando, Miguel. *The Cuban Americans.* Westport, CT: Greenwood Press, 1998.

Hall-Russell, Cheryl. *Racial and Ethnic Diversity.* Ithaca, NY: New Strategist Publications, 1998.

Hall-Russell, Cheryl, and Robert H. Kasberg. *African American Traditions of Giving and Serving: A Midwest Perspective.* Indianapolis: Indiana University Center on Philanthropy, 1997.

Hammack, David C., ed. *Making the Nonprofit Sector in the United States.* Bloomington: Indiana University Press, 1998.

Harris, Thomas. *International Fund Raising for Not-for-Profits: A Country by Country Profile.* New York: Wiley, 1999.

Hirschfelder, Arlene, and Marta Kreipe de Montano. *The Native American Almanac: A Portrait of Native America Today.* New York: Macmillan USA, 1993.

Inada, Lawon Fusao, ed. *Only What We Could Carry: The Japanese Internment Experience.* Berkeley, CA: Heyday Books, 2000.

"Invisible and in Need: Philanthropic Giving to Asian American and Pacific Islanders." *Asian Americans and Pacific Islanders in Philanthropy.* New York: 1992.

Jaffe, A. J. *The First Immigrants for Asia: A Population History of the North American Indians.* New York: Plenum Press, 1992.

Joseph, James A. *Remaking America: How the Benevolent Traditions of Many Cultures Are Transforming Our National Life.* San Francisco: Jossey-Bass, 1995.

Katz, William Loren. *Black Indians: A Hidden Heritage.* New York: Aladdin Paperbacks, 1997.

Kidwell, Clara Sue. "True Indian Giving." *Foundation News and Commentary,* v. 31, n. 3 (May/June 1990).

Kim, Hyung-chan, ed. *The Korean Diaspora.* Santa Barbara, CA: ABC-Clio, 1977.

Kitano, H. L. *Japanese Americans: Evolution of a Subculture.* Englewood Cliffs, NJ: Prentice-Hall, 1976.

Kitano, Harry H. L., and Roger Daniels. *Asian Americans: Emerging Minorities.* Englewood Cliffs, NJ: Prentice-Hall, 1995.

Kyle-Brown, Ann. "Understanding Multiculturalism: Corporate Response and Innovation." New York: Council on Foundations, 1992.

Lai, Him Mark, Genny Lim, and Judy Yung. *Island: Poetry and History of Chinese Immigrants on Angel Island, 1910–1940.* Seattle: University of Washington Press, 1980.

Lee, Robert. *Guide to Chinese American Philanthropy and Charitable Giving Patterns.* San Rafael, CA: Pathway Press, 1990.

Leonard, Karen Isaksen. *The South Asian Americans.* Westport, CT: Greenwood Press, 1997.

Levine, Daniel. "Immigrant/Ethnic Mutual Aid Societies, c.1880s–1920: A Proposal for Typology." Indianapolis: Indiana University Center on Philanthropy, 1995.

Levy, Richard H. "Give Them Some Credit." *American Demographics* (May 1999).

Loewen, James W. *The Mississippi Chinese: Between Black and White.* Cambridge, MA: Harvard University Press, 1971.

Lyman, Stanford M. *The Asian in North America.* Santa Barbara, CA: ABC-Clio, Inc., 1970.

___. *Chinese Americans.* New York: Random House, 1974.

McClain, Charles Jr. "The Chinese Struggle for Civil Rights in Nineteenth Century America: The First Phase, 1850–1870." *California Law Review,* v. 72 (1984).

Meier, Matt S., and Feliciano Ribera. *Mexican Americans/American Mexicans: From Conquistadors to Chicanos.* Revised edition. New York: Hill and Wang, 1993.

Melendy, H. Brett. *Asians in America: Filipinos, Koreans and East Indians.* Boston: Twayne, 1977.

Miller, Stuart C. *The Unwelcome Immigrant: The American Image of the Chinese, 1752–1882.* Berkeley: University of California, 1888.

National Committee for Responsive Philanthropy. "Grants: Corporate Grantmaking for Racial and Ethnic Communities." Wakefield, RI: Moyer Bell Publishers, 2000.

Neusner, Jacob, ed. *World Religions in America: An Introduction.* Louisville, KY: Westminster John Knox Press, 2000.

Novas, Himilce. *Everything You Need to Know About Latino History.* Revised edition. New York: Penguin Group, 1998.

O'Neill, Michael, and William L. Roberts. *Giving and Volunteering in California.* San Francisco: University of San Francisco, 1995.

Olson, James S. *The Ethnic Dimension in American History.* 3rd ed. St. James, NY: Brandywine Press, 1999.

Olson, James S., and Judith E. Olson. *Cuban Americans: From Trauma to Triumph.* New York: Twayne Publishers, 1995.

Ong, Paul, ed. "The State of Asian Pacific America: Economic Diversity Issues and Policies." LEAP, Asian Pacific American Public Policy Institute. Los Angeles, CA: UCLA, 1994.

Ong Hing, Bill, and Ronald Lee, eds. "The State of Asian Pacific American: Reframing the Immigration Debate." LEAP, Asian Pacific American Public Policy Institute. Los Angeles, CA: UCLA, 2000.

Ostrower, Francie. *Why the Wealthy Give: The Culture of Elite Philanthropy.* Princeton, NJ: Princeton University Press, 1995

Papdemetriou, Demetrios G. "Myths and Realities." *UNESCO Courier* (November 1998).

Pearson, Birger A. "Ancient Roots of Western Philanthropy." Indianapolis: Indiana University Center on Philanthropy, 1997.

Prince, Russ Alan, and Karen Maru File. *The Seven Faces of Philanthropy: A New Approach to Cultivating Major Donors.* San Francisco: Jossey-Bass, 1994.

Pusch, Margaret, ed. *Multicultural Education.* Intercultural Network, 1981.

Radice, Michael L. "Pursuing the Culturally Specific Donor." Garden City, NJ: *Fund Raising Management*, May, 2000.

Ramos, Henry A. J. "Latino Philanthropy: Expanding U.S. Models of Giving and Civic Participation." *Cultures of Caring: Philanthropy in Diverse American Communities.* Washington, D.C.: Council on Foundations, 1999.

Rivas-Vazquez, Ana Gloria. "New Pools of Latino Wealth: A Case Study of Donors and Potential Donors in U.S. Hispanic/Latino Communities." In *Nuevos Senderos: Reflections on Hispanics and Philanthropy.* Ed. Diana Campoamor, William A. Diaz, and Henry J. Ramos. Houston, TX: Arte Publico Press, 1999.

Root, Maria P. P., ed. *Filipino Americans: Transformation and Identity.* Thousand Oaks, CA: Sage Publications, 1997.

Rose, Kenneth W., Thomas E. Rosenbaum, Pecolia Rieder, and Gretchen Koerpel, comp. "A Survey of Sources at the Rockefeller Archive Center for the Study of African-American History and Race Relations." Indianapolis: Indiana University Center on Philanthropy, 1993.

Saillant, John. "Black, White, and 'The Charitable Blessed': Race and Philanthropy in the American Early Republic." Indianapolis: Indiana University Center on Philanthropy, 1993.

Sanchez, George J. *Becoming Mexican American: Ethnicity, Culture and Identity in Chicano Los Angeles, 1900–1945.* New York: Oxford University Press, 1993.

Scanlan, Joanne. *Cultures of Caring: Philanthropy in Diverse American Communities.* Washington, D.C.: Council on Foundations, 1999.

Shao, Stella. "Asian American Giving: Issues and Challenges (A Practitioner's Perspective)." *Cultures of Giving II: How Heritage, Gender, Wealth, and Values Influence Philanthropy.* Ed. Charles H. Hamilton and Warren F. Ilchman. San Francisco: Jossey-Bass, 1995.

Sims, Bennett J. *Servanthood: Leadership for the Third Millennium.* Cambridge, MA: Cowley Publications, 1997.

Singh, Nikky-Guninder Kaur. *Sikhism: World Religions.* New York: Facts on File, Inc., 1993.

Smith, Bradford. *Americans from Japan.* Philadelphia: J.B. Lippincott Company, 1948.

Smith, Bradford, et al. *Philanthropy in Communities of Color.* Bloomington: Indiana University Press, 1999.

Smurl, James F. "Three Religious Views About the Responsibilities of Wealth." Indianapolis: Indiana University Center on Philanthropy, 1991.

Spickard, Paul R. *Japanese Americans: The Formation and Transformation of an Ethnic Group.* New York: Twayne, 1996.

Takaki, Ronald. *A Different Mirror: A History of Multicultural America.* Boston: Little, Brown and Company, 1993.

____. *A Larger Memory: A History of Our Diversity, with Voices.* Boston: Little, Brown and Company, 1998.

____. *In the Heart of Filipino America.* New York: Chelsea House Publishers, 1995.

Thomas, R. Roosevelt, Jr. *Beyond Race and Gender.* New York: AMACOM, 1991.

Thorpe, Dagmar. "Looking at Philanthropy Through Native American Eyes." *The Journal.* Alexandria, VA: National Society of Fund Raising Executives, Autumn 1989.

Tobin, Jacqueline L., and Raymond G. Dobard. *Hidden in Plain View: The Secret of Quilts and the Underground Railroad.* New York: Doubleday, 1999.

Tonai, Rosalyn Miyoko. "Asian American Charitable Gving." San Francisco: University of San Francisco, 1988.

Torres-Saillant, Silvio, and Ramona Hernandez. *The Dominican Americans.* Westport, CT: Greenwood Press, 1998.

Wells, Ronald Austin. *The Honor of Giving: Philanthropy in Native America.* Indianapolis: Indiana Center on Philanthropy, 1998.

Wesley, Charles H., Ph.D. *The History of Alpha Phi Alpha: A Development in College Life,* 5th edition. Washington, D.C.: Howard University Press, 1957.

Wiley, Peter Booth. *A Free Library in This City: The Illustrated History of the San Francisco Public Library.* San Francisco: Weldon Owen, Inc., 1996.

Willey, Gordon R. *An Introduction to American Archaeology: North and Middle America,* Vol. 1. Englewood Cliffs, NJ: Prentice-Hall, 1966.

Winters, Mary-Frances. "Reflections on Endowment Building in the African-American Community." *Cultures of Caring: Philanthropy in Diverse American Communities.* Washington, D.C.: Council on Foundations, 1999.

Yanagisako, Sylvia Junko. *Transforming the Past: Tradition and Kinship Among Japanese Americans.* Stanford, CA: Stanford University Press, 1985.

Yellow Bird, Michael. "What We Want to Be Called." *American Indian Quarterly.* University of Nebraska Press (Spring 1999).

Index